Call to Order

Call to Order

Floor Politics in the House and Senate

STEVEN S. SMITH

The Brookings Institution
Washington, D.C.

Library of Congress Cataloging-in-Publication Data

Smith, Steven S., 1953–
    Call to order : floor politics in the House and Senate / Steven S.
Smith.
        p.   cm.
    Includes index.
    ISBN 0-8157-8014-1 (alk. paper). ISBN 0-8157-8013-3
(pbk. : alk. paper) :
        1. United States. Congress—Decision making. 2. United States—
Politics and government—1945—Decision making. 3. Legislation—
United States. 4. United States. Congress—Rules and practice.
I. Title
JK1096.S58   1989
328.73'077—dc20   89-9802
                                                              CIP

        9 8 7 6 5 4 3 2

Typeset in Linotron Aldus with Palatino Display
Composition by Graphic Composition, Inc.
Athens, Georgia
Printing by R. R. Donnelley and Sons, Co.
Harrisonburg, Virginia
Book design by Ken Sabol

THE BROOKINGS INSTITUTION

The Brookings Institution is an independent organization devoted to nonpartisan research, education, and publication in economics, government, foreign policy, and the social sciences generally. Its principal purposes are to aid in the development of sound public policies and to promote public understanding of issues of national importance.

The Institution was founded on December 8, 1927, to merge the activities of the Institute for Government Research, founded in 1916, the Institute of Economics, founded in 1922, and the Robert Brookings Graduate School of Economics and Government, founded in 1924.

The Board of Trustees is responsible for the general administration of the Institution, while the immediate direction of the policies, program, and staff is vested in the President, assisted by an advisory committee of the officers and staff. The by-laws of the Institution state: "It is the function of the Trustees to make possible the conduct of scientific research, and publication, under the most favorable conditions, and to safeguard the independence of the research staff in the pursuit of their studies and in the publication of the results of such studies. It is not a part of their function to determine, control, or influence the conduct of particular investigations or the conclusions reached."

The President bears final responsibility for the decision to publish a manuscript as a Brookings book. In reaching his judgment on the competence, accuracy, and objectivity of each study, the President is advised by the director of the appropriate research program and weighs the views of a panel of expert outside readers who report to him in confidence on the quality of the work. Publication of a work signifies that it is deemed a competent treatment worthy of public consideration but does not imply endorsement of conclusions or recommendations.

The Institution maintains its position of neutrality on issues of public policy in order to safeguard the intellectual freedom of the staff. Hence interpretations or conclusions in Brookings publications should be understood to be solely those of the authors and should not be attributed to the Institution, to its trustees, officers, or other staff members, or to the organizations that support its research.

To Barbara and Ty

Foreword

CONGRESS is a remarkably different institution today from what it was in the 1950s. Some of the important ways are widely recognized: a larger staff, empowered subcommittees, a new budget process, and a more assertive membership. During the 1960s and 1970s Congress became a more collegial institution, with far more members able to influence important policy decisions. By the late 1970s, however, members, journalists, and academic observers shared a common set of descriptive terms for Congress: decentralized, chaotic, fragmented, unworkable. The diffusion of power was accompanied by scheduling problems for both the leadership and the rank and file, and by serious threats to the autonomy of major committees. Even the location of key decisions became less predictable. Party and committee leaders in both chambers struggled to adapt to the new conditions.

In this book, Steven S. Smith addresses a little-studied aspect of change in Congress since the 1950s: the greater importance of floor decisionmaking. The number of floor amendments to committee bills began to grow in the 1960s and skyrocketed in the early 1970s. This development was central to the challenges to the old regime and contributed to the sense of uncertainty and instability that was pervasive in the mid-1970s. Smith investigates how the House and the Senate, in their separate ways, responded to the changing character of floor activity. He argues that the House developed new strategies to reduce the hazards that expanding floor activity had created for the majority and the standing committees, whereas the Senate continues to struggle with obstructionism and rampant individualism. The author concludes with an analysis of how developments on the chamber floors have affected committee power. He shows that while congressional committees have lost much of their former autonomy, they still are robust forces in policymaking.

Steven S. Smith, a former senior fellow in the Brookings Governmental Studies program, is associate professor of political science at the University of Minnesota. He wishes to express his appreciation to Stanley Bach, Richard F. Fenno, Jr., Thomas E. Mann, David W. Rohde, and Barry R. Weingast for their advice and friendship. He also is indebted to Paul E. Peterson for his encouragement to pursue the project. The author gives special thanks to the many members of Congress and staff professionals who shared their experiences with him.

Many others contributed in important ways to the book. Marcus Flathman, Forrest Maltzman, Judy Newman, Morton Soerensen, and Thomas Weko provided research assistance, as did a team of Brookings interns: Jim Gold, Radhika Karmarker, Don Kennedy, Carolyn Klinger, Tom Lininger, Carrleigh MacLeish, Ben Page, Clint Stinger, Karen Voghel, Mark Watts, and Emily Zimmerman. Nancy D. Davidson edited the manuscript; Sandra Z. Riegler provided administrative assistance; and Renuka D. Deonarain, Ellen P. Isan, and Vida R. Megahed provided secretarial assistance. Peter Dombrowski verified the factual statements and citations, Susan L. Woollen prepared the manuscript for typesetting, and Max Franke prepared the index.

The author and the Brookings Institution would like to thank the Dillon Fund and the Everett McKinley Dirksen Congressional Research Center for support for parts of this project. The interpretations and conclusions in this book are those of the author and should not be ascribed to the persons and organizations acknowledged above or to the trustees, officers, or staff members of the Brookings Institution.

BRUCE K. MACLAURY
President

April 1989
Washington, D.C.

Contents

-»>X<«-

1. Floor Politics in Transition   1
   The Contours of Congressional Decisionmaking Processes   3
   Context   6
   Additional Themes   11

2. Revolution in the House   15
   An Overview of House Amending Activity   16
   Domination by Committee Chairmen before Reform   20
   Steps toward a More Collegial Process, 1970–73   24
   A First Look at the Effects of the Reforms   28
   Reactions to Collegial Decisionmaking   35
   An Unsettled House   45

3. Counterrevolution in the House?   49
   Budget Politics and the House Floor   50
   Appropriations Riders   59
   Televising House Floor Sessions   62
   Innovation in Special Rules   69
   Interpreting Change in the House   83

4. Evolution in the Senate   86
   Senate Amending Activity   88
   Cloture and Unanimous Consent   94
   The Use of Complex Unanimous Consent Agreements   99
   Pressure to Elaborate the Formal Rules   119
   Budget Politics and Senate Amending Activity   123
   Televising Senate Floor Sessions   125
   House and Senate Differences Reconsidered   127

5. Why Don't We Do It on the Floor?   130
   Norms and Floor Activity   131
   Party, Apprenticeship, and Committee Deference   146
   The Hyperactives   153

A Closer Look at the 99th Congress   158
Conclusion   166

6. Floor Power, Committee Power   168
   Sources of Committee Power   170
   Committees and Floor Amending Activity   176
   Counteramendments   183
   Restrictive Rules and House Committees   188
   Conclusion   195

7. Conferences and Committee Power   197
   Committee Autonomy in Conference   198
   Reforms of Conference Procedures   199
   Resolving Differences between the Chambers   204
   Conference Composition   209
   The Case of House Defense Authorization Bills   216
   Roll Call Vote Challenges to Conference Committees   223
   Conclusion   231

8. Debate, Deliberation, and Reform   233
   Central Arguments   234
   Debate and Deliberation on the Floor   236
   Reform Proposals   246
   A New Equilibrium?   250

Appendix 1: Introduction to Floor Procedure   253
   The House   253
   The Senate   257

Appendix 2: Notes on Data Collection   260

Index   263

Tables

-»X«-

2-1. Final Disposition of House Floor Amendments, by Type of Vote, Selected Congresses, 1955–86   31

2-2. House Amendments Adopted, by Method of Final Disposition, Selected Congresses, 1955–86   33

2-3. Amending Activity by House Republicans, Selected Congresses, 1955–86   34

3-1. Types of Special Rules Adopted by the House, by Type of Measure, 94th–99th Congresses (1975–86)   75

3-2. House Floor Amendments, by Type of Measure and Rule, 94th–99th Congresses (1975–86)   82

3-3. Percentage of Amendments Adopted in the House, by Type of Measure and Rule, 94th–99th Congresses (1975–86)   83

4-1. Amendments Adopted and Contested in the Senate, by Type of Vote, Selected Congresses, 1955–86   91

4-2. Motions to Table Amendments in the Senate, Selected Congresses, 1955–86   106

4-3. Complex Unanimous Consent Agreements, Selected Congresses, 1955–84   114

4-4. Debate Limitations in Complex Unanimous Consent Agreements, Selected Congresses, 1955–84   116

4-5. Debate Limitations on Individual Amendments in Complex Unanimous Consent Agreements for Key Vote Measures, Selected Congresses, 1955–84   117

4-6. Restrictions on Amendments in Complex Unanimous Consent Agreements, Selected Congresses, 1955–84   118

5-1. Per Capita Amendment Sponsorship in the House and Senate, by Seniority, Selected Congresses, 1955–86   136

5-2. Amendments Adopted in the House and Senate, by Seniority of Sponsors, Selected Congresses, 1955–86   138

5-3. Estimates of the Effects of Committee Activity, Committee Position, Seniority, and Party on Amending Activity in the House, by Committee Membership, 99th Congress   160

5-4. Estimates of the Effects of Committee Activity, Committee Position, Seniority, and Party on Amending Activity in the House, by Type of Rule, 99th Congress   164

5-5. Estimates of the Effects of Committee Activity, Committee Position, Seniority, and Party on Amending Activity in the Senate, by Committee Membership, 99th Congress   165

6-1. Index of Floor Amending Activity for House Committees, Selected Congresses, 1955–86   178

6-2. Index of Floor Amending Activity for Senate Committees, Selected Congresses, 1955–86   179

6-3. Secondary Amendments Subject to a Recorded Vote, House and Senate, Combined 96th and 99th Congresses, 1979–80, 1985–86   185

6-4. Percentage of House Special Rules that Were Restrictive or Closed, by Committee, Selected Congresses, 1975–80, 1981–86   189

6-5. House Amending Activity Conducted under Restrictive Special Rules, by Committee, Selected Congresses, 1975–80, 1981–86   192

7-1. Methods of Resolving Differences between the Chambers, by Type of Measure, Selected Congresses, 1955–86   206

7-2. Size of Conference Delegations, Selected Congresses, 1955–86   210

7-3. Conferences with Noncommittee and Limited-Purpose Conferees, Selected Congresses, 1955–86   212

7-4. Percentage of Conferences Subject to Roll Call Votes on Motions to Adopt Report, Instruct Conferees, or Recommit Report, Selected Congresses, 1955–86   226

Figures

-->>X<<-

1-1. Alternative Models of Decisionmaking   4

2-1. House Floor Amendments, by Type of Measure, Selected Congresses, 1955–86   16

2-2. Measures Subject to Floor Amendments in the House, Selected Congresses, 1955–86   18

2-3. House Amendments Adopted, by Type of Measure, Selected Congresses, 1955–86   19

2-4. Mean Turnout for Amendment Votes, by Type of Vote, Selected Congresses, 1955–86   22

3-1. Number of Limitation Amendments Offered to House Appropriations Bills, 88th–99th Congresses (1963–84)   60

4-1. Number of Senate Floor Amendments, by Type of Measure, Selected Congresses, 1955–86   89

4-2. Measures Subject to Floor Amendments in the Senate, Selected Congresses, 1955–86   90

4-3. Amending Activity in the House and Senate, Selected Congresses, 1955–86   93

5-1. Percentage of Floor Amendments Sponsored by a Member Not Sitting on the Committee of Origin, by Chamber, Selected Congresses, 1955–86   143

5-2. Percentage of Members Sponsoring Floor Amendments to Measures from Committees Other than Their Own, by Chamber, Selected Congresses, 1955–86   144

5-3. Percentage of Floor Amendments Adopted, by Sponsors' Committee Membership and Chamber, Selected Congresses, 1955–86   145

5-4. Per Capita Amendment Sponsorship, by Party and Chamber, Selected Congresses, 1955–86   148

5-5. Percentage of Amendments Adopted, by Sponsors' Party and Chamber, Selected Congresses, 1955-86   149

5-6. Percentage of Amendments Adopted in House, by
     Sponsors' Seniority and Party, Selected Congresses,
     1955–86   150

5-7. Percentage of Amendments Adopted in House, by
     Sponsors' Committee Membership and Party, Selected
     Congresses, 1955–86   151

5-8. Members' Amending Activity, by Chamber, Selected
     Congresses, 1955–86   152

7-1. House Floor Amendments Offered to Defense
     Authorization Bills, 87th–99th Congresses (1961–86)   217

Call to Order

CHAPTER ONE

Floor Politics in Transition

IN LIGHT OF what has been written about Congress over the decades, it may seem foolish to write about the importance of its chambers' floors in policymaking. The conventional wisdom, well grounded in experience, is that the power of Congress is vested in its standing committees. As Woodrow Wilson put it in 1885, "It is not far from the truth to say that Congress in session is Congress on public exhibition, whilst Congress in its committee-rooms is Congress at work."[1] This conventional wisdom is a cornerstone of studies of the modern Congress as well. Donald Matthews began his 1960 examination of Senate committees this way: "'The committees are where the *real* work of the Senate is done,' so goes a familiar Capitol Hill refrain. Its constant repetition seems justifiable."[2]

I argue here, however, that during the 1960s and 1970s the House and Senate floors were transformed into far more important arenas of substantive policymaking. As a result, decisionmaking in Congress took on a more collegial character, one in which rank-and-file and minority party members took advantage of new opportunities on the floor to exercise their formal equality as partners in policymaking. The transformation of floor decisionmaking had unanticipated consequences and stimulated countermoves to moderate its effects. Neither chamber had fully adjusted to the changes by the late 1970s, although the House was in the process of doing so. By the late 1980s, House decisionmaking had been reshaped by new legislative procedures and strategies, giving the House a different character than it had in the 1970s, while the Senate continued to struggle with an unpredictable, floor-oriented process.

The dramatic changes in the character of floor politics were illustrated in April 1988, when the annual defense authorization bill came to the House floor. By the time the House prepared to debate the bill on the floor,

1. Woodrow Wilson, *Congressional Government* (New York: Meridian, 1956), p. 69.
2. Donald R. Matthews, *U.S. Senators and Their World* (Vintage Books, 1960), p. 147.

240 amendments had been submitted for consideration. Amendments concerned such complex and important topics as the strategic defense initiative, chemical weapons, U.S. obligations to NATO, and the MX and Midgetman missile programs. The House adopted amendments that enforced the numerical limits on nuclear weapons specified by the unratified 1979 SALT II treaty, cut spending on the strategic defense initiative, and restricted tests of space-based weapons that are not consistent with Congress's interpretation of the antiballistic missile treaty. Armed Services Chairman Les Aspin took the challenges to his committee's recommendations well. "There was a race to see if we could get to 600 amendments before the Navy got 600 ships," Aspin said, referring to the Reagan administration's defense goals, adding that "I think we're going to beat them. We'll get to 600 by 1991 for sure."[3] The 1988 floor experience contrasted sharply with the treatment of defense legislation in the 1950s and 1960s. During 1961–66, for example, the first five years in which defense authorization bills were adopted annually, only three floor amendments were offered in the Senate and only seven in the House, and only three minor amendments were adopted.

The history of defense authorization bills is part of a much larger transformation in the character of floor decisionmaking. Between the mid-1950s and the late 1970s, the total number of floor amendments expanded from just over 400 to nearly 1,700 per Congress in the House and from about 600 to 1,800 in the Senate. Many things had changed by the late 1970s, not the least of which was the willingness of the parent chambers to challenge committee recommendations.

But Congress did not stand still in the 1980s. In fact, it is now well into a new era of floor decisionmaking, its third distinct era since the 1950s. The three eras were more clearly delineated in the House, where the fairly stable pattern of the 1950s and early 1960s erupted into the turbulent reform period of the 1970s and then settled into yet another distinctive pattern in the 1980s. In the Senate, too, the 1980s have had a special character, as budget politics have altered the structure of the congressional agenda. In both houses, amending activity subsided somewhat in the 1980s, but not to the level of the 1960s. These patterns of change in congressional floor politics since the 1950s require important qualifications of the standard propositions about the distribution of power in Congress. This book identifies the ways congressional decisionmaking has changed and offers a new, more accurate view of the structure of power in Congress.

---

3. "Amendment City," *The New York Times*, April 21, 1988, p. A28.

The Contours of Congressional Decisionmaking Processes

In a broad sense, this book is about the changing contours of decision-making processes in Congress. Unfortunately, characterizing the ways in which Congress makes policy decisions is a tricky business. Although the basic mechanics of the legislative process are familiar to most readers of this book, even the casual observer of Congress recognizes that there are many procedural variations in the treatment of major legislation. The role of subcommittees varies from measure to measure, full committee scrutiny varies, floor procedure is adjusted to individual measures, conference committees are sometimes crucial and sometimes avoided, and party leadership involvement is sometimes extensive and sometimes negligible.[4] Many generalizations about congressional politics tend to obscure the great variety in the legislative routes taken by bills and resolutions.

Nevertheless, a general framework that abstracts from the mechanics of legislative procedure will prove useful. Two central features of any decisionmaking process are the number of participants and the number of decisionmaking units that structure their participation. The conventional wisdom about the modern Congress is that a very large number of members are active participants but their contributions are made within the committees or subcommittees on which they serve. The scope of congressional activity is partitioned into dozens of committee and subcommittee jurisdictions in order to create a division of labor. In this particular combination of participants and units, the process appears to be very decentralized—the terms "committee government" or even "subcommittee government" are used to highlight the location in the process where most decisions are made. This combination is depicted in the upper right quadrant of figure 1-1.

At the other extreme, a single participant might determine policy outcomes for the body. All power is centralized in the holder of a single office. In a hierarchical bureaucracy, all decisions may flow upward but ultimately are controlled by a central decisionmaker. In Congress, this could be a party leader, although a fully centralized process is difficult to imagine, in part because of the bicameral structure of Congress.

Congressional decisionmaking processes often are characterized as being at some location on the continuum running from centralized to decentral-

4. On the remarkable number of ways legislation is brought to, and considered on, the House floor, see Stanley Bach, "Patterns of Floor Consideration in the House of Representatives," paper prepared for the Center for American Political Studies, Harvard University, December 9, 1988.

FIGURE 1-1. *Alternative Models of Decisionmaking*

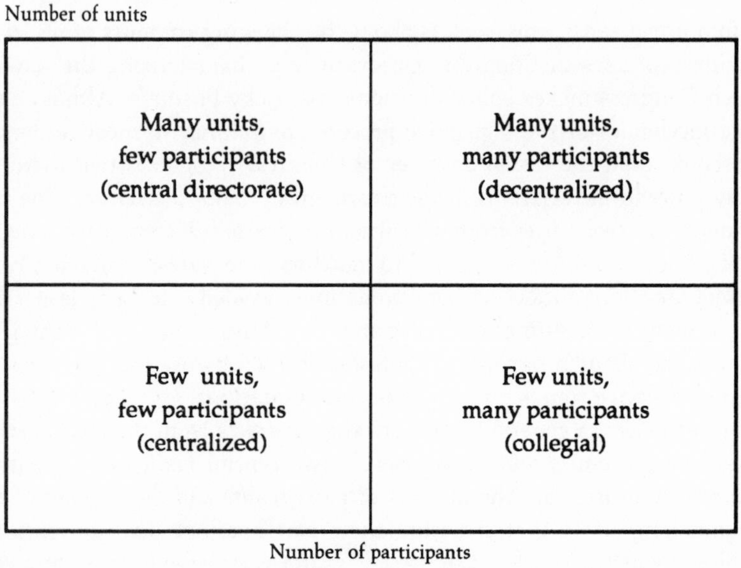

Number of units

Many units, few participants (central directorate)	Many units, many participants (decentralized)
Few units, few participants (centralized)	Few units, many participants (collegial)

Number of participants

ized (lower left to upper right quadrants of figure 1-1). But figure 1-1 suggests that there are important other possibilities that must be considered. The combination of few participants operating through many different organizational units (upper left in figure 1-1) has never been common to Congress. The closest Congress has come to such a form was when a handful of senators served as both committee chairmen and party leaders during the late nineteenth century.

The collegial pattern, however, is a possibility in Congress. The collegial pattern reflects broad participation within one or few organizational units. The chamber floors, for example, may give all members an opportunity to offer proposals in the form of amendments and to join in the debate or deliberations about proposals.[5] Pure collegial decisionmaking is grounded in egalitarian norms that encourage and tolerate the full participation of any member seeking to influence outcomes. Because of various rules and

5. In order to avoid confusion, it is worth noting that the term "the floor" is used in three related senses on Capitol Hill and in this book. The most obvious sense is the physical location in the Capitol building. A second sense refers to a specific stage in the legislative process that normally follows a report from a standing committee recommending a measure for enactment. And a third sense is as a synonym for a parent chamber, the collectivity of representatives or senators. All three senses are implied in most uses of the term in this book, except where the context makes clear a narrower meaning. To speak of the growing importance of the floor, then, is to imply that the parent chambers, usually meeting at a certain place and a certain stage in the legislative process, are more decisive in shaping policy outcomes.

informal practices structuring agendas and limiting participation, few decisionmaking bodies achieve the pure collegial form, but it is an ideal that many pursue. The ideal type is reflected in most congressional discussions about reform, as well as in members' everyday discourse.

Powerful forces propel Congress toward a decentralized pattern of decisionmaking. A complex division of labor is required to manage the tremendous work load of the institution. Members' attention must necessarily be focused on the work of their own committees and subcommittees; thus few members can regularly scrutinize the work of other committees and subcommittees. The political interests of individual members reinforce the institutional pressures toward decentralization. Factors such as geographically segregated constituencies, frequent elections, and weak national parties foster parochialism. Parochialism, in turn, encourages members to prefer a fragmented, decentralized decisionmaking process that allows them to focus their energies on matters important to their home districts and states.

But counterbalancing forces are present as well. A fully decentralized system limits the ability of members to influence decisions on matters that do not fall within the jurisdiction of their committees or subcommittees. Members with wide-ranging personal and constituency interests may find a collegial process better suited to their needs. This would be a more floor-oriented process in which the ability to challenge committee recommendations was preserved by formal rules, informal norms, and the distribution of resources.

A tension between preferences for a decentralized form and preferences for a collegial form of decisionmaking will exist in any legislative body in which individual members care about a wide range of issues but must take a special interest in decisions affecting local constituencies or must manage large work loads. Further tensions will arise when legislators become concerned about coherent and rapid action on policy problems, which usually leads to preferences for a more centralized process. The pieces of a policy can be integrated more fully and decisions made more expeditiously when a central decisionmaker controls the process. The tensions among these competing preferences produce a restlessness in Congress about its own decisionmaking processes.

This book's central argument is that decisionmaking has moved in the direction of a more collegial form since the 1950s, but this movement has been far from complete and has been arrested in the House of the 1980s. The pattern of change differs in the two chambers of Congress, and change has sometimes occurred gradually and sometimes in fits and starts in both chambers. The underlying tensions among the three forms of decisionmaking have continued to tug at the House and Senate. And pressures for change continue as institutional and individual needs evolve. But the overall pattern since the 1950s is unmistakable. Decisionmaking in both chambers now is substantially more floor-oriented than it was at mid-century.

Context

Many forces of change in American politics converged to expand the number and the importance of decisions made on the House and Senate floors in recent decades. Demands from a rapidly changing external environment, shifting internal incentives, and expanding resources all played an important role in altering the importance of floor decisions in Congress.

Unfortunately, pinpointing the particular contribution of each of these forces to congressional change is not possible. Reciprocal and reinforcing effects abound, making causal linkages among the forces of change difficult to demonstrate. Congress's extreme permeability further complicates matters. No central authority in Congress determines who gets elected to it; no one in Congress meaningfully regulates who has access to its members; no one in Congress single-handedly arranges the institution's policy agenda. As a result, the boundaries between Congress and its environment, the identity of its effective decisionmakers, the nature of the tasks performed, and other features are considerably more ambiguous and variable than in many other institutional or organizational settings.

Nevertheless, important developments external and internal to Congress clearly have altered members' preferences for how they conduct their affairs. Since the 1950s, an important thrust of the change has been for a more collegial process—one in which members not holding formal leadership positions, particularly committee chairmanships, have a substantial voice in shaping policy outcomes. A brief review of these developments will set the stage for the examination of the changing decisionmaking patterns in subsequent chapters.

External Changes

Perhaps the most important developments molding congressional decisionmaking practices were dramatic changes in the policy problems the institution faced. The volume, complexity, and controversy of issues on the national agenda are manifested on the floors of Congress. The 1960s and 1970s brought a succession of issues—civil rights, poverty, the Vietnam war, consumer protection, nuclear weapons, energy—that engendered intense, polarized floor action in the House and Senate. Most major issues eventually find their way to the floor of both chambers, even though the committee and party systems serve to screen and focus issues before they reach the floor. Such issues not only stimulate the personal interest of members of Congress, but also restructure the political environment of Congress, which in turn reshapes the incentives and disincentives that influence members' behavior.

Demands from constituents to pursue more issues on the floor are now much greater than they were in the 1950s. Members have much larger and more heterogeneous constituencies. The average House district has grown since the 1950s from 345,000 to 520,000, while the average senator must now serve a constituency that averages over 4.5 million people. Thanks to new communications technology, far more home newspapers and television stations cover members' Washington activity, often with the help of the many Washington news services. And winning reelection costs much more for most members and involves greater competition for campaign contributions. Each one of these developments increased the incentives for members to champion causes and demonstrate responsiveness to the various constituencies.

New issues, an expanded federal government, and technological developments have helped to stimulate a remarkable surge in the number and variety of organized interest groups in Washington. In the early 1980s, about 30 percent of all national nonprofit organizations had their headquarters in Washington, up from about 20 percent in the early 1970s.[6] More corporations and state and local governments opened offices in Washington as well. Washington representation for corporations and other organizations also was boosted by the growth of political action committees in the aftermath of the campaign finance reforms of the early 1970s. In short, the number and organizational capacity of outsiders seeking members' time and effort increased dramatically in the 1960s and 1970s, intensifying the pressure on members to respond to the entreaties of outside groups looking for legislators to champion their causes.

Not surprisingly, Congress's work load has grown tremendously since the 1950s. Probably the best indicator is the total number of pages enacted into law in each Congress. In the Congresses of the 1950s the average was 1,908 pages, a figure that increased to 2,439 in the 1960s and 4,049 in the 1970s.[7] Floor amendments certainly contributed to the number of pages

---

6. Robert H. Salisbury, "Washington Lobbyists: A Collective Portrait," in Allan J. Cigler and Burdett A. Loomis, eds., *Interest Group Politics*, 2d ed. (Washington: CQ Press, 1986), p. 149. Also see Jack L. Walker, "The Origins and Maintenance of Interest Groups in America," *American Political Science Review*, vol. 77 (June 1983), pp. 390–406.

7. Norman J. Ornstein, Thomas E. Mann, and Michael J. Malbin, *Vital Statistics on Congress, 1987–1988* (Washington: Congressional Quarterly, 1987), p. 170.

enacted into law, but the larger, more complex legislation reported from committees also created bigger targets for floor amendments. Whatever the cause, floor sessions consumed many more hours as the work load expanded. In the 1950s the House averaged 1,064 hours of floor session a Congress, which increased to 1,447 hours in the 1960s and 1,695 in the 1970s. Senate sessions lengthened from 1,809 hours to 2,137 hours to 2,273 hours in the same three decades.[8]

It would be surprising if such changes in the policy environment and legislative responsibilities did not affect the kind of people attracted to service in Congress. A common observation, and an accurate one, is that the type of politicians elected to Congress has changed. Senate liberals elected between 1958 and 1964 were the first to be singled out as a "new breed."[9] They were noted for their policy activism, their interest in self-promotion, and their commitment to challenging the established power structure in Congress. Similarly, many House Democrats elected in the early 1970s have been labeled a new breed, as have many Republicans elected to both chambers more recently.[10] One long-time observer of congressional politics described the new-breed member this way: "His absorbing interest is governmental policy. He came to Congress with a sense of mission, even a mandate, to have an impact on the legislative process. He is impatient . . . [and] has no habit of being deferential to the established and the powerful, and he will not be so in Congress, either in committee or on the floor."[11] Whatever the causes for the change—less dependence on parties for election and reelection and more independent entrepreneurialism top the list— it is clear that members are now far more assertive in nearly all aspects of daily activity than their predecessors of the 1950s.

Internal Changes

Several developments internal to Congress altered the context of floor decisionmaking as well. Perhaps what is most important, the prefloor stages of the process were subject to significant reforms, particularly in the House. The grip of House committee chairmen over decisions of their committees was loosened considerably by the reforms of the 1970s.[12] Chair-

8. Ornstein and others, *Vital Statistics*, pp. 165–67.

9. See Michael Foley, *The New Senate: Liberal Influence on a Conservative Institution, 1959–1972* (Yale University Press, 1980), especially chap. 4.

10. For example, see Richard E. Cohen, "Strains Appear as 'New Breed' Democrats Move to Control Party in the House," *National Journal*, June 25, 1983, pp. 1328–31.

11. James L. Sundquist, *The Decline and Resurgence of Congress* (Brookings, 1981), p. 371.

12. For discussions of these reforms, see Roger H. Davidson and Walter J. Oleszek, *Con-*

men could no longer withhold legislation from the floor single-handedly, a self-selection process for subcommittee assignments was instituted by House Democrats, and subcommittee chairmanships became elective. With the exception of the smallest committees, committees were required to establish subcommittees with fixed, written jurisdictions. And, unless a committee majority decides otherwise, chairmen were required to refer legislation to subcommittees. The Senate never adopted reforms of committee procedure as sweeping as those in the House, although it did adopt rules changes requiring open meetings, limiting proxy voting, and providing for recorded voting in committees.

The demise of autocratic chairmen was accompanied by improved opportunities for rank-and-file members to participate in committee decisionmaking. In both chambers, committees were expanded in size to accommodate members seeking more opportunities to pursue their policy and political interests. Between 1955 and 1987, the average number of standing committee assignments for members grew from 1.2 to over 1.7 in the House and from 2.2 to 2.9 in the Senate. At the same time, the number and average size of subcommittees expanded, creating new opportunities within committees for rank-and-file members. The average number of subcommittee assignments increased from 1.6 to 3.8 in the House. The Senate average grew from 4.8 subcommittee assignments in 1955 to 7.0 in 1987.[13] Of course, as the number of subcommittees increased, so did the number of subcommittee leadership positions. About half the majority party representatives now hold a committee or subcommittee chairmanship, while nearly all majority party senators hold at least one chairmanship.

These changes in committee decisionmaking practices had profound implications for floor politics. Weaker full committee chairmen were less able to mold consensus positions in their committees, making it more likely that disputes among committee members would spill onto the floor. Subcommittee chairmen, who assumed more responsibility for managing legislation on the floor, often lacked the experience and political clout to take over where the full committee chairmen left off. As a result, unfriendly amendments were more likely to go unanticipated by committee leaders, and committees appeared to be more vulnerable to attack. Moreover, rank-and-file members, with more committee and subcommittee assignments, were more likely to have a committee-based connection to an issue, to de-

gress Against Itself (Indiana University Press, 1977); and Steven S. Smith and Christopher J. Deering, Committees in Congress (Washington: CQ Press, 1984), chap. 2.

13. Ornstein and others, Vital Statistics, p. 130.

velop a wide range of personal and political interests, and therefore to have a reason for offering amendments on the floor.

Improved staff resources reinforced the stimulative effects of environmental and intracommittee developments on floor amending activity. Personal staff allotments increased greatly. In the House, the cap on personal staff increased from eight to ten in 1965 and to eighteen in 1975. In the Senate, the average personal office grew from twelve staff members in 1957 to thirty-nine in 1980.[14] Committee staffs also expanded in both chambers, with subcommittee as well as minority party leaders on committees gaining staff assistance. In the Senate, each senator gained additional personal staff to help manage committee responsibilities, a practice that has been adopted for a few committees in the House as well. And all members have access to the expanded services of the Congressional Research Service, the General Accounting Office, and other congressional service units. Thus nearly all members gained the means to write amendments, publicize their proposals, prepare for floor debate, and attract support.

New issues, larger constituencies, more pressure groups, a heavier work load, less cohesive committees, improved resources, and more assertive members have all played a part in stimulating more floor activity in the decades since the 1950s. As powerful as the effects of changes in incentives and capacity are, they are not the whole story. There must be opportunities for the new mix of incentives and resources to manifest itself. Formal floor procedures and associated informal practices structure those opportunities.

Rules do many things in Congress, as in all institutions. In addition to establishing the most visible structural features of an institution (committees, leadership positions), rules define policy and procedural jurisdictions, establish sequences or stages that relate the decisions of the various units to each other, specify criteria for making decisions at the various stages, and limit the content and timing of policy proposals. For members pursuing their own political goals, rules create opportunities and impose constraints, sometimes producing distinct advantages for certain members and disadvantages for others. Consequently, rules affect members' strategies by shaping their expectations about others' behavior. Among the affected strategic decisions are decisions to go to the floor.

Over time, formal rules and informal practices adjust to each other and to changing political conditions. At some points, chamber majorities (or supermajorities) become intolerant of the advantage gained by a minority from a particular rule or practice, and they force a change. Procedural reform may have repercussions for the effect of other rules and practices,

14. Ornstein and others, *Vital Statistics*, p. 142.

stimulate alterations in legislative strategies, affect the kinds of political objectives it is feasible to pursue, and, ultimately, reshape policy outcomes.

As the next three chapters will explore, changing rules and associated practices have played an important role in shaping floor activity. In the House, reform of voting methods, special rules, and other procedural changes have affected the opportunities and constraints for using the floor to pursue political goals. Change in the Senate has been less directly tied to reform of formal rules, although the adjustments in the cloture rule and related leadership practices have changed the incentives and disincentives for the use of the floor.

In sum, both internal incentives and resources and external pressures have driven more important policy decisions to the floors of the House and Senate. All pressures for change have not been relieved, however. To the contrary, the collegial elements of decisionmaking processes in the House and Senate often are somewhat inconsistent with the continuing bias in favor of a decentralized system. The egalitarianism of a collegial process often conflicts with the special status granted to committee chairmen in a decentralized process. And both collegial and decentralized processes conflict with the occasional interest in centralizing some policymaking functions in central party leaders in order to produce timely and coherent policy. In an institution where internal processes ultimately are determined by the collective membership and where there is great variation in the' policy and political tasks that must be managed, the result is a nearly continuous tug-of-war about how the institution should conduct its affairs.

Additional Themes

The substantive focus on the floors of the House and Senate, so conceived, still may appear to be an unnecessarily confining approach to addressing the broad patterns of change in congressional decisionmaking, but that focus turns out to be useful. All legislation eventually must be approved on the House and Senate floors, where voting alignments, amending activity, and patterns of participation tend to reflect the forces shaping congressional politics generally. It is where much public discussion on major issues takes place in Congress; the advent of televised floor sessions makes it all the more important that the function of floor activity be properly understood. And the floor is the one place where all members of each chamber are formally equal. Each member has one vote at the floor stage, regardless of seniority, party affiliation, or committee assignment. At other stages—in committee meetings, party caucuses, or conference sessions—participation is restricted in some way. Thus, while a sweeping analysis of prefloor and postfloor politics is not attempted here, observations of the floor will permit some informed interpretation of broader changes in Congress. A relatively rich literature on committees, leaders, and parties already exists and will contribute to the interpretations offered throughout the book.

Assessing the importance of floor decisionmaking is not easy. Ideally, the contribution of each stage of the legislative process to the ultimate legislative product could be determined, assigning weights to the various provisions of the legislation according to some measure of their policy significance. Generalizing about all legislation in a Congress by assigning weights to the individual measures according to their significance would be the first step in assessing the relative importance of the various stages of the process. Even this first step is impractical, if not impossible.

Other evidence also would be required to make inferences about the role of the floor. Knowledge of the policy preferences of the participants at each stage would be required. Without some direct evidence of policy preferences, inferences about who wins or loses and about the location of vital decisions would have to be highly qualified. For example, floor concurrence with committee recommendations may reflect the power of committees to extract support from potential opponents on the floor, the ability of the floor to manipulate wayward committees to report measures the floor approves, or genuine policy agreement between the committee and the floor. Thus, even if the content of policy decisions at each stage could be evaluated, inferring the influence of the floor would remain a very hazardous enterprise. Unfortunately, gathering systematic data on members' policy preferences over many issues and years is not possible.

I have pursued several less than ideal alternative strategies. Central to the study is the record of floor amending activity in the House and Senate. The amending record has very seldom been exploited, but it offers a view of floor activity essential to understanding how the role of the floor has changed. Appendix 1 provides a primer on floor procedures for readers not familiar with them; appendix 2 outlines how I gathered amending data.

The relationship between amending activity, politics, and procedures is an intriguing subject for both politicians and political scientists. Daily participants in congressional politics recognize that process matters because it may create advantages for the proponents of some policy interests at the expense of others. Knowledge of the implications of process is gathered through hard experience, accumulated and sometimes passed on from one politician to another. Political scientists have sought to formulate more systematic theories about the effects of process on policy outcomes. In recent years, investigators have pursued deductive, and sometimes mathematical, models of the connection, often seeking to draw a parallel between the operation of the models and the workings of Congress.

The ways in which the two chambers manage and limit floor amending activity is of special interest because floor procedures, both formally and informally defined, have evolved in important ways since the 1950s. In the House, especially, the methods by which bills are considered and amended on the floor have changed in ways that directly affect the volume and success of amending activity. In chapters 2-4 I explore the aggregate patterns of amending action in the two chambers.

A secondary theme in chapters 2-4 is the role of the two parties in each chamber. Particularly in the House, the ebbs and flows in the character of floor decisionmaking were a response to interparty competition. In fact, the search for procedural advantage by the two parties in the majoritarian House has been a driving force behind much of the change in the use of the floor as an arena for policymaking since the 1950s. Interparty competition was also important in the Senate, but the Senate's dependence on extraordinary majorities and unanimous consent for many decisions reduces the probability that change in formal and informal practices will advantage one party over the other.

In chapters 5-7 I disaggregate some of the broad patterns addressed in chapters 2-4 and provide important qualifications on the nature of change in congressional decisionmaking practices. The changing patterns of participation among individual members of Congress are investigated in chapter 5. During the 1950s, widely recognized norms of apprenticeship and committee deference served to limit effective participation to a few senior committee leaders. Moreover, the distribution of resources and parliamentary prerogatives advantaged senior, majority party, committee chairmen in both chambers. Changing norms, resources, and procedures have affected nearly every stage in congressional decisionmaking processes, but they have not been examined systematically for their effects on floor participation in either the House or Senate.

In chapter 6 I demonstrate that the pattern of change in floor experience has varied considerably among the committees of Congress. Some committees have managed to escape waves of floor amendments, while others frequently have their legislation picked apart by opponents on the floor. These differences caution against broad statements about committee power. Interpreting the implications of floor developments for committee power is a delicate problem. The strategic, highly complex, and ever-changing context of congressional politics makes definitive assessments of winning and losing, degrees of autonomy, and relative power nearly impossible.

Activity at subsequent stages in the legislative process, particularly at the conference stage, is examined in chapter 7. The relationship between the floors and conference committees is vital to understanding the importance of the developments on the floors themselves. Dominance of conferences by senior members of the committees originating the legislation necessarily calls into question the significance of floor amending activity. The losses committees suffer on the floor may in many circumstances be recouped in conference, leaving floor amendments with little net effect on policy outcomes. But here, too, committee autonomy has been challenged.

A framework for evaluating reform proposals is the subject of chapter 8. Neither chamber's floor operates in a manner consistent with ideal forms of discussion and debate, but the chambers exhibit distinctive preferences for the type of discussion their members consider most appropriate. The excesses of each type are the primary targets of internal and external criticism. A different mix of reform is required in each chamber.

To put the central issues more concretely, the book seeks answers to the following questions: Do the patterns of increased amending activity represent a significant change in the importance of the chamber floors as arenas for policymaking? What consequences did formal and informal changes in floor procedure have for the function of the floors in the legislative process? Is there evidence from floor behavior to support the view that prescriptive norms restraining participation have disintegrated? Did committee autonomy decline? How have committees responded to the new patterns of decisionmaking? Has there been a convergence in the procedure, function, and importance of floor decisionmaking in the House and Senate, or are differences between the chambers so great that generalizations about the importance of the floor stage must always be qualified in chamber-specific ways? Answers to these questions will not be concise and unequivocal, but they are vital to understanding the character of the modern Congress.

CHAPTER TWO

Revolution in the House

THE HOUSE of Representatives has passed through two phases in the nature of floor activity during the past four decades, and it now is well into a third phase. The first phase, running from the 1950s to the early 1970s, was characterized by a mushrooming congressional agenda, gradually expanding floor activity, and the absence of recorded voting in the Committee of the Whole.[1] The second phase began quite abruptly in 1973 with the full implementation of rules providing for recorded electronic voting in the Committee of the Whole. The current and third phase was in full bloom by 1981, the first year of the Reagan administration, although elements of this new phase began to accumulate in the late 1970s.

The shift from the first to the second phase in the early 1970s represented a revolutionary change in floor politics. The number of floor amendments skyrocketed when members looked to the floor as a new outlet for expression and as a court to which committee decisions might be appealed. Relations between the parties, between junior and senior members, and between committees and the floor were altered with the help of important structural and procedural reforms. House decisionmaking became far less predictable as nearly all members had more opportunities to offer floor amendments with some hope of success. The tidy decentralized process characterizing the first phase was transformed into a somewhat strained combination of decentralized and collegial elements. The distinctively committee-centered politics of the House became more fluid. Most policy decisions continued to be made in committee or subcommittee, but more decisions were challenged on the floor. The strains produced a decade of move and countermove, as the parties, factions, and leaders of the House adapted to the postreform environment of floor decisionmaking. The transformation from the first to the second phase is the subject of this chapter.

---

1. See appendix 1 for a brief review of floor procedures in both chambers.

FIGURE 2-1. *House Floor Amendments, by Type of Measure, Selected Congresses, 1955–86*

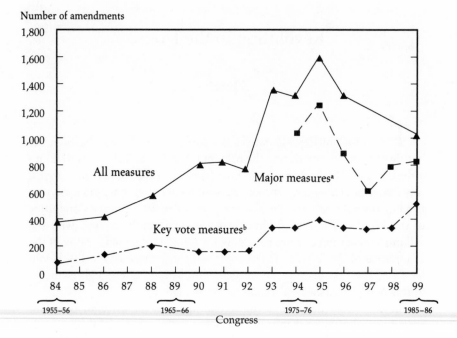

Number of amendments

SOURCE: See appendix 2.
   a. Measures that received a special rule for initial floor consideration.
   b. Measures associated with a "key vote" as identified by *Congressional Quarterly*.

An Overview of House Amending Activity

The explosion of floor amendments is a core feature of changing House politics since the 1950s. This development is so rich and varied that it is worth examining it from several points of view.

The most obvious features of the pattern of expanding amending activity are the break points denoting the three phases (figure 2-1). The first phase, the period up to the 92d Congress (1971–72), shows a gradual increase in amending activity, reaching a plateau in the late 1960s. The second phase follows the explosion of amending activity in the 93d Congress (1973–74), with a peak in the 95th Congress (1977–78)—President Jimmy Carter's first Congress and Thomas P. "Tip" O'Neill's first Congress as Speaker of the House. The third phase is in full view by the 97th Congress (1981–82), when there was a substantial drop in amending activity, followed by a partial recovery in the 98th and 99th.[2] The 1980s represent a distinctive pattern that contrasts sharply with the hyperactivity of the 1970s.

These patterns also are reflected in the amending activity on politically significant legislation. One way to identify the most important issues is to draw upon measures subject to a "key vote." In each Congress, the *Congressional Quarterly Almanac* reports twenty-five to thirty issues its editors consider to be of greatest national political or policy significance.[3] The measures associated with key votes constitute a thin layer of major legislation that tends to receive the personal attention of presidents and congressional party leaders. They are seldom more than 1 or 2 percent of all measures considered on the floor. Another way to identify important measures is to consider measures that receive a special rule for initial floor consideration ("major measures" in figure 2-1). This broader band of legislation comprises about 20 percent of all legislation reaching the House floor. Special rule measures are the targets of more than three-quarters of all floor amendments in recent years. On average, however, key vote measures stimulate even more amending activity than special rule legislation.

In the key vote stratum, the break between the first and second phases is just as sharp as for all legislation, but the break between the second and third phases is not visible. If anything, the trend toward more amending activity continues in the 1980s for the upper stratum of key vote measures. In contrast, the broader band of major measures faced significantly fewer floor amendments in the 1980s than in the 1970s, which is consistent with the view that the Congresses of the 1980s comprise a distinctive era. Just why and how the 1980s are so distinctive is the subject of the next chapter.

A different perspective is offered by the proportion of measures considered on the floor to which amendments were offered, as figure 2-2 shows. The proportion increased nearly monotonically during the late 1950s and 1960s, peaked in the mid-1970s, and remained between 15 and 20 percent

2. While the number of amendments for all measures was not collected for the 97th and 98th Congresses (1981–1984), the pattern of a dip in the 97th Congress and some recovery thereafter is visible in the number of recorded votes, which tracks well with the number of amendments. In the four Congresses of the 1979–86 period, the number of recorded votes was 1,276, 812, 906, and 890, respectively. Appendix 2 provides estimates of the number of amendments for the Congresses for which data were not collected. See Norman J. Ornstein, Thomas E. Mann, and Michael J. Malbin, *Vital Statistics on Congress, 1987–1988* (Washington: Congressional Quarterly, 1987), p. 165.

3. Key votes are not without their problems, of course. Over the years, the criteria employed for the selection of key votes have varied somewhat. Moreover, there is no practical way to examine the reliability of the application of the criteria specified. For some background, see Steven A. Shull and James M. Vanderleeuw, "What Do Key Votes Measure?" *Legislative Studies Quarterly*, vol. 12 (November 1987), pp. 573–82.

FIGURE 2-2. *Measures Subject to Floor Amendments in the House, Selected Congresses, 1955–86*

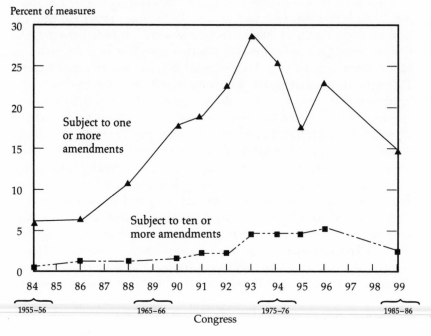

Percent of measures

SOURCE: See appendix 2.

thereafter. The proportion then declined further in the 1980s, consistent with the contraction in the total number of amendments. This pattern is due, at least in major part, to innovations in the special rules governing the amendment stage in the Committee of the Whole and a contraction in Congress's policy agenda, as chapter 3 will explore.

Not all amendments are successful or important. Indeed, it is conceivable that the proportion of successful amendments declined as the number of amendments increased. Just the opposite happened during the 1970s, as figure 2-3 shows. The success rates both for all amendments and for amendments to major legislation increased while the volume of amending activity increased. Another possibility is that a large portion of amending activity since the early 1970s has been trivial, producing amendments that were more successful but of lesser political import. There is some evidence that this is the case. One indication is that there has been a slight increase in the percentage of amendments disposed of by voice vote.[4] Another in-

4. Amendments voted on by voice votes averaged 64 percent of all amendments in the five

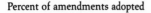

FIGURE 2-3. *House Amendments Adopted, by Type of Measure, Selected Congresses, 1955–86*

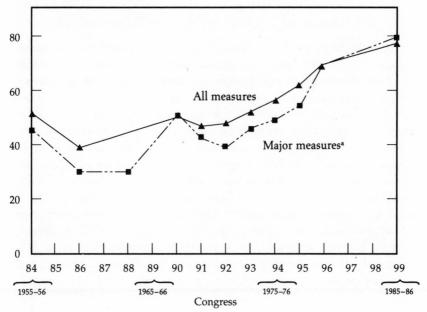

Percent of amendments adopted

SOURCE: See appendix 2.
a. Measures that received a special rule for initial floor consideration.

dication is that the percentage of amendments leading to a contested vote—a 60–40 split or closer—has dropped a little since the mid-1970s.[5] But the change in neither indicator is large enough to account for the increase in successful amendments.

The case seems overwhelming that the floor has become a more important location for policymaking in the House of Representatives. Moreover, the aggregate patterns of floor amendment activity show distinctive periods in the nature of floor decisionmaking. And yet, because of the complexity

---

post-1973 Congresses for which data are available; they averaged 60 percent in the six Congresses in the pre-1973 period.

5. The six pre-1973 Congresses for which data are available had a mean of 18.0 percent contested amendments, while the five post-1973 Congresses had a mean of 14.9 percent, dropping all the way to 11.4 percent in the 99th Congress. Contested amendments are defined throughout the book as amendments that were subject to a teller or recorded vote for which the vote split was 60–40 (or 40–60) or closer.

of change that underlies these straightforward patterns, it will pay to suspend judgment until more of the evidence is considered.

Domination by Committee Chairmen before Reform

Power in the House of the 1950s centered in the chairmen of its standing committees. The Legislative Reorganization Act of 1946 had consolidated the House committee system into nineteen standing committees, each with a fairly large jurisdiction. The 1946 act also guaranteed professional staff assistance to all standing committees. Committees varied widely in their internal organization and decisionmaking processes, but the formal power to organize the staff and subcommittees, as well as to set agendas and control the flow of legislation, resided with the full committee chairmen, with only a few exceptions. A disproportionate number of chairmanships were held by southern Democrats, by virtue of their committee seniority. Largely conservative in ideological outlook, the southerners managed to bottle up much of the legislation proposed by House liberals. To make matters worse for liberals, the Rules Committee was in the firm control of a bloc of southern Democrats and Republicans, a coalition that often blocked floor consideration of major bills reported by other committees. The Speaker, Sam Rayburn of Texas, tended to avoid conflict by supporting decisions of the committees, although he occasionally managed to push legislation through obstructionist committees by force of personality, appeals to friendship, and accumulated favors.

In fits and starts, and only in certain places, the domination by committees and their chairmen began to give way in the 1960s. In 1961 the Rules Committee was expanded to include more liberals, paving the way for floor consideration of legislation dealing with civil rights, education, and other domestic issues in the following years. Intracommittee revolts against some committee chairmen loosened their stranglehold on legislation. Members' personal staff allotments grew, improving their ability to participate in committee and floor action. And the Speaker during the 1960s, John McCormack of Massachusetts, was more in tune with the policy preferences of his party's liberal majority. He also was much less assertive than Rayburn in defending the prerogatives of the standing committees.

Committees and their chairmen retained important procedural advantages throughout the 1950s and 1960s, of course. Committees could block nearly any legislation they opposed. Discharging legislation from committees remained very difficult. Tight germaneness rules usually made it impossible to circumvent a committee by offering a bill as a floor amendment to another measure. The near-monopoly of "proposing power" gave, and still gives, committees an important source of bargaining leverage.

On the floor, full committee chairmen managed most legislation, giving them control of the time during general debate. Amending procedures in the Committee of the Whole reinforced their control. House precedent that committee amendments be considered before others' amendments gave chairmen the opportunity to modify their legislation to forestall unfriendly challenges. Chairmen also knew that if they survived the Committee of the Whole they would succeed in the House because amendments defeated in the Committee of the Whole could not be reconsidered by the House.[6]

Moreover, voting procedures in the Committee of the Whole were stacked in favor of the chairmen. By virtue of a precedent dating back to 1840, no recorded voting was permitted in the Committee of the Whole.[7] At best, members could demand a teller vote, in which members walk up the center aisle, first those voting aye and then those voting nay, and are counted by two members appointed as "tellers." Neither members' presence nor their vote was recorded—but the chairmen could carefully observe members queuing up to march by the tellers. Chairmen sometimes could be seen standing shoulder-to-shoulder with the tellers in order to very conspicuously scrutinize each member approaching them.[8] Furthermore, chairmen and other bill managers could easily gain recognition to offer second-degree amendments to dilute unfriendly first-degree amendments or to offer a motion to cut off debate on amendments, making it impossible for amendment sponsors to explain their amendments and solicit support.

The absence of recorded voting and the advantages of committee chairmen undercut the incentives for members to be in attendance during floor debate and votes on amendments. This is plain in the turnout for standing division votes on amendments. Division votes were, and still are, conducted without ringing the bells that notify members of a teller or recorded vote. As a result, turnout on division votes for amendments provides a good

6. Amendments adopted in the Committee of the Whole must be approved by the House before the passage of the measure.

7. See Norman J. Ornstein and David W. Rohde, "The Strategy of Reform: Recorded Teller Voting in the U.S. House of Representatives," paper prepared for the 1974 annual meeting of the Midwest Political Science Association, p. 1.

8. The system not only helped chairmen to get their way, but also made it relatively easy for a member to ignore commitments to constituents or pressure groups. In his autobiography, Tip O'Neill called teller voting "a cowardly system. It was embarrassingly easy for a member to duck a vote because he had made promises to both sides—and even to lie about it afterward, because there was no way anybody could check." See Thomas P. O'Neill, Jr., with William Novak, *Man of the House: The Life and Political Memoirs of Speaker Tip O'Neill* (Random House, 1987), p. 204.

FIGURE 2-4. *Mean Turnout for Amendment Votes, by Type of Vote, Selected Congresses, 1955–86*

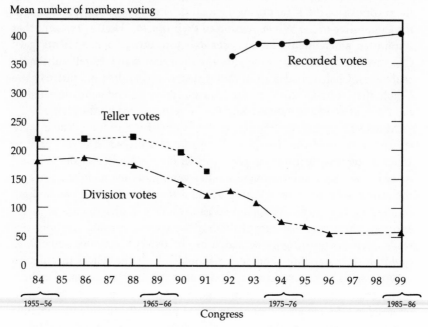

Mean number of members voting

SOURCE: See appendix 2.

indication of the number of members that were on or near the floor during routine debate on amendments in the Committee of the Whole. Before the advent of recorded voting in 1971, far less than half of the House voted on amendments disposed of by a standing division. Average turnout peaked at about 42 percent for five pre-1970 Congresses (see figure 2-4). Even on amendments subject to a teller vote, for which the bells rang in the office buildings, only about half of the members cast votes, on the average, in the prereform Congresses. In the last prereform Congress, the 91st (1969–70), turnout was lower for teller votes than it was for division votes a decade earlier. Hale Boggs, the majority whip in the late 1960s, stated flatly, "The truth is, the system of teller voting is a major contributor to absenteeism."[9]

The importance of turnout is that it can affect vote outcomes.[10] Stories

9. *Congressional Record*, July 27, 1970, p. 25800.
10. During the debate on reforming the teller voting rule, Representative James Burke of Massachusetts commented that absentees "are usually the cause of the outcome of the teller

abound of the manipulation of turnout for political advantage under teller voting.[11] Those members with the organizational support and staff resources to stimulate timely turnout, particularly party and committee leaders, were at a real advantage. With a very short voting period, votes on amendments had to be anticipated in advance and an effective communications system was required to round up the last few supporters on close votes. Liberal Democrats generally were at a disadvantage; indeed, they were notorious for spending little time on the floor and losing at a disproportionate rate. The liberal Democratic Study Group (DSG), organized in the late 1950s, worked hard to compensate with its own whip system, but it worked well only for the most significant issues.[12]

Reinforcing—and probably reflecting—committees' procedural advantages were informal norms about appropriate behavior on the floor.[13] An apprenticeship norm called for new members to spend an unspecified period learning from senior members before actively participating in decisionmaking. A committee deference norm called for members to defer to the recommendations of committees, which were presumed to reflect their members' special expertise. Apprenticeships served to build expertise, and expertise underpinned deference to committees. Such norms helped to reduce the number of challenges, particularly successful ones, to committee recommendations. The norms were further reinforced by the low frequency and success rates of challenges to committees.

To the extent that floor experience—familiarity with parliamentary procedure, responsibility for building coalitions—breeds success, rank-and-file members of the 1950s were severely handicapped. To the extent that success, or expected success, encourages participation, there was not much success to offer encouragement. The cards were held by the committees and their chairmen, and rank-and-file members had insufficient incentives to challenge them on the floor in most situations. The result was captured in Lewis Froman's description of the House floor in the mid-1960s:

> The floor of the House of Representatives appears, to the casual observer sitting in the gallery, to be a very confusing, noisy, and unexciting place

---

vote by failing to be present on the floor of the House." He exaggerated, of course, but his point is clear. *Congressional Record*, July 27, 1970, p. 25797.

11. For example, see Lewis A. Froman, Jr., *The Congressional Process: Strategies, Rules, and Procedures* (Little, Brown, 1967), pp. 80–82, on the 1964 antipoverty bill.

12. Froman, *Congressional Process*, pp. 77–78. Ornstein and Rohde calculated that the success rate of amendments sponsored by the most conservative members was 54.5 percent in 1969–70, compared with only 15.6 percent for liberal members. See Ornstein and Rohde, "The Strategy of Reform," p. 3.

13. Chapter 5 will evaluate the change in informal norms limiting floor participation.

compared with the Senate. There are 435 members of the House and most are little known, even, in many cases, in their own constituencies. Members are constantly streaming on and off the floor, talking with one another in their seats or smoking behind the rail, and the unpracticed eye will usually miss the significance of the activities that are occurring on the floor. . . . From this chapter, a picture will emerge of the House of Representatives as a well-ordered, well-managed, sensible set of activities, as members, having differing preferences about the legislation before them, clash with each other over important matters within a very strict set of rules.[14]

Confusing and noisy, but well ordered and well managed.

The events of the 1960s provided the necessary incentives for change in the role of the floor. Both the volume and divisiveness of the issues led members to pursue their legislative causes to the floor more frequently. For example, the debate on the Civil Rights Act of 1964 produced 126 floor amendments, setting a record for its time. Even without recorded voting in the Committee of the Whole, the extraordinary polarization of views produced waves of amendments on some issues.

Despite these developments, there appeared to be an effective cap on the volume and success of amending activity in the first phase. The last two Congresses of the 1960s and the first Congress of the 1970s—the 90th, 91st, and 92d—each had around 800 amendments and amendment success rates just below 50 percent. The invisible threshold was reflected in the frustration of House liberals, who believed that teller voting advantaged conservative committee chairmen. In 1970, for example, votes on the antiballistic missile system, school desegregation, the supersonic transport, and the Cambodian invasion were conducted with tellers.[15] The liberals lost each of those votes, and each time some of them blamed the outcome on the absence of a public voting record.[16] Their frustration played a major role in stimulating reform of voting procedures.

Steps toward a More Collegial Process, 1970–73

The political forces in and out of Congress straining the institution in the late 1960s and early 1970s were noted in chapter 1. The period's politics were dominated by tension between the branches. Both Congress as

14. Froman, *Congressional Process*, p. 62.
15. See *Congressional Quarterly Almanac, 1970*, vol. 26 (1971), p. 454.
16. For example, Tip O'Neill commented during the 1970 debate on reforming the teller vote rule that "if we were recording these votes, if the people at home knew how we actually voted, I believe we probably would have had some different results." *Congressional Record*, July 27, 1970, p. 25797.

an institution and individual members of Congress sought to reestablish their role in the political system.[17] Congress passed the War Powers Resolution over the president's veto in 1973, adopted the Congressional Budget and Impoundment Control Act in 1974, moved to improve oversight of executive branch activities in the Legislative Reorganization Act of 1970 and the Committee Reform Amendments of 1974, required the executive branch to notify Congress about executive agreements with foreign countries in 1972 and about covert activity in 1974, and increased the use of legislative veto provisions. This turmoil in Congress's political environment intensified frustrations among rank-and-file members of the House about their limited influence in shaping policy. For many, a major part of the solution was structural and procedural reform in Congress.

Several reform efforts came to fruition in the early and mid-1970s. A central thrust of the reforms was to force full committee chairmen to share power with committee colleagues, particularly subcommittee chairmen, leading observers to label decisionmaking in the postreform House "subcommittee government."[18] Among other things, subcommittees were guaranteed referral of legislation, fixed jurisdictions, and their own staff. Other reforms sought to strengthen the Speaker's hand. The Speaker gained the authority to nominate the Democratic members of the Rules Committee in 1973 and obtained a more central role in making other committee assignments. In 1974 the Speaker was granted authority to refer legislation to more than one committee, which permitted the Speaker to structure more carefully committee review of complex legislation.

Reforms of floor procedure also proved crucial to redistributing influence in the House. The Legislative Reorganization Act of 1970, an overhaul of many congressional rules and practices, provided for recorded teller voting in the Committee of the Whole. Implemented in the 92d Congress (1971–72), the new rule provided that twenty members could request a recorded vote, which was conducted by members signing green or red cards (yea or nay) and depositing them in a box for the clerks to count. Since members' names were written on the cards, clerks could then record indi-

---

17. James L. Sundquist, *The Decline and Resurgence of Congress* (Brookings, 1981).

18. For summaries of the subcommittee reforms, see Roger H. Davidson and Walter J. Oleszek, *Congress Against Itself* (Indiana University Press, 1977), especially chap. 7; Stephen H. Haeberle, "The Institutionalization of the Subcommittee in the United States House of Representatives," *Journal of Politics*, vol. 40 (November 1978), pp. 1054–65; Norman J. Ornstein, "Causes and Consequences of Congressional Change: Subcommittee Reforms in the House of Representatives, 1970–73," in Norman J. Ornstein, ed., *Congress in Change: Evolution and Reform* (Praeger, 1975), pp. 88–114; Leroy N. Rieselbach, *Congressional Reform* (Washington: CQ Press, 1986), chap. 3; and Steven S. Smith and Christopher J. Deering, *Committees in Congress* (Washington: CQ Press, 1984), chap. 2.

viduals' votes for the House *Journal, Congressional Record,* and other publications. The rule established a twelve-minute voting period in order to guarantee that voting was not cut off arbitrarily.[19]

The sponsors of voting reform hoped that recorded voting would improve the accountability of members to their constituents, increase attendance, and, most important, change some vote outcomes.[20] But supporters of the reform differed in their estimates of the more general effects of recorded voting. O'Neill, the author of the recorded voting amendment, dismissed predictions that members would be compelled to spend more time on the floor by suggesting that recorded votes would be demanded on only fifteen or so issues each year.[21] He suspected that attendance would improve and that outcomes on a few important issues would change, but he went out of his way to allay fears that recorded voting would radically alter members' daily routines.

In contrast, Richard Bolling argued that the new rule ultimately would produce fundamental changes in the conduct of business in the House. Bolling predicted that

> inevitably we are going to arrive at the time when members will know that we will be voting on amendments; they will be on the floor of the House waiting the recorded votes on amendments, and the whole method of operation of the institution will change. . . . I believe we should come to that. I believe we will come to that. It will massively change the way in which this institution works.[22]

Many opponents of reform shared Bolling's view, but Bolling saw virtue where opponents saw vice. Bolling believed that past practice had been working to the advantage of a conservative minority faction.[23] New rules that encouraged better attendance and promoted accountability would, in his view, enhance control of policy outcomes by the liberal majority of the Democratic party.

19. O'Neill also proposed an amendment that would have allowed a recorded vote in the House on any amendment rejected in the Committee of the Whole by a teller vote. The amendment was rejected on a point of order. In addition, the House rejected an amendment to provide for immediate implementation of an electronic voting system. Electronic voting was approved two years later. For an account of the passage of the Legislative Reorganization Act, see John F. Bibby and Roger H. Davidson, *On Capitol Hill: Studies in the Legislative Process,* 2d ed. (Hinsdale, Ill.: Dryden Press, 1972), pp. 251–80.

20. See the floor debate, *Congressional Record,* July 27, 1970, pp. 25796–818. For additional background on the reformers' objectives and strategies, see Ornstein and Rohde, "The Strategy of Reform."

21. *Congressional Record,* July 27, 1970, p. 25797.

22. *Congressional Record,* July 27, 1970, p. 25804.

23. See Richard Bolling, *House Out of Order* (Dutton, 1965), and *Power in the House: A History of the Leadership of the House of Representatives* (Dutton, 1968).

The 1970 act also guaranteed at least ten minutes of debate on any amendment printed in the *Record* at least one day in advance.[24] Previously, a successful motion to limit debate on amendments, usually offered by the committee bill manager, could prevent or limit further debate on amendments. While it did not prevent votes on amendments, such a motion made it difficult to explain amendments, which sometimes made it impossible to attract support. The procedure worked to the advantage of the committee seeking to defeat unfriendly amendments.[25] As a result of the new rule, amendment sponsors could, with a little advance planning, reserve the right to be recognized in order to describe their "prenoticed" amendments. Objections to the rule were heard from members who feared that amendments would be offered to delay action on measures and who insisted that a majority should retain the right to close debate and proceed to voting on amendments. However, the rule was easily adopted by a voice vote.

The effects of recorded teller voting were felt immediately. In the 92d Congress (1971–72), there were very few unrecorded teller votes on amendments in the Committee of the Whole as the demand for a recorded vote became a standard feature of requests for teller votes. Indeed, O'Neill's prediction of only fifteen recorded votes each year proved to be one of the worst forecasts in the history of congressional rulemaking. His prognostication for attendance was on target, however, as turnout for teller votes on amendments shot upward. The average turnout for recorded teller votes on amendments was 360 in the 92d Congress, compared with 163 for unrecorded teller votes on amendments in the 91st Congress (figure 2-4). Furthermore, and O'Neill later claimed great foresight on this count, it appeared that recorded voting played a role in overturning earlier votes on the supersonic transport and other issues in the 92d Congress.[26] The success rate of amendments subject to a recorded vote was 29 percent, compared with 22 percent in the 90th Congress and 20 percent in the 91st Congress for amendments subject to unrecorded tellers.

Despite all of these changes, the advent of recorded teller voting did not appear to stimulate more amending activity, at least by itself. The number of floor amendments was slightly lower in the 92d Congress than in the 91st (figure 2-1). Moreover, the proportion of contested amendments—perhaps an indicator of politically significant amendments—was not much different than in previous Congresses.

The 1971–72 experiment with recorded tellers was a brief transition in voting procedures. At the beginning of the 93d Congress in 1973, the

24. *Congressional Record,* July 27, 1970, pp. 25789–95.
25. See Froman, *Congressional Process,* p. 79.
26. *Congressional Quarterly Almanac, 1973,* vol. 29 (1974), p. 782.

House instituted electronic voting for recorded votes, in both the Committee of the Whole and the House. The major argument in favor of electronic voting was that the new system would cut the time required to conduct roll call votes and quorum calls, which normally took over thirty minutes under the old procedure. A fifteen-minute voting period was established for recorded votes, with members casting their votes by inserting a wallet-size identification card into one of forty-eight voting consoles scattered around the chamber. Both sides of the chamber were equipped with computer terminals allowing leaders to identify immediately how individuals or groups voted. Boards showing the running tally and individuals' votes were installed on the walls in the gallery at the front of the chamber.

At about the same time, the Democratic Caucus moved to regulate closed rules—rules that prohibited floor amendments. Unhappiness with special rules barring floor amendments, particularly for bills from the Committee on Ways and Means, led the caucus to require chairmen to give advance notice to the House of their intention to request a closed rule. The rule gave the caucus the authority to instruct Rules Committee Democrats to report a rule permitting certain amendments to be considered on the floor. The caucus regulations reflected a new caucus commitment to broader participation in House decisionmaking.

A First Look at the Effects of the Reforms

By January 1973 the House had substantially revamped floor voting procedures. The most obvious result was an avalanche of floor amendments in early 1973. As I already have mentioned, the surge in amending activity was accompanied by higher amendment success rates and no dramatic shift in the proportion of contested votes on amendments. Bolling was close to the mark in predicting a major change in the way the House conducted its business on the floor. Before considering the reaction to the new conditions on the floor, a closer look at some of the effects of reform is in order.

The break in the pattern of amending activity in 1973 is hard to explain without giving primary emphasis to the role of electronic recorded voting in the Committee of the Whole. It is somewhat perplexing that the surge in amending activity did not appear until recorded voting in the Committee of the Whole, implemented in 1971, was supplemented by the electronic voting system two years later. The political incentives to offer amendments seem more strongly related to recorded voting than to the device used to record votes. That is, the special value of putting oneself, or one's opponents, on the record should have encouraged additional amending activity by itself. No single explanation appears to be adequate for the delayed increase, but several factors probably played a role.

One important factor is the dip in the work load of the House in the 92d Congress (1971–72). One study indicates that the number of measures considered in the Committee of the Whole was substantially lower in the first session of the 92d Congress than in the first session of the 93d.[27] In fact, during the 92d Congress the administration sent relatively few messages to Congress, the number of public bills enacted was below that in the surrounding Congresses, and the number of pages of legislation was relatively low.[28] With fewer targets for amendments, the total number of amendments might have been temporarily depressed in the 92d Congress.

In addition, the speed and ease of electronic voting probably made it easier to acquire support for a request for a recorded vote. Under the old procedures, casting a vote could be a time-consuming process. Even recorded tellers required members to wait their turn to deposit their ballots in the box in the well of the House, where members often were subject to vigorous buttonholing by party and committee leaders. In contrast, the burden of time and arm-twisting on the individual members is minimal with recorded voting by electronic device. Members may enter the chamber from seven different doors. Some of them have been known to choose the door through which they will be least conspicuous to a solicitous party or committee leader. And the act of voting takes only a few seconds. Voting consoles are scattered throughout the chamber, permitting members to enter the chamber, vote by inserting their identification card and punching a button, and exit very quickly.[29] Consequently, the installation of the electronic system may have eliminated most of the remaining resistance to recorded voting. If so, electronic voting made possible the full exploitation of floor amendments as political tools by the rank-and-file membership.

Finally, it is important to keep in mind that floor amendments often breed additional amendments. As bill managers and others seek to modify amendments, the number of floor amendments grows more rapidly than the first-order stimuli of recorded voting, electronic voting, and other fac-

27. CQ Almanac, 1973, p. 782. The study was conducted by the staff of the Democratic Study Group.

28. Roger H. Davidson, "The Legislative Work of Congress," paper prepared for the 1986 annual meeting of the American Political Science Association, pp. 44, 52.

29. Members would later blame electronic voting for making it more difficult for them to get to know each other. Because individual names are no longer called out during a recorded vote, new members' faces and names are not matched by many members unless they happen to share committee assignments or other common responsibilities. See Jayne O'Donnell, "So Many Lawmakers, So Little Time," Roll Call, April 3, 1988, p. 11.

tors might suggest. Thus, whatever combination of forces produced a surge in amendments, its effect was compounded by a second-order response. In the 96th Congress (1979–80) and 99th Congress (1985–86), for example, almost one-fifth of all amendments subject to a recorded vote were amendments to amendments.

The political incentives of recorded voting and the ease of electronic voting seemed to open the floodgates of amending activity in the 93d and the following Congresses. One consequence was that the House did not realize most of the anticipated time savings of electronic voting. On recorded votes for motions other than amendments, the House saved at most sixty-eight hours of floor time during the 93d Congress (1973–74).[30] However, the House conducted recorded votes on 158 more amendments in the 93d Congress than in the 92d, many of which might have been stimulated by the new voting procedures. Debate on those 158 amendments consumed a minimum of twenty-six hours and voting on them consumed a minimum of forty hours, for a minimum of sixty-six additional hours.[31] In short, the net savings by the move to recorded electronic voting probably were not positive. In fact, the House spent twenty more days in session in the 93d than in the 92d Congress.

Not only was there an escalation of amending activity in the 93d Congress, there also was an expansion of the number and proportion of amendments pushed to the most advanced form of voting. Members exhausted their parliamentary options more frequently after recorded voting in the Committee of the Whole was introduced (table 2-1). A possible explanation is that the number of contested amendments had increased, stimulating amendment supporters and opponents to seek a more definitive vote count—but the number of contested amendments did *not* increase. The pattern suggests that the ability to establish a public record had a strong independent influence on voting tactics, reducing reliance on division votes to dispose of amendments.

Yet not all of the increase in amending activity can be attributed to recorded electronic voting. The absolute number of amendments subject only

30. The number of recorded votes not directly on amendments increased from 456 to 727 between the 92d and 93d Congresses, an increase of 271 amendments. Many of these votes were associated with amending activity, much of which probably was stimulated by the new procedures. If each of the votes on these additional amendments consumed fifteen minutes, the normal voting period, something just less than sixty-eight hours was actually saved by the new electronic system.

31. The estimate is based on ten minutes of debate for each amendment. The estimate would be much higher if it included time on amendments not subject to recorded votes that may have been by-products of recorded-vote amendments, time spent on pro forma amendments, and time devoted to recorded votes on procedural motions related to the additional amendments.

TABLE 2-1. *Final Disposition of House Floor Amendments, by Type of Vote, Selected Congresses, 1955–86*[a]

Percent

Congress	Method of final disposition				
	Voice vote	Division vote	Unrecorded teller vote	Recorded vote	Total
84th (1955–56)	60.5	25.9	9.9	3.7	100.0
	(245)	(105)	(40)	(15)	(405)
86th (1959–60)	58.1	28.2	10.1	3.6	100.0
	(258)	(125)	(45)	(16)	(444)
88th (1963–64)	60.1	23.1	15.8	1.0	100.0
	(369)	(142)	(97)	(6)	(614)
90th (1967–68)	61.5	20.7	13.3	4.5	100.0
	(521)	(175)	(113)	(38)	(847)
91st (1969–70)	64.4	22.6	11.1	1.9	100.0
	(565)	(198)	(97)	(17)	(877)
92d (1971–72)	56.9	18.4	0.3	24.4	100.0
	(451)	(146)	(2)	(193)	(792)
93d (1973–74)	62.1	13.3	. . .	24.6	100.0
	(885)	(189)	. . .	(351)	(1,425)
94th (1975–76)	58.4	14.3	. . .	27.2	99.9
	(798)	(196)	. . .	(372)	(1,366)
95th (1977–78)	60.9	13.1	. . .	26.0	100.0
	(1,028)	(221)	. . .	(439)	(1,688)
96th (1979–80)	66.0	8.5	. . .	25.5	100.0
	(909)	(117)	. . .	(351)	(1,377)
99th (1985–86)	71.6	0.5	. . .	27.9	100.0
	(767)	(5)	. . .	(299)	(1,071)

SOURCE: See appendix 2.

a. Number of amendments in parentheses.

to a voice vote nearly doubled between the 92d and 93d Congresses, and the proportion of voice-vote amendments was actually somewhat higher in the late 1970s and 1980s than in the 1950s and 1960s. Some of the voice-vote amendments may have been by-products of other amendments pushed to recorded votes. Amendments designed to preempt other amendments and second-degree amendments frequently have this character. But the tremendous growth of voice-vote amendments suggests that forces beyond procedural change played an important role as well. A very different environment had emerged on the floor of the House.[32]

In this new environment, the pattern of attendance on the floor contin-

32. One consequence of the use of recorded voting was the gradual demise of standing division votes as a method of disposing of amendments. In recent Congresses, two-thirds or more of all amendments received voice votes exclusively, with most of the rest pushed to recorded votes. As will be discussed later, there is a similar pattern in the Senate, where recorded voting has been allowed on amendments all along.

ued to change. Fewer members attended floor sessions to listen to the debate. Again, an important clue lies in the turnout for standing division votes on amendments. Turnout on division votes continued a long-term decline in the 1970s, reaching a remarkably low point of less than 15 percent in the 96th Congress (1979–80), as figure 2-4 indicates. Slipping floor attendance was due, in part, to the increasing burden of committee responsibilities and other duties. Between 1955–56 and 1969–70, the number of committee and subcommittee meetings grew from 3,210 to 5,066, and by 1979–80 it had reached 7,022.[33] Of course, floor activity itself became more burdensome. The sheer density of floor decisionmaking grew tremendously in the 1970s. In the prereform period, about two amendments a day were considered on average, or nearly one amendment every two hours and twenty minutes of session. The House of the 1970s considered four or five amendments a day, about one amendment every hour and twenty minutes. That is, the House not only made more discrete amendment decisions, but also reserved less time, on average, for each decision. The tremendous burden of running to and from the floor began to consume a much larger part of members' daily routines.[34] Few members could afford to spend time on the floor listening to floor debate on minor amendments. Instead, most members came to assume that amendments of any importance would be subject to a recorded vote and that the bell system would call them to the floor in time to vote.

O'Neill's prediction that recorded voting would change some outcomes is consistent with the evidence. Amendments subject to recorded votes in the postreform period were about 10 percent more likely to pass than were their teller-vote ancestors (table 2-2). In addition, declining turnout for division votes meant that division-vote outcomes were less likely to reflect chamber preferences accurately. As a result, a higher proportion of division votes were appealed to recorded votes in the postreform period and more division-vote outcomes were overturned.[35]

Recorded voting also magnified the difficulty members faced in explaining their votes at home. Nearly every issue of any importance now was

33. Ornstein and others, *Vital Statistics on Congress, 1987–1988*, p. 165.

34. In addition, the House adopted new rules governing quorum calls in 1974 and 1977, which made it more difficult for members to slow down the business of the House by noticing the absence of a quorum while a vote is pending. One effect, no doubt, was to reduce the number of members on the floor during division votes. Representative Robert Bauman made this point, for example. See *Congressional Record*, May 11, 1978, p. 13307.

35. About 22 percent of division votes were appealed to a teller vote on average in the prereform period, while about 33 percent were appealed to a recorded vote in the postreform period. For the Congresses examined, the percentage of division votes overturned in the pre- and postreform eras averaged about 16 and 29 percent, respectively.

TABLE 2-2. *House Amendments Adopted, by Method of Final Disposition, Selected Congresses, 1955–86*[a]

Percent

	Method of final disposition			
Congress	Voice vote	Division vote	Unrecorded teller vote	Recorded vote
84th (1955–56)	69.8 (245)	21.0 (105)	25.0 (40)	46.7 (15)
86th (1959–60)	49.2 (258)	15.2 (125)	24.4 (45)	68.8 (16)
88th (1963–64)	58.5 (369)	9.9 (142)	29.9 (97)	33.3 (6)
90th (1967–68)	58.5 (521)	22.3 (175)	38.1 (113)	84.2 (38)
91st (1969–70)	58.9 (565)	19.7 (198)	19.6 (97)	64.7 (17)
92d (1971–72)	62.1 (451)	24.0 (146)	50.0 (2)	29.0 (193)
93d (1973–74)	62.1 (885)	25.9 (189)	. . .	41.0 (351)
94th (1975–76)	70.3 (798)	29.6 (196)	. . .	34.4 (372)
95th (1977–78)	77.0 (1,028)	31.2 (221)	. . .	37.4 (439)
96th (1979–80)	84.7 (909)	34.2 (117)	. . .	39.6 (351)
99th (1985–86)	92.3 (767)	40.0 (5)	. . .	37.5 (299)

SOURCE: See appendix 2.

a. Number of amendments in parentheses.

subject to a recorded vote that could come back to haunt them at election time. Particularly for the majority party Democrats, the diversity of constituencies created pressures to ignore the entreaties of party and committee leaders and to vote the way electoral considerations demanded. In combination with new cross-cutting issues, the result was greater cohesiveness among Republicans, less cohesiveness among Democrats, and considerably greater difficulty for Democratic leaders in building majority coalitions.[36]

And perhaps most important, the partisan character of amending activity changed suddenly with the advent of recorded electronic voting. As table 2-3 indicates, minority party Republicans sponsored a disproportion-

36. For a superb review of the evidence on this point, see Barbara Sinclair, "Coping with Uncertainty: Building Coalitions in the House and the Senate," in Thomas E. Mann and Norman J. Ornstein, eds., *The New Congress* (Washington: American Enterprise Institute for Public Policy Research, 1981), pp. 178–220.

TABLE 2-3. *Amending Activity by House Republicans,*
Selected Congresses, 1955–86

Congress	Republican percentage in House	Percent of amendments sponsored by Republicans		
		All amendments	Teller-vote amendments	Recorded-vote amendments
84th (1955–56)	47	37.0	52.5	*
86th (1959–60)	35	43.9	51.1	*
88th (1963–64)	41	46.9	61.9	*
90th (1967–68)	43	46.5	69.0	*
91st (1969–70)	44	31.6	38.1	*
92d (1971–72)	41	28.9	*	37.3
93d (1973–74)	43	44.1	*	50.1
94th (1975–76)	33	39.1	*	49.2
95th (1977–78)	33	44.4	*	52.4
96th (1979–80)	36	41.2	*	51.3
99th (1985–86)	42	40.8	*	52.5

SOURCE: See appendix 2.
*Fewer than five amendments.

ate number of the amendments pushed to a recorded vote. It was not unusual for the minority party to offer a disproportionate share of all floor amendments in the prereform period. After all, minority party members were most likely to be dissatisfied with voice- and division-vote outcomes on their amendments. But with new voting procedures in the 1970s, Republicans could force Democrats to go on the record, often repeatedly, on divisive amendments. As will be explored further in chapter 5, per capita amending activity and success rates for Republicans also shot upward in the 93d Congress as Republicans disproportionately took advantage of the new voting procedures.

A few Republicans became self-appointed floor watchdogs. H. R. Gross of Iowa was renowned for his floor amendments in the prereform era. When he retired in 1974, his role was filled, with vigor, by John Ashbrook and John Rousselot of California and Robert Bauman of Maryland. The three firebrand Republicans had been active organizers of conservative organizations; Bauman chaired the American Conservative Union in the 1970s. They actively sought ways to challenge committee products, raise ideologically charged issues, and force recorded votes. Bauman even entertained requests for recorded-vote amendments from Republican challengers to Democratic incumbents in order to compel Democrats to take politically dangerous public positions.[37] The effect, quite naturally, was to heighten the personal and partisan conflict on the floor.

37. Interview with Robert Bauman, July 16, 1987.

In retrospect, it is clear that Bolling's thesis that recorded voting would transform floor politics was far more accurate than O'Neill's thesis of incremental change. The burst of amending activity was accompanied by altered uses of voting options, changing patterns of attendance, and an intensified partisan cast to floor action. Norman Ornstein, describing these changes, concluded:

> Now the House floor is often a free-for-all, rarely a ratification point for decisions pre-structured by one or two specialists. Carefully crafted legislation is not the only, or the highest, priority of the House. During the floor debate and amendment process, making ideological points for national groups or constituencies, protecting the interests of particular groups, asserting an individual prerogative, or altering a broader policy direction (with deep regard for the specific piece of legislation under consideration) are all competing priorities of significant rank.[38]

In the context of House politics, a revolution had occurred in floor decisionmaking.

The political import of these developments is that they reflect a substantial expansion of the scope of political conflict on the House floor, and expanding the scope of conflict seldom has neutral effects.[39] By enlarging the range of interests represented in decisionmaking on the floor, the reforms of the early 1970s frequently had the effect of shifting the balance of power in the House and changing the location of key decisions from committees to the floor. In doing so, these developments opened the door for groups and factions, such as elements of the minority party, to exercise more influence over policy outcomes.

Reactions to Collegial Decisionmaking

Reactions to the dramatic changes in floor practice came quickly and continued for several years. The reactions reflected the deepening uncertainty about floor activity among committee and party leaders, as well as the rank and file. On several dimensions—who would offer amendments, on what subjects, with what vote outcomes, with what policy consequences—there was greater unpredictability to floor activity. Deals struck in committee could easily come unglued when the parties to the deal were forced to cast recorded votes on an unanticipated floor amendment. Reelec-

38. Norman J. Ornstein, "The House and the Senate in a New Congress," in Mann and Ornstein, eds., *The New Congress*, pp. 368–69.

39. E. E. Schattschneider, *The Semisovereign People: A Realist's View of Democracy in America* (Hinsdale, Ill.: Dryden Press, 1975), chaps. 1, 2.

tion prospects could change as members were forced to cast repeated recorded votes on divisive issues. And scheduling legislation for the floor became hazardous as the length of debate on legislation became difficult to predict. Rank-and-file members complained that chairmen had lost control of their bills, chairmen complained that party leaders had lost control of the rank and file, and nearly everyone complained about the long hours it took to dispose of floor amendments. In response, the House, particularly the Democrats, moved incrementally to corral amending activity in the Committee of the Whole.

Recorded Votes

The immediate and most obvious target of complaints about floor developments was the rule providing for recorded voting in the Committee of the Whole. Within a few months of the introduction of electronic voting in January 1973, many members were complaining that the number of recorded votes was forcing them to spend more time on the floor, the number of minor amendments was increasing, and the floor schedule and the nature of amendments were less predictable. Resolutions to raise the number of members required to support a request for a recorded vote from twenty to forty-four were introduced by Rules Committee Chairman Ray Madden and a senior southern Democrat, Sonny Montgomery. The Rules Committee eventually settled on forty as the number required, but the provision was defeated by a coalition of junior Democrats and most Republicans when the Rules proposal reached the floor in April 1974. Montgomery's compromise proposal, which would have set the threshold at thirty-three, was rejected by a lopsided voice vote.[40]

In December 1978, after suffering a record number of floor amendments in the 95th Congress, the Democratic Caucus settled on a package of rules changes to reduce the burden of recorded voting. A very modest increase to twenty-five in the number of members required to support a request for a recorded vote was included in the package. The package also provided that only one vote approving the *Journal* for the previous day was permitted, that a recorded vote on an amendment could be limited to five minutes if preceded by a recorded quorum call, and that the Speaker could cluster a set of five-minute recorded votes on final passage of bills and adoption of special rules. The package was adopted by the House on a party-line vote in January 1979.[41]

---

40. *Congressional Quarterly Almanac, 1974,* vol. 30 (1975), p. 671.

41. *Congressional Record,* January 15, 1979, pp. 7–17. For background, see Ann Cooper, "Democrats Soften Proposed Ethics Changes," *Congressional Quarterly Weekly Report,* December 9, 1978, pp. 3405–06; and Cooper, "Congress' First Days Quiet, Fights to Come," *Congressional Quarterly Weekly Report,* January 20, 1979, pp. 75–77.

Suspension of the Rules

A more direct and efficient way to reduce the dangers of amending activity is to use a device that avoids the amendment stage altogether. One such device is suspension of the rules, a motion that simultaneously suspends the rules of the House and provides for the adoption of the measure and any amendments included in the motion.[42] The Speaker exercises complete discretion in recognizing members for the purpose of offering suspension motions, although he may do so only on certain days. Debate on the motion is limited to forty minutes, and the motion requires a two-thirds majority of those voting to pass. But measures considered under suspension of the rules may not be amended, except by amendments included in the motion itself. It is not very surprising that bill managers and majority party leaders would look to suspension motions as a partial solution to unpredictable and unfriendly amending activity.[43]

Suspension of the rules generally has been, and still is, intended for minor, noncontroversial bills. It is particularly useful at the end of a Congress when the House is anxious to clear a backlog of legislation before adjourning.[44] The standing rules of the House do not limit the kind of legislation that may be considered under suspension, so the Speaker exercises great discretion in choosing the legislation to be considered in this way. The Speaker sometimes is subject to great pressure from chairmen and other bill sponsors to schedule their bills on the suspension calendar.

In the span of just six years, 1973–79, the House changed the rule governing suspension motions four times. In 1973 the House adopted a proposal to increase the number of days on which the Speaker may entertain suspension motions from just two days a month to every other Monday and Tuesday. Democratic leaders argued, with some validity, that the additional days were necessary to handle the large work load and to distribute the consideration of minor bills more evenly throughout each month. Republicans objected on the grounds that the majority party would have more time in which to push through bills shielded from floor amendments.

42. A motion to suspend the rules has the effect of waiving points of order against the measures and any amendments included in the motion and of providing for immediate consideration of the measure. Under certain circumstances, a request for a vote to second the motion is in order.

43. An excellent discussion of the suspension procedure is provided by Stanley Bach, "Suspension of the Rules in the House of Representatives," report 86–103 GOV, Congressional Research Service, May 12, 1986.

44. In fact, under a long-standing rule, the Speaker is free to recognize members for suspension motions any time during the last six days of a Congress as long as the two chambers have approved a resolution setting the adjournment date. When an adjournment is not set, and even at other times, the Speaker may receive unanimous consent to entertain motions to suspend the rules.

O'Neill, then majority leader, indicated that the Democrats' practice of consulting with the minority leader or the ranking committee Republican would continue, but his assurances did not satisfy most Republicans. The effect of the rule was felt quickly: the number of suspension motions considered rose from 194 in 1971–72 to 255 in 1973–74, and then to 325 in 1975–76.[45]

A 1974 rule permitted the Speaker to defer votes on suspension motions and to cluster several of them at five-minute intervals at convenient times, sparing members many trips to the floor. By separating most debates on suspension motions from the votes on the motions by several hours, and sometimes by a day or more, cluster voting made it less likely that members would know much about the legislation on which they were voting. Members were forced to rely more on the recommendations of party and committee leaders, a dependence that clearly advantaged the majority party Democrats. The use of suspension motions worked so well that the Democrats modified the rule again in 1977 to permit suspension motions every Monday and Tuesday, redoubling the number of suspension days. Republican protests fell on deaf majority party ears once again.[46] During 1977–78 the number of suspension motions shot up to 453, an increase of 128 over the previous Congress.[47]

It is not merely coincidental that suspension motions became more popular in the same Congress that set the record for the number of floor amendments. In fact, it is likely that this combination—frequent use of suspension of the rules and mushrooming amending activity—explains the paradoxical pattern of amending activity in the 95th Congress (1977–78): both voluminous amending activity and a dip in the proportion of measures subject to amendment (figures 2-1 and 2-2). As bill sponsors saw others' bills picked apart with floor amendments, they began to look for alternative routes to floor passage. Indeed, many significant bills were brought to the floor by motions to suspend the rules in the 95th Congress, including several expensive health bills, a highly controversial education bill, and an authorization bill for hydroelectric plants.[48]

The vast majority of suspension motions continued to be adopted, although Republican objections began to have some effect in the 95th Congress. They frequently punctuated their protests by demanding time-consuming recorded votes on seconding motions to the suspension mo-

45. Bach, "Suspension of the Rules," p. 62.
46. See the debate, *Congressional Record*, January 24, 1977, pp. 53–69.
47. Bach, "Suspension of the Rules," p. 62.
48. Ann Cooper, "Legislative Parkinson's Law: House Use of Suspensions Grows Drastically," *Congressional Quarterly Weekly Report*, September 30, 1978, pp. 2693–95.

tions, which usually had been adopted by unanimous consent. Even many Democrats started to resent the circumvention of the amending process, the truncated debate, and abbreviated votes, particularly for some of the not-so-minor bills. In fact, several suspension motions were defeated with the help of a few defecting Democrats. About 8 percent of the suspension motions were rejected in the 94th Congress (1975–76), and 7 percent were rejected in the 95th (1977–78), nearly double the rate of the preceding Congresses.[49] The affected measures still could be considered by some other means, such as by special rule, but the pattern reflected a concern that Democratic party and committee leaders had abused the mechanism to avoid unfriendly amendments.

The complaints produced action by the Democratic Caucus in December 1978. To avoid irritating recorded votes on seconding motions, the caucus proposed to set aside the requirement of a seconding motion if printed copies of the measures and any amendments thereto were available one legislative day in advance. With a little foresight, then, bill sponsors could avoid a separate vote on whether to consider a suspension motion, which is what the seconding motion provided. The proposal was adopted as a part of the Democrats' rules package in January 1979.

In response to complaints about the kinds of bills passed under suspension of the rules, the Democratic Caucus decided to adopt its own restrictions. No bill authorizing or appropriating more than $100 million for a year could be placed on the suspension calendar without special approval by the party's Steering and Policy Committee.[50] As a party rule, rather than a standing rule of the House, the rule could not be enforced by a point of order on the floor. The caucus rule restrained the use of suspension motions as long as Democrats chose to observe it.[51]

With the exception of the 97th Congress (1971–72), in which the number of bills considered was far below normal, the number of suspension motions has remained much higher than in the prereform Congresses. Suspension of the rules became the vehicle of choice for many bill sponsors seeking quick and predictable floor action, as well as for majority party leaders seeking to expedite floor consideration of measures without signif-

49. Bach, "Suspension of the Rules," p. 62.

50. The new rule also required that the Speaker give a three-day advance notice to the House that a measure was scheduled for consideration under suspension of the rules. The original version required notice of three legislative days, but this was later relaxed to three calendar days. This rule also was a caucus rule and has been ignored by the Speaker at times.

51. Complaints about the use of suspension of the rules continued to surface from time to time in the 1980s. In late 1987, for example, Republicans complained that reform of the Hatch Act was considered under suspension of the rules. *Congressional Record*, daily edition, November 17, 1987, pp. H10045–72.

icant opposition. By retaining party control over important conditions on the use of suspension motions, House Democrats managed to construct a tool for avoiding floor amendments, at least for measures for which they could attract the necessary two-thirds support to adopt suspension motions.

Special Rules

Even after adjustments in the rules governing recorded voting and suspension motions were in place, most major legislation remained vulnerable to unfriendly floor amendments. The number of members required to support a request for a recorded vote could usually be obtained for most amendments, and major legislation could not meet the $100 million test or attract the two-thirds support required for suspension motions. The only predictable aspect of floor consideration of most important legislation was that many amendments were waiting to be offered. The first budget resolution of 1979, for example, was treated to more than three dozen first- and second-degree amendments on the House floor. The experience led Rules Committee Chairman Richard Bolling to declare, "We have to devise a technique whereby those who wish to use the budget process as a means of making political points are limited to making political points on macro issues."[52] More than tinkering with the formal rules was required, in the view of many House Democrats.

Frustration with floor amending activity reached the boiling point late in 1979. Floor amendments were undermining House action on President Jimmy Carter's legislative program, time-consuming floor activity was extending the length of the session, and the Democrats suffered some major defeats in September.[53] Democrats' frustration was reflected in an August 1979 letter directed to the Speaker and the Rules chairman, drafted by Representative John LaFalce of New York and signed by over forty of his Democratic colleagues. The letter is worth quoting at length:

> In light of daily sessions from 10:00 to 8:00 or 10:00 P.M. or later, in light of debate of a week or more over a single bill, and in light of the year long sessions we have had so often in the recent past and we are likely to have this year, the time to put the institution[al] process first is now.
>
> And the vehicle for doing this is available now. It is the modified open rule, an approach permitting reasonable proposed amendments to bills on

52. Quoted in "Process Questioned: Budget Making Is 'Devilishly Difficult Thing,' House Finds," *Congressional Quarterly Weekly Report*, May 12, 1979, p. 879.
53. See Mary Russell, "O'Neill Rebounds From Setbacks in Party and on Floor," *Washington Post*, November 22, 1979, p. A3.

the floor but limiting the number of such amendments, and the time permitted for debate on the amendments. This technique has proven effective in dealing with tax bills; there is no reason why it shouldn't be used in other areas as well. To be sure, use of this approach would have to be judicious and sensitive to the rights of the minority, but we are confident the Rules Committee and the Leadership could and would work with the leading proponents and opponents of bills and amendments and exercise prudent judgment in formulating modified open rules. If a particular modified rule did not adequately protect minority rights, we could always defeat the rule. . . .

Some will cry out that the Leadership is trying to institute "gag rules" or worse, but in our judgment this issue is too important and we should tolerate the criticism for the good of the House, its Membership, and the country. For without relief of some kind, we won't be able to do the jobs for which we were elected and the ultimate result will be inefficient Members in an inefficient institution. Neither is desirable; both are avoidable.[54]

LaFalce was recommending a solution to a problem that was, in part, a collective action problem for the Democrats. Although most Democrats had an interest in suppressing repetitive, divisive Republican amendments, many of the same Democrats also had taken advantage of the opportunities to offer floor amendments. Self-restraint proved difficult to exercise in the mid-1970s when so many others were scoring political points at home and in Washington by sponsoring floor amendments. In fact, several of the Democrats signing the LaFalce letter were among the most active sponsors of floor amendments themselves. But by 1979 the Democrats had become painfully aware of the political dangers and practical problems of unlimited floor amendments. The LaFalce letter stated the issue in institutional terms: the efficiency of the House and the burden of unpredictably long floor sessions. The letter also could have mentioned the costs of amending activity for Democratic legislation and the political price that Democrats were paying collectively for casting votes on divisive issues raised by Republican amendments. These Democrats were expressing their willingness to take steps to restrain amending activity, even if it meant that their own opportunities to offer amendments sometimes would be restricted.

For Democratic activists, the dilemma posed by Republican amending activity was not as severe as it would have been a decade earlier. During the 1970s, liberal Democrats gained control of several of the key committees that earlier had been dominated by conservative chairmen. In fact, by 1977 committee and subcommittee chairmen had become more supportive

54. Letter dated August 2, 1979.

of party positions on the floor than the average Democrat.[55] Consequently, the ability to freely offer floor amendments was no longer as vital to the pursuit of liberals' policy interests as it had been in the late 1960s. The LaFalce group was not proposing that the party turn back the clock on the committee reforms; instead, they were proposing to reduce the damage done to committee products and their personal schedules by often unpredictable floor amendments.

Special rules were well suited to the task because of their great flexibility. Most major legislation, the kind concerning the LaFalce group, is brought to the floor through special rules. Special rules are resolutions, reported by the Committee on Rules, that provide for the consideration of legislation on the floor.[56] They may supplement or even supplant the standing rules of the House. For example, special rules may structure the amending process in the Committee of the Whole by ordering amendments, barring certain amendments, or allowing certain amendments that otherwise could not be considered. While rules must be adopted by majority vote before they take effect, they create the possibility of custom-tailoring the amendment process to individual measures.

The solution proposed by LaFalce—designing special rules to limit floor amendments—was ready-made because of the firm control of the Rules Committee by the Democrats and their Speaker. Had there been much doubt about who controlled Rules, the LaFalce group probably would not have turned to special rules. Indeed, senior Rules Democrats Richard Bolling and Gillis Long also were supporting more creative use of special rules by the Democratic leadership and had been urging O'Neill to take advantage of the opportunities special rules represented.[57] Ironically, some of the liberals who sought in the early 1970s to assert party control over special rules in order to check the use of closed rules now were seeking to limit amendments through restrictive rules. In response to the LaFalce letter, as well as to his own observations, no doubt, Speaker O'Neill conferred with Rules Democrats, who proceeded to report more special rules with restrictions on amendments.[58]

The viability of this shift in strategy was dependent on the cohesiveness of the Democratic party in the House. Because special rules require a majority vote on the House floor and Republicans could be expected to object to particularly restrictive rules, Democratic leaders and the Rules Commit-

---

55. See Smith and Deering, *Committees in Congress*, pp. 193–94.
56. See appendix 1 for more detail.
57. Interview with Richard Bolling, October 28, 1986.
58. Russell, "O'Neill Rebounds from Setbacks." Also see Richard E. Cohen, "Filling the Leadership Vacuum," *National Journal*, January 12, 1980, p. 63.

tee would have to design special rules that could attract the support of the vast majority of Democrats. The traditional ideological diversity among Democrats might have made such support quite problematic, but the ideological gap between northern and southern Democrats was closing during the late 1970s. In 1971–72 only 29 percent of southern Democrats supported the party's position on "party votes" 60 percent or more of the time; in 1979–80, 54 percent of the southern Democrats did so.[59] The declining internal polarization made it considerably easier for the Democratic leadership and the Rules Committee to adopt a strategy that would often require party cohesiveness on the floor.

The use of restrictive special rules was not new to the House in 1979, of course. As LaFalce noted, restrictive rules had been employed for tax bills and other legislation from Ways and Means for many years. Rules restricting amendments only to a certain degree were uncommon in other areas—but not unknown. A few restrictive rules—that is, rules that limit but do not prohibit amendments—had been employed in the 94th and 95th Congresses.[60] In 1977, for example, the complex energy package came to the floor under a particularly complicated restrictive rule. In the view of a senior aide to Speaker O'Neill, the successful experience with the 1977 rule left the Democratic leadership receptive to the idea of employing restrictive rules more frequently.[61]

The move to more restrictive rules was aided by Richard Bolling's elevation to the Rules Committee chairmanship in 1979. Bolling, a close friend of Speaker O'Neill, asserted himself in the design of special rules.

59. See David W. Rohde, "Variations in Partisanship in the House of Representatives, 1953–1988: Southern Democrats, Realignment and Agenda Change," paper prepared for the 1988 annual meeting of the American Political Science Association, tables 1, 2, 3. Also see his "Something's Happening Here; What It Is Ain't Exactly Clear: Southern Democrats in the House of Representatives," in Morris P. Fiorina and David W. Rohde, eds., *Home Style and Washington Work: Studies of Congressional Politics* (University of Michigan Press, forthcoming). "Party votes" are roll call votes on which a majority of Democrats vote against a majority of Republicans.

60. Table 3-1 in the next chapter reports the number and types of rules employed between 1975 and 1986. Robinson reports that between 1939 and 1960, 87 of 1,215 rules—7.2 percent—were "closed," a category that appears to include both closed and modified (restrictive) rules. For the four Congresses of 1967–74, Bach reports that restrictive and closed rules comprised 6 percent, 13 percent, 12 percent, and 12 percent, respectively, of all rules. While Bach's figures were not calculated in exactly the same way as those reported here, they suggest that there was some movement to more restrictive rules in the late 1960s and late 1970s, even though their frequency pales in comparison with that of the 96th Congress (1979–80). See James A. Robinson, *The House Rules Committee* (Bobbs-Merrill, 1963), pp. 43–44; and Stanley Bach, "Special Rules in the House of Representatives: Themes and Contemporary Variations," *Congressional Studies*, vol. 8, no. 2 (1981), table 1, p. 43.

61. Interview with Ari Weiss, former executive director of the House Democratic Steering and Policy Committee, July 19, 1987.

"My technique," Bolling explains, "was to take the responsibility and to take my lumps when things went wrong." [62] Bolling took the lead in crafting restrictive rules, frequently coaching bill managers on the type of rule to request of the Rules Committee. Bolling developed a good working relationship with Ari Weiss, O'Neill's chief legislative strategist, and together they helped to reshape special rules in the 96th Congress.

While the number of special rules with restrictive provisions increased somewhat in the 96th Congress, an equally important change occurred in the nature of the restrictive provisions employed. [63] In the 94th and 95th Congresses, about a third of the restrictive rules listed the specific amendments that would be in order on the floor; the remainder protected selected sections of bills from amendment, permitted amendments on only certain sections, or merely required advance notice of amendments to be offered. In the 96th Congress, for the first time, a majority of the restrictive rules specified the particular amendments that would be permitted on the floor. Moreover, of the amendment-specific rules in the 96th Congress, a majority permitted only one or two amendments, a much higher proportion than in the 94th and 95th Congresses. And, in the 96th Congress, the percentage of rules that were fully closed peaked after such rules had been used very sparingly during the preceding Congresses.

Thus Democratic leaders and Rules members began to design some special rules that virtually eliminated uncertainty about the amendments that would be offered in the Committee of the Whole. When such a rule is a possibility, prospective amendment sponsors normally have to prepare their amendments well in advance, appear before the Rules Committee to explain the importance of their amendments and why they should be included in the rule, and perhaps appeal to the Democratic leadership for assistance in getting the amendments to the floor. Because the content and consequences of various amendments are discussed at length among the interested parties, much of the uncertainty about floor amendments is eliminated even if the reported rule does not severely restrict amendments. Restrictive rules provide insulation from unanticipated votes on divisive issues, reduce scheduling burdens, and permit more effective targeting of resources against unfriendly amendments.

Republican reaction to the shift to more restrictive special rules was swift and predictable. One of the first major bills to receive a restrictive rule in the fall of 1979 was the Carter administration's welfare reform

62. Interview with Richard Bolling, October 24, 1986.

63. Chapter 3 extends the discussion of restrictive rules into the 1980s. Also see Stanley Bach and Steven S. Smith, *Managing Uncertainty in the House of Representatives: Adaptation and Innovation in Special Rules* (Brookings, 1988), chap. 3.

legislation. During the debate on the rule, Republican Robert Bauman, the newest member of Rules, protested bitterly:

> The only reason that this bill is being brought to us under a closed rule, allowing one relatively minor amendment, is that apparently the majority on the Ways and Means Subcommittee that controls this legislation does not want to be bothered with the nuisance of having members of the House being able to offer amendments and to vote on them on the floor. . . . This is a continuing trend that we have seen in recent weeks.[64]

Bauman later wrote:

> This new restrictive procedure on offering amendments on the House floor is the most serious and scandalous blow struck against democratic procedures in the House to date, for it effectively disfranchises all 435 members by denying them the opportunity to offer, consider, and vote on amendments to legislation when it comes to the House floor. In addition to being undemocratic, this restrictive approach is based on the assumption that the judgments of our committees are somehow infallible and therefore beyond question or alteration.[65]

Unfortunately for the Republicans, they generally lacked the votes required to defeat or amend the restrictive special rules reported from the Rules Committee.

An Unsettled House

On several counts, the 96th Congress (1979–80) proved to be a transitional one. Tinkering with the rules governing recorded voting and suspension motions was finished, at least for the time being, and the tactical adaptation of special rules was under way. The mix reflected ambivalence about the reforms of the early 1970s. While a few members waxed poetic about the good old days, recorded voting in the Committee of the Whole was in no danger of being repealed. Even House Democrats continued to offer floor amendments in droves whenever they had the opportunity. And the move toward opening floor activity to public view took another step with the inauguration of televised floor sessions in 1979. On the other hand, many members of the House, especially Democrats, had reached a point of satiation with floor amending activity. The frustration with devel-

---

64. *Congressional Record,* November 1, 1979, p. 30554.
65. Robert E. Bauman, "Majority Tyranny in the House," in John H. Rousselot and Richard T. Schulze, eds., *View from the Capitol Dome (Looking Right)* (Ottawa, Ill.: Green Hill Publishers, 1980), p. 11.

opments on the floor ran through the Democratic rank and file as well as the leadership, as the LaFalce appeal indicated. The Democratic Caucus readily endorsed the plans to tighten the rules for recorded voting and to expand the use of suspension motions. Most Democrats approved of the effort to create a more predictable floor schedule and to gain some insulation from unfriendly (usually Republican) amendments.

Assessing the effect on amending activity of any one of the changes of the 96th Congress is very difficult, given the number of nearly simultaneous adjustments that were made.[66] Amending activity was down in the 96th from the astounding level in the previous Congress. Furthermore, amending activity among Republicans dipped far more than among Democrats (see chapter 5). Nevertheless, amending activity in the 96th Congress did not differ much from that in the 93d and 94th Congresses, suggesting that the immediate effects of the adjustments were modest in the 96th.[67]

By 1980 much of the conventional wisdom about the House had been turned on its head. Congress in session was no longer merely Congress on exhibition. A relatively closed, committee-oriented system had become a more open, floor-oriented system for much legislation. Committees surely remained the single most important feature of House policymaking, but bill managers could less frequently take floor action for granted. Dismayed party and committee leaders moved to manage the uncertainty of floor decisionmaking and insulate some of their most important legislation from unfriendly amendments.

The developments on the floor had mixed effects for the decisionmaking processes within the House. In the first place, floor developments were integral to the changes within committees that followed the reforms of the early 1970s. Most obviously, the expansion of amending opportunities

66. Increasing the number of members required to request a recorded vote probably had a very modest effect. Republican activist Robert Bauman asserts that, given the poor attendance on the floor during most floor debate, the new threshold was sufficient for a few requests for recorded votes to be turned down (interview, July 16, 1987). No count of rejected requests is available, however, so a more definitive evaluation is not possible. In any case, there is no evidence—and no informed opinion that I have been able to uncover—that the higher threshold reduced the volume or success of amending activity.

67. The effect of televising floor sessions is considered at greater length in the next chapter, but it is worth noting that the advent of House television in March 1979 was not associated with a surge in amending activity. The ability to appear on television, all things being equal, may increase the political value of going to the floor with amendments for most members. And yet the number of floor amendments fell in the 96th Congress and again in the 97th Congress, indicating that whatever stimulus television may have provided, its effect on the volume of amending activity was overwhelmed by the effects of other developments.

made it easier for committee members to challenge their chairmen on the floor. The reforms left chairmen weaker but not disarmed, for they retained day-to-day control of committee agendas, large staffs, and a reservoir of expertise and political connections. Even for subcommittee chairmen, a viable floor option is vital to their intracommittee influence. The reforms of the early 1970s created independent but not wholly autonomous subcommittees, whose recommendations are frequently challenged at the full committee stage. Thus in many circumstances the decentralization of intracommittee processes was reinforced by the new opportunities on the floor.

In a broader sense, however, developments on the floor served to check the extent of decentralization in the House. Floor amending activity potentially undermines the autonomy of committees regardless of the degree of decentralization within them. By forcing committee members—whether the full committee chairman, a subcommittee chairman, or a junior minority party subcommittee member—to look ahead and outward to the floor, the developments of the 1970s expanded the range of interests involved in committee deliberations and added new uncertainties to committee members' political calculations. Consequently, the independence that subcommittees gained cannot be translated as subcommittee autonomy within the House.

To the contrary, the decentralization of committee decisionmaking was, in many respects, inconsistent with the thrust of the reforms of floor procedure, even though both committee and floor reforms were efforts to curtail the power of full committee chairmen. The new opportunities and uses of the House floor served to enhance the power of rank-and-file and minority party members, thus moving the House toward a more collegial style of decisionmaking. The need for party, committee, and subcommittee leaders to anticipate and even consult rank-and-file members more regularly gave junior and minority party members much more influence on policy and strategy. Majority party leaders were stimulated to institutionalize this emerging relationship through more frequent use of task forces, an expanded whip system, and more frequent caucus meetings. But these developments undermined the autonomy of the newly empowered subcommittees and their chairmen. In short, the strategic setting of the postreform House was altered in a fundamental way by the new combination of decentralized committees and more active rank-and-file members on the chamber floor.

What began in the early 1970s as an effort to weaken the stranglehold of committee chairmen over House policymaking ended as an effort to minimize the damage of unforeseen consequences for majority party and committee control. The reform of floor voting procedure had consequences unanticipated by many of its promoters, with the majority party suffering along with the committees it dominated. The response, which took the form of further innovation and elaboration in floor procedure, was initiated by the majority party and its leaders. The result helped to reestablish some predictability in floor activity but left the key feature of the reform—recorded voting—in place.

CHAPTER THREE

Counterrevolution in the House?

THE INGREDIENTS for a new era of floor decisionmaking were accumulating in the House throughout the 1970s. Majority party Democrats were incrementally adjusting floor procedures and their own strategies to the conditions of the postreform House. The full effect of the evolving procedures and practices was not felt until the 1980s, however, when the political environment of the House changed radically. The 1980 elections brought Republican control of the White House and the Senate, which thrust House Democrats into a defensive position. The congressional agenda shifted from an array of welfare, energy, environmental, health, and consumer issues to a focus on budgetary issues. These developments intensified the importance of controlling floor action for the House Democrats. By the end of the 1980s, the floor retained a far more important role than it had in the prereform House, but evolving majority party attitudes about unrestrained floor amending activity yielded major changes in practice. The drive to more collegial forms of decisionmaking ended and a new balance in patterns of decisionmaking emerged.

This chapter explores the current era by examining the consequences of four developments for floor decisionmaking. First, I consider the effect of budget politics on floor decisionmaking. An agenda dominated by the budget deficit reduced the number of targets for amending activity and stimulated the use of even more protective rules for much of the remaining floor agenda. Second, I discuss the Democrats' steps to limit appropriations riders—amendments to appropriations bills that seek to alter public policy by barring spending for certain purposes. Third, I review the effects of televised floor sessions on floor activity. The expected stimulative effect of television on amending activity was not realized, but there were other consequences of television for floor activity. Finally, the character of special rules is investigated further. Inventiveness marked the design of special rules in the 1980s, sometimes as a direct consequence of developments in budget politics. Innovations in special rules played a central role in curbing floor amending activity.

Budget Politics and the House Floor

Starting in 1980, the congressional agenda was transformed by the politics of reducing federal budget deficits. Budget politics permeated all issues, narrowed policy options, and further intensified partisanship. Budget politics altered relations between the parties, between Congress and the White House, between the House and Senate, and among committees, party leaders, and the floor in both chambers. Understanding these developments is the first step to understanding floor activity in the 1980s.

At first, large budget deficits put House Democrats on the defensive, reinforcing their leadership's interest in carefully regulating unfriendly floor amending activity. Throughout the 1980s, budgetary constraints limited new legislative initiatives and reduced the number of bills coming to the floor, thereby reducing the number of targets for amendments. Amending targets were further pruned as the legislative vehicles for making fiscal decisions took on greater importance. Much legislation that normally would have been considered as separate bills was folded into omnibus budget measures. Furthermore, the politics and time constraints of budget decisions produced even more restrictive rules for floor consideration of money bills. These developments altered the kinds, location, and sequence of vital policy decisions made by the House.

The Budget Process and the Role of the Floor

During the 1970s the budget process did not fundamentally change the power of standing committees and their relations with the chamber floors. As envisioned by the Congressional Budget and Impoundment Control Act of 1974, Congress would adopt its own budget, with the new Budget committees assigned the responsibility of designing the resolutions that would embody the budget. A first budget resolution was to be adopted in May of each year, setting nonbinding targets for the spending and revenue decisions of the authorization, appropriation, and tax bills to follow. The initiative for binding spending decisions remained with the authorization and appropriations committees, whose legislation would be considered on the floor during the summer months. A second budget resolution was to be adopted in September, which was to be binding because it could order particular committees to report legislation reconciling spending under their jurisdiction with the resolution. Meaningful "reconciliation" instructions were not included in House budget resolutions of the 1970s, however. The House tended to endorse the decisions of the summer months in the second budget resolutions, preserving the autonomy of the standing committees in setting budgetary policy.

Budget resolutions of the 1970s were treated like most other measures when they reached the House floor. That is, they were subject to dozens of amendments under open rules. The floor continued to be an open appeals court, in this case open to the appeals of committees distressed by Budget Committee decisions as well as to the amendments of the rank and file. Under such conditions, the Budget Committee was very sensitive to the preferences of committees and the House in writing the resolutions in the first place.[1]

In 1980, when the federal government faced an unexpectedly large budget deficit, congressional Democrats in both chambers agreed to add some teeth to the budget process. They did so by including reconciliation instructions in the first budget resolution, ordering several standing committees to report legislation that would cut spending in the next fiscal year. Since budget resolutions must be approved on the floor, incorporating reconciliation instructions in the first resolution put the floor ahead of the committees in the decisionmaking sequence on spending policy. The legislative initiative shifted from the standing committees to those writing the version of the first budget resolution that could attract majority support on the floor—whether they were Budget Committee members, party leaders, or the administration.[2] House Democrats justified such an infringement on the autonomy of the standing committees on the basis of the severity of the deficit problem and the threat the deficit represented to the party's collective well-being.

House Democrats found themselves in radically different circumstances after the 1980 elections. Ronald Reagan swept Jimmy Carter out of the White House with a policy platform that challenged the core of the Democratic legacy of the previous two decades. Just as important and much more surprising, the Republicans wrested majority control of the Senate from the Democrats. And to make matters worse for the Democrats, Republicans won a net gain of thirty-four additional House seats, which would soon permit the new administration to forge a majority coalition of Republicans and conservative Democrats for its preferred versions of the

1. For background on the origins of the 1974 budget act and its implementation during the 1970s, see Allen Schick, *Congress and Money: Budgeting, Spending, and Taxing* (Washington: Urban Institute Press, 1980).

2. For background on the use of reconciliation, see John W. Ellwood, "The Great Exception: The Congressional Budget Process in an Age of Decentralization," in Lawrence C. Dodd and Bruce I. Oppenheimer, eds., *Congress Reconsidered*, 3d ed. (Washington: CQ Press, 1985), pp. 315–42. Not surprisingly, the first use of reconciliation instructions in the first budget resolution received little support from senior committee members or the members of the affected committees. See "Junior Members Back Reconciliation Plan," *Congressional Quarterly Weekly Report*, May 10, 1980, p. 1229.

first budget resolution and reconciliation package in 1981. The new reconciliation procedure provided the means for the conservative coalition to impose its will, by a majority vote on the floor, on the Democratically controlled standing committees.[3]

The political position of the Democratic leadership improved as President Reagan's sway with conservative Democrats weakened after 1981, giving the majority party leadership a stronger hand in shaping spending priorities. Nevertheless, skyrocketing deficits in the following years led Congress to continue to write reconciliation instructions into first budget resolutions.[4] Persistent deadlock over how to set spending and revenue priorities caused recurring delays in the consideration of budget resolutions and reconciliation packages and yielded reconciliation instructions requiring substantially smaller savings than in the 1981 package.[5] As a result, the grip of reconciliation on the decisions of standing committees proved to be less firm in the five years following 1981.

Frustration with continuing high deficits and political stalemate led Congress to adopt the Gramm-Rudman-Hollings procedure in 1985. The new procedure provided across-the-board cuts in spending (shielding a few programs from the cuts) if Congress and the president could not agree on the means to cut spending by specified amounts in each of the next five years. After the Supreme Court ruled unconstitutional a key mechanism of the procedure—the role of the comptroller general in triggering the across-the-board cuts—Congress modified the procedure in 1987. The effect of both versions of the procedure was to reinforce the reconciliation procedure and the appropriations targets of the first budget resolution and, in the absence of successful deficit reduction, to take individual spending decisions out of the hands of Congress—committees, leaders, and the floors—and of the president.

Omnibus Legislating

Even though the reconciliation process lost much of its bite after 1981, the major spending and tax measures continued to dominate the congres-

---

3. Criticisms of the use of reconciliation in 1981 can be found in *Congressional Budget Process*, Hearings before the Task Force on the Budget Process of the House Committee on Rules, 97 Cong. 2 sess. (Government Printing Office, 1983).

4. Since 1982 the requirement for a second budget resolution has been circumvented by making the first budget resolution's targets binding at the start of the fiscal year if Congress fails to adopt a separate second resolution. This provision merely acknowledges that placing reconciliation instructions in the first resolution makes the first resolution binding.

5. For a synopsis of the budget stalemate of the 1980s, see John R. Cranford, "Budget Standoffs Characterize Reagan Years," *Congressional Quarterly Weekly Report*, October 24, 1987, p. 2572.

sional agenda. Increasingly, committees, party leaders, and rank-and-file members saw two types of measures—reconciliation bills and continuing appropriations resolutions—as vehicles for passing legislation normally considered as separate bills. The Democratic House, in particular, recognized that attaching other legislation to necessary money legislation was a way to compel the Republican Senate and White House to consider its legislation. The result was more reliance on "omnibus" measures.[6] Omnibus measures reduced the number of separate measures taken to the floor, reshaped the normal targets for floor amendments, and altered the strategic setting in which the two parties, rank-and-file members, and the standing committees interacted.

Right from the start, reconciliation packages included items unrelated to budget savings. The 1980 reconciliation bill included many provisions expanding health benefits under the medicare and medicaid programs, which stimulated Ways and Means' ranking Republican, Barber Conable, to complain, "I am deeply disturbed that it seems to have become a new mechanism for holding the government hostage, agglomerating a lot of very important substantive issues in the name of reconciliation."[7] The 1981 Republican reconciliation package, adopted on the floor instead of the version put together by the House committees, made dozens of sweeping changes in policy that Republicans had pursued with separate bills for many years. The changes so outraged Democrats that many of them swore that they would never permit such a subversion of committee jurisdiction in the future. Yet many of the same Democrats recognized the political cover that the reconciliation process would provide and included major nonbudgetary items in the Democratic version that was defeated on the floor.[8] Conable voted for the Republican package.

Since 1981 reconciliation bills have been smaller, but only in the sense that they have provided for smaller savings in spending.[9] Each one affected

6. On the move to omnibus legislating, see Dale Tate, "Retrenchment Tool: Use of Omnibus Bills Burgeons Despite Members' Misgivings; Long-Term Impact Disputed," *Congressional Quarterly Weekly Report*, September 25, 1982, pp. 2379–83; and Allen Schick, "The Whole and the Parts: Piecemeal and Integrated Approaches to Congressional Budgeting," prepared for the Task Force on the Budget Process, House Committee on the Budget, Serial No. CP-3 (GPO, 1987).

7. Quoted in Dale Tate, "$8.2 Billion Reconciliation Bill Cleared," *Congressional Quarterly Weekly Report*, December 6, 1980, pp. 3487–88. Other provisions added benefits in child nutrition programs, including one important item that was added in conference.

8. For a summary of the 1981 House reconciliation bill's provisions, see "Summary of Differences in Reconciliation Measures," *Congressional Quarterly Weekly Report*, July 4, 1981, pp. 1170–78.

9. In recent years, the House also has employed several separate bills to handle reconciliation packages of the various committees.

at least seven House committees and incorporated major authorization items that previously would have been considered in separate legislation, if at all. In 1982, for example, Ways and Means incorporated in its reconciliation package the text of a bill providing for an extension of unemployment compensation benefits. As a separate bill, the extension faced a nearly certain presidential veto; as a part of the deficit reduction package, the president was forced to sign it into law. In 1984, when the House passed a reconciliation bill before acting on the first budget resolution to avoid delays in an election year, the House package included a previously rejected health program for poor pregnant women and their children and expanded medicaid coverage.[10] Nonbudget items also made up a large part of the 1985 and 1986 reconciliation packages.[11]

Despite vigorous criticism of these uses of reconciliation, efforts to keep reconciliation bills free of nonbudget items usually failed.[12] Many committees mastered the technique of loading their reconciliation recommendations with unrelated provisions. In a decade when new program initiatives usually had little chance of enactment as freestanding measures, committees did not want to give up one of the few legislative vehicles for getting their proposals to the president's desk. As one congressional observer put it, "At a time when there are only a handful of legislative trains leaving the station, few want to see any of them derailed."[13]

Continuing appropriations resolutions, or "CRs" as they often are called, also became central features of the congressional agenda in the 1980s. Continuing resolutions are required when one or more of the thirteen regular appropriations bills is not enacted by October 1, the start of

10. In 1984 both chambers acted upon reconciliation and appropriations legislation before final approval of the first budget resolution, turning inside out what little remained of an orderly process. Floor consideration of appropriations bills before final action on a first budget resolution required waivers of a provision of the 1974 budget act. See Dale Tate, "Changes Being Considered: Hill Budget Process Working to Force Economic Decisions," *Congressional Quarterly Weekly Report*, August 18, 1984, pp. 2015–20.

11. For example, a 1985 House reconciliation bill included a reauthorization of Amtrak and the text of a $14.3 billion bill reauthorizing federal subsidized housing programs as well as creating new programs. Although the housing strategy did not work in the end, House Democrats hoped to force the Republican Senate to act on the controversial bill by including it in the reconciliation package. The 1986 reconciliation bill included a highly controversial provision to expand AFDC benefits to two-parent families, a complex Conrail sale package, and many health program items. In 1987 the Democrats attempted to include a major welfare reform package in the reconciliation bill, but the rule for the bill was defeated. After the welfare reform package was removed, the bill passed.

12. House Republicans, for example, have proposed that committees be prohibited from including items such as general authorization legislation in their reconciliation packages. See *Congressional Record*, daily edition, January 6, 1987, pp. H8–9.

13. Alan Ehrenhalt, "Media, Power Shifts Dominate O'Neill's House," *Congressional Quarterly Weekly Report*, September 13, 1986, p. 2137.

the new fiscal year. They need be only one- or two-page interim measures extending spending authority during the period before the regular bill is enacted. When it becomes clear that one or more of the regular bills is never going to be adopted, a year-long continuing resolution must be approved.

In the 1970s it was common for one or two of the regular appropriations bills not to be enacted before Congress adjourned at the end of the calendar year. In the 1980s delays in approval of budget resolutions and spending policy stalemates repeatedly disrupted the normal appropriations process. In 1982, 1984, and 1985, over half of the regular bills were not enacted by the end of the year. In 1986 and 1987, none of the regular bills was enacted, requiring Congress to adopt mammoth catchall continuing resolutions. Members seeking to influence policy through appropriations measures were forced to do so in the continuing resolutions. As essential measures, they also attracted members looking for ways to get nonappropriations items into law when there was no time for separate action late in the sessions. Conveniently, continuing resolutions may contain any manner of legislation, unlike regular appropriations bills, for which strict germaneness rules apply.[14] As a result, continuing resolutions became critical battlefields on both budget and nonbudget matters.[15]

The effects of omnibus legislating and budgetary constraints on the structure of the floor agenda were unmistakable. The most obvious was a significant contraction in the number of major bills reaching the House floor. A good barometer of the number of major bills before the House is the number of measures reaching the floor under a special rule. In the Congresses between 1975 and 1980, an average of 205 bills was brought to the floor under special rules. In contrast, the first three Congresses of the 1980s averaged only 110 such measures. At the same time, the average size of measures eventually enacted into law shot upward. In 1975–80, the average length of enacted measures was 7.9 pages, compared with 9.3 pages during the next six years.[16]

Omnibus legislating also transformed the nature of amending opportu-

14. Under House precedents, continuing resolutions are not considered "general appropriations" measures, which may not include legislative authorizations.

15. Republicans also have proposed to limit the uses of continuing resolutions. In 1987 they proposed that continuing resolutions be limited to thirty-day periods or less and use set formulas for determining appropriations levels. They recommended that special rules for continuing resolutions permit amendments to those sections not previously adopted by the House and that the rules could not waive points of order against continuing resolutions without a two-thirds majority vote. *Congressional Record*, daily edition, January 6, 1987, pp. H8–9.

16. See Norman J. Ornstein, Thomas E. Mann, and Michael J. Malbin, *Vital Statistics on Congress, 1987–1988* (Washington: Congressional Quarterly, 1987), p. 170.

nities on the floor. Fewer but larger measures, usually considered under severe time pressures, cut down on the number of separate targets for amending activity on the floor. This was most obvious in the 97th and 98th Congresses, when even the total number of pages of enacted legislation was down from the level of the late 1970s.[17] Large, complex bills, with many provisions drafted at the last minute by various committees and sub-committees, also put rank-and-file members on the floor at a severe informational disadvantage. When a major continuing resolution was considered on the floor in 1986, a senior member, referring to the chairman (James Whitten) and ranking Republican (Silvio Conte) of the Appropriations Committee, griped, "Jamie knows all. Sil knows some. The average member knows zip."[18] Even if they had been permitted to offer floor amendments at will, most members would not have been in a position to take advantage of the opportunity.

Budget Measures, Restrictive Rules, and Amending Activity

Omnibus legislating appears even more consequential for floor amending activity once the special rules for budget measures are considered. Time constraints, volatile issues, and partisan politics prompted the Democratic leadership and the Rules Committee to carefully frame the special rules for budget measures. Without exception, budget resolutions, reconciliation bills, and year-long continuing resolutions of the 1980s were subject to special rules severely limiting floor amendments. In fact, reconciliation measures and continuing resolutions drew completely closed rules on several occasions during the 1980s.

The consequences of restrictive rules and omnibus packages for amending activity were quite dramatic. For example, the number of separate amendments on first budget resolutions averaged nearly twenty between 1975 and 1979. In contrast, between 1981 and 1986 the average was just over three amendments for the adopted resolutions, nearly all of which were comprehensive substitutes.[19] The effect on appropriations amending activity was less dramatic because many bills included in continuing appropriations are considered separately on the floor in advance.[20] Nevertheless,

---

17. Ornstein and others, *Vital Statistics*, p. 170.

18. Quoted in Elizabeth Wehr, "Congress Clears $576 Billion Spending Measure," *Congressional Quarterly Weekly Report*, October 18, 1986, p. 2585.

19. The first version of the first budget resolution for fiscal 1983 was defeated after none of the substitute alternatives was adopted. The number of amendments considered on the floor, including the substitutes and amendments thereto, totaled forty-nine.

20. That is, the House often passes appropriations bills for which there is no Senate or conference action; this requires that the bills' text eventually be included in continuing resolutions.

swollen continuing resolutions and protective rules have reduced dramatically the volume of appropriations amending activity. In the six years before 1981, 815 amendments were offered to appropriations measures, while in the following six years only 502 amendments were offered.[21]

Budget measures' restrictive rules, combined with the necessity that they be enacted, gave committee draftsmen of the measures greater autonomy. The House was presented with many take-it-or-leave-it choices on deficit reduction and appropriations packages loaded with nonbudget items. Members frequently complained about their limited choices, as well as their inability to learn what was in large, often hastily drafted, bills. Republicans repeatedly lambasted the Democrats for barring them from offering meaningful amendments.

The take-it-or-leave-it nature of omnibus legislating was taken one step further in late 1987. Just before a joint White House-congressional negotiating team on the budget deficit reached a compromise, House Democrats managed to get the House to pass a reconciliation package, which was considered under a rule permitting only a Republican substitute. The compromise package produced by the negotiating group called for changes in the mix of spending cuts and taxes contained in the House-passed version, prompting Republicans to call for a new bill. House Democrats, however, decided to take the House-passed version to conference, modify it there, and leave the House with an up-or-down decision on the product of the conference committee negotiations. As a result, no one had an opportunity to amend the new version on the House floor.[22]

In many respects, then, omnibus legislating and restrictive rules allowed some authorizing committees and especially the Appropriations Committee to recover some autonomy lost in the 1970s. But such a simplistic interpretation about committee power would be unwise. While some committees' adaptations to deficit politics were important, the net effect of the developments in the 1980s is quite ambiguous. The need for omnibus measures in the first place is the result of a spending policy gridlock and highly constrained spending choices. For Appropriations and other committees, what they gain in protection from unfriendly amendments to items attached to omnibus measures may be trivial when matched against their losses due to budget constraints on new initiatives and spending levels.

21. About half of the decline in appropriations amendments in the 98th and 99th Congresses is due to a new rule on appropriations riders, as is discussed below. It also is worth noting that even when all thirteen regular appropriations fail to be taken to the floor, funding for governmental functions still is provided in continuing resolutions. Thus the number of potential targets for floor amendments remains fairly constant from year to year.

22. See Elizabeth Wehr, "Turning Budget Pact into Law Won't Be Easy," *Congressional Quarterly Weekly Report*, November 28, 1987, pp. 2929–30.

Thus, while a few committees gained autonomy in relation to their parent chamber, the negative-sum nature of the budget game left the net value for most House committees quite ambiguous.

Moreover, some of the developments had counterbalancing effects. For example, some authorization committees that gained a modicum of protection from floor amendments under the special rules for reconciliation legislation found that continuing resolutions, with protective rules, could be used to circumvent the authorization stage altogether. Appropriations members occasionally incorporated nonappropriations provisions in continuing resolutions in order to modify policies in ways that the relevant authorization committee would not support. For many authorizing committees, therefore, there was great uncertainty about the structure of the legislative game they would play each year.[23]

The most unambiguous effect of reliance on omnibus budget measures was to enhance the position of the Appropriations committees relative to most other standing committees. In general, authorizing committees benefited from continuing resolutions only to the extent that they acquired the cooperation of the appropriators. Appropriators were in a position to resist the inclusion of certain authorization provisions in continuing resolutions. Sometimes appropriators could even assume the role of authorization committees in devising legislative language for the continuing resolutions. The parliamentary location of the appropriators also gave them some additional leverage over authorization committees on matters the authorization committees were handling in nonappropriations measures. The return to regular appropriations bills in 1988 served to avert the confrontation between appropriations and authorization committees that appeared inevitable in 1987.

It should not be assumed that any gains in committee autonomy will have lasting value. In January 1988, in the aftermath of embarrassing news stories about items included in the 1987 continuing resolution, forty-nine House Democrats wrote Speaker James Wright that they would not "support the use of the continuing resolution as an end-of-session fiscal year catch-all legislative vehicle."[24] The letter said that "to do so is destructive of the jurisdictions of the authorization committees and prevents the orderly consideration of individual appropriations bills." The letter followed

23. For additional background on authorizations and omnibus legislating, see Lawrence J. Haas, "Unauthorized Action," *National Journal*, January 2, 1988, pp. 17–21.

24. Letter dated January 7, 1988, drafted and circulated by Representatives Buddy MacKay, George Miller, and Charles W. Stenholm. For background, see Tom Kenworthy, "49 Say Nay to Catchall Spending Bills: Hill Democrats Send Pledge to Wright," *Washington Post*, February 1, 1988, p. A13.

a December 1987 meeting of committee chairmen with the Speaker during which the chairmen complained bitterly about violations of their jurisdictions in the 1987 continuing resolution.[25] Wright agreed to do what he could to avoid another massive continuing resolution. With the help of President Reagan's subsequent vow to veto future omnibus continuing resolutions, all thirteen regular appropriations bills had passed the House by the end of 1988. The future of mammoth continuing resolutions is uncertain.

Appropriations Riders

Even with omnibus spending bills, most appropriations bills continued to reach the House floor for separate consideration during the 1980s. Many of them were later folded into continuing resolutions because they failed to receive timely Senate or conference action, but they were first subject to floor amendments as separate bills in the House. As a result, appropriations "riders" continued to be a nagging problem for House Democrats and the Appropriations Committee. Riders are amendments, added in committee or on the floor, that come in one of two forms. "Legislative riders" change existing law in some way. Unless protected by a special rule or adopted by unanimous consent, legislative riders are prohibited by House rules. "Limitation amendments" place temporary restrictions on the purposes for which spending is authorized without altering any other existing law. House precedents permit such amendments to appropriations bills, even though they often have important policy implications. Authorizing committees have complained for decades that riders undermine their jurisdiction, while others, including Appropriations members, have found the annual appropriations bills to be useful vehicles for pursuing their policy objectives.

A part of the proliferation of floor amendments in the 1970s was an expansion in the number of limitation riders offered on the floor (figure 3-1). The number of riders peaked in the 96th Congress (1979–80), when

25. See "Democrats Protest Catchall Bills," *Congressional Quarterly Weekly Report*, January 16, 1988, p. 126. President Ronald Reagan also protested large continuing resolutions in his 1988 state of the union address. See Janet Hook, "Reagan's Attack on Pork-Fed Mega-Bills Strikes a Responsive Chord in Congress," *Congressional Quarterly Weekly Report*, January 30, 1988, pp. 190–91. Even Appropriations Committee members recognized the potential for a revolt against continuing resolutions. One Appropriations Democrat said that "there's been a revulsion against the process this year. Even members of the Committee don't like it. . . . We're already talking about how we can prevent it in the future." Quoted in Jacqueline Calmes, "Fights on Contra Aid, Fairness Doctrine: Big Spending Decisions Go Down to the Wire," *Congressional Quarterly Weekly Report*, December 19, 1987, p. 3117.

FIGURE 3-1. *Number of Limitation Amendments Offered to House Appropriations Bills, 88th–98th Congresses (1963–84)*

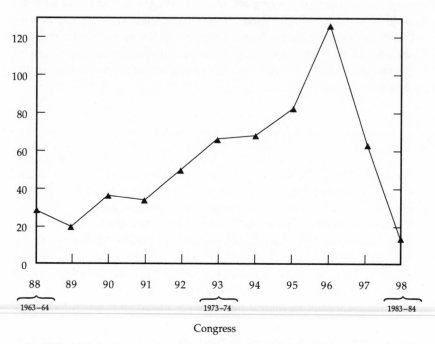

Congress

SOURCE:Richard C. Sachs, "Limitation Amendments to Appropriations Bills: The Implementation of House Rule XXI(2)(d) in the Ninety-Eighth Congress," Congressional Research Service, December 14, 1984.

126 were offered. Limitation riders were used disproportionately by Republicans and Democratic conservatives who lacked votes in the committees.[26] Riders on such highly controversial issues as abortion, school busing, schools, and job safety regulations forced members to cast recorded votes, often repeatedly, on politically sensitive matters.

The Democratic leadership gave serious consideration to a rules change to prohibit or limit the use of riders in late 1980.[27] The outcome of the 1980 elections, which made southern Democrats the pivotal bloc on budget and tax policy decisions, led Speaker O'Neill to put off any change to avoid

26. Alan Murray, "'Vampire Politics': House Funding Bill Riders Become Potent Policy Force," *Congressional Quarterly Weekly Report*, November 1, 1980, pp. 3251–55.

27. Barring limitation amendments was a part of the recommendations of the last reform committee of the 1970s. See *Final Report*, House Select Committee on Committees, 96 Cong. 2 sess. Report 96-866 (GPO, 1980), pp. 80–83.

alienating the southern conservatives. During the 97th Congress (1981–82), the number of limitation amendments dropped considerably, due primarily to omnibus legislating and restrictive rules, but they continued to be offered in substantial numbers. After Democratic strength was reinforced by the outcome of the 1982 elections, the Democrats imposed a new rule on riders.[28]

The new rule, adopted by the House in January 1983, requires that members seeking to offer limitation amendments to an appropriations bill must wait until all other amendments are considered. Even then, a limitation amendment may not be offered if the bill manager makes a successful motion that the Committee of the Whole rise and report the bill to the House, which ends the amending process. Only if the motion to rise fails may a member be recognized to offer a limitation amendment. The motion to rise is not debatable, so a member who intends to offer a limitation amendment must make advance preparations to prevent his or her colleagues from supporting a motion to rise. Only one limitation amendment is permitted after each motion to rise fails, so it is easy for a chamber majority to avoid voting on controversial amendments. Of course, a special rule may put in order a limitation amendment during the regular amending stage in the Committee of the Whole.

Limitation amendments were virtually eliminated from the House floor by the new rule. A survey of appropriations amendments uncovered only six limitation amendments in 1983 and five in 1984.[29] Three of the eleven amendments had been granted a waiver of the new rule in a special rule adopted by the House. On four other occasions, a limitation amendment was turned away by a successful motion to rise. Rules Committee Democrats receive few inquiries about waivers of the rule, which might be included in a special rule, suggesting that House members expect Rules to be quite frugal in granting their requests. Rules Republicans, not surprisingly, are questioned more frequently about the possibility of a waiver, but they are seldom optimistic about the prospects of obtaining one.[30] The near

28. Under the old rule, known as the "Holman rule," amendments to appropriations bills that limited expenditures for purposes that otherwise were permitted in law were allowed as long as they reduced expenditures. See Stanley Bach, "The Status of Limitation Amendments under the Rules of the House of Representatives for the 98th Congress," Congressional Research Service, February 7, 1983.

29. Richard C. Sachs, "Limitation Amendments to Appropriations Bills: The Implementation of House Rule XXI(2)(d) in the Ninety-Eighth Congress," Congressional Research Service, December 14, 1984.

30. An aide to Representative James Quillen, Rules' ranking Republican, reports that he receives several inquiries per week when general appropriations bills are on the floor, but

abandonment of limitation amendments is a significant part of the drop in appropriations amending activity since 1983.

The new rule has not purged appropriations measures of limitation provisions, however. The rule does not affect the ability of the Appropriations Committee to include such language in the bills it reports to the floor.[31] As long as there is majority support for the committee bill and the motion to rise, the new mechanism retains committee discretion but limits amending opportunities for members on the floor. Thus the union of very restrictive rules for continuing resolutions and a ban on floor limitation amendments substantially strengthened the hand of the Appropriations Committee on the floor of the House. But again, the difficulty of weighing these gains in autonomy against the losses imposed by spending constraints precludes a tidy interpretation of the net effect of 1980s budget politics on the Appropriations Committee's power.

Televising House Floor Sessions

The most conspicuous aspect of floor activity in the 1980s is the presence of television. Many opponents argued that televising floor sessions would produce more grandstanding and generate more amending activity. They suggested that televised sessions would enhance members' ability to reach an outside audience by offering and debating floor amendments. Television also would make it easier to keep abreast of floor developments and to become familiar with floor procedure. A 1980 survey, in which members were asked about their use of the television signal cabled to their offices, confirmed that television was aiding members in these ways.[32] Moreover, televised sessions might be expected to sensitize everyone—members, staff, lobbyists, the national media, and the general public—to developments on the House floor, thereby increasing the political import of floor decisions. But it turns out, at least so far, that it is unlikely that this most conspicuous change on the House floor had a significant effect on substantive floor activity.

That conclusion was not obvious at first. Indeed, the first major legislative trial for the new system, the debate on the first budget resolution in May 1979, seemed to confirm the worst fears of television's opponents.

---

indicates that "most of them won't bother to ask Rules for a waiver if they do not have a chance of getting it." Interview with Michael Hynes, August 6, 1987.

31. See Bach, "The Status of Limitation Amendments," pp. 13–14.

32. The study was conducted by the Committee on House Administration. Cited and discussed in Ronald Garay, *Congressional Television: A Legislative History* (Westport, Conn.: Greenwood Press, 1984), p. 142.

The budget resolution was the first bill of genuinely national import to come to the floor after the cameras were turned on. To Speaker O'Neill's chagrin, the resolution faced forty-one first- and second-degree amendments and the debate stretched over three weeks, setting records for budget resolution debates in the House. O'Neill attributed the multitude of amendments to the presence of television cameras.[33] There is little doubt that several amendments were offered for symbolic purposes, but attributing the activity to television is very difficult. Television probably added little to the symbolic value of amendment sponsorship and recorded votes. The building intensity of the budget debate and the difficulty of the choices may have led the amendment sponsors to the same actions.[34]

The effects on amending activity of televised sessions, which began in March 1979, were never given a chance to materialize fully. Beginning in late 1979, the shift to more restrictive special rules for major bills prevented the members from fully exploiting the opportunities created by House television. Even so, the incentives to use a floor amendment to get television time were not as great as they seemed at first. Several factors must be kept in mind.

First, the audience for television coverage of the floor is quite small. The number of local cable television systems carrying C-SPAN, which provides gavel-to-gavel coverage of House and Senate floor sessions, increased from 700 in 1980 to 1,300 in 1984 and recently reached 1,900. About a quarter of House members' districts had no cable systems during the early 1980s, and in most districts cable television is not available to most constituents.[35] Moreover, most amending activity is conducted during afternoon hours rather than during the prime-time evening hours. Only four in ten cable viewers watch C-SPAN at all, and those four report a mean of only twelve viewing hours each month.[36]

Second, the use of taped portions of floor debate in local newscasts is very limited. On occasion, some members notify local broadcast stations of their floor activity in advance so the local news editor can have it recorded for news program use. But seldom does prospective local-station use play much of a role in members' decisions to sponsor amendments. Members know that the probability is small that taped segments of floor sessions will be used. Many amendments are not newsworthy, amendments come up when it is too late to be used on the local news, and not all local

33. Garay, *Congressional Television*, p. 138.
34. See "Process Questioned: Budget Making Is 'Devilishly Difficult Thing,' House Finds," *Congressional Quarterly Weekly Report*, May 12, 1979, pp. 878–79.
35. See Garay, *Congressional Television*, p. 143.
36. *C-SPAN Update*, January 14, 1985, special supplement, pp. 2–3.

stations have the technical capacity to receive the satellite signals from the floor. When local stations are notified, it tends to be as an afterthought. A 1984 survey of House press secretaries showed that televised floor proceedings ranked at the bottom of a list of thirteen alternative media outlets for members.[37]

Third, use of taped floor speeches in campaign advertising is prohibited by House rules, precluding the most obvious use of taped debate on floor amendments. Nonincumbents are not covered by the House rules, however, and there have been a few instances in which challengers have used tapes of floor sessions against incumbents. House Republicans began storing tapes of floor sessions for use by challengers to incumbent Democrats in 1983, and the Democrats followed suit in 1984. Republican leader Robert Michel's 1984 challenger used clips of Michel in negative campaign ads, stimulating both parties' campaign chairmen to take some interest in penalizing challengers who use the tapes in ads. Despite some bipartisan interest in adopting regulations of broader scope, partisan bickering has prevented agreement on the appropriate action.[38]

Fourth, floor amendments are only one way, and not the easiest way, to gain the floor for attracting media attention. The House offers members numerous opportunities to give speeches. Each floor session begins with a period in which members may give one-minute speeches on any subject. Members also may offer pro forma amendments during floor debate on most bills in order to acquire time to speak before the cameras. The House also permits "special-order" speeches by members at the end of each day's session.

Finally, the nature of the live coverage limits some of its potential political uses. The Speaker of the House supervises the in-house television system, from which the signal is fed to C-SPAN and other outlets. Speaker O'Neill established, and Speaker Wright has continued, guidelines to preserve the decorum of floor sessions, such as limiting the size of visual displays and banning legible lapel buttons. Whenever there is a recorded vote, members' individual votes are not shown and members' activity in the chamber during the vote is difficult to observe. Consequently, tapes of the session cannot be used to document a particular member's absence, vote, or floor behavior during a recorded vote.

37. Timothy Cook, "Press Secretaries and Media Strategies in the House of Representatives: Deciding Whom to Pursue," *American Journal of Political Science*, vol. 32 (November 1988), p. 1054, table 1.

38. Diane Granat, "Free Hand for Non-Incumbents: Political Uses of House Tapes Generating Inter-Party Static," *Congressional Quarterly Weekly Report*, May 12, 1984, pp. 1129–30.

Unfortunately, there has been no systematic study of the use of House television by the national networks. What little evidence is available suggests that national media outlets concentrate their coverage on members holding formal positions of responsibility in the House and Senate, leaving little time for rank-and-file members.[39] Of the attention given to rank-and-file members, it is safe to say that little is given to their floor amending activity. It is even more certain that very few of the major amendments attracting such network coverage were motivated by the prospect of television coverage.

More typical of network coverage of House floor activity was the use of Speaker Jim Wright's floor speech on October 20, 1987. The day after the crash of the stock market, Wright used the floor to communicate his demand for a summit with the president on the budget deficit. The network evening news programs used clips of Wright's emotional floor speech to note both the demand for a summit and the intensity of congressional reaction to the previous day's events. A formal legislative action of the House was not involved. Rather, a major event, not necessarily a legislative one, led the networks to look for a visual way to air alternative views. Televised floor speeches often are well suited to the task.

Partisan Use of House Television

Not surprisingly, members of both parties have attempted to exploit televised floor sessions to raise issues and criticize the opposition. Bill Alexander, then the Democratic chief deputy whip, attempted in 1981 to organize one-minute speeches by party colleagues to bring attention to the consequences of the spending cuts proposed by the Reagan administration. He did so again in 1984, when he also sought to stimulate and organize special-order speeches by Democrats.[40] Neither effort worked very well.

The most notable use of the floor, and House television, was the 1984 effort by a group of conservative Republicans, who had dubbed themselves the Conservative Opportunity Society (COS) the previous year.[41] In the face of restrictive special rules and a truncated congressional agenda, conservative Republicans sought ways to raise their own issues and exact a price from Democrats for placing obstacles in their path. Their effort had two components. The first was to pursue obstructionist parliamentary tac-

---

39. Cook, "Press Secretaries and Media Strategies"; also see Joe S. Foote, "SIUC 99th Congress New Visibility Study," Southern Illinois University, August 18, 1987; and Andrew Rosenthal, "All Whom TV Deems Quotable," *New York Times*, August 17, 1987, p. B6.

40. On the 1984 effort, see Granat, "Free Hand for Non-Incumbents," p. 1130.

41. For background on the Republican effort, see Diane Granat, "Televised Partisan Skirmishes Erupt in House," *Congressional Quarterly Weekly Report*, February 11, 1984, pp. 246–49.

tics at every turn, including repeated unanimous consent requests to take up controversial legislation and demands for recorded votes on normally routine procedural motions. They hoped to build a record of opposition to their causes among marginal House Democrats who might be vulnerable to charges of support for liberal leadership positions.[42] The House Republicans' campaign committee and outside conservative groups worked with the COS to publicize the effort and its products.

A closely related effort was to use House television to promote their views and embarrass the Democrats. They unsuccessfully sought unanimous consent to reserve four hours each day throughout the session for their own special-order speeches. Not discouraged, the core COS group of a dozen or so members continued to use one-minute and special-order speeches to chide the Democrats. Their effort exhausted Democrats' tolerance on May 8, when Republicans Newt Gingrich and Robert Walker used a special order to read a report critical of Democratic foreign policy that named nearly fifty individual Democrats. Many of the named Democrats thought they were treated unfairly in the report and resented the use of a special-order speech to single them out. Many of them demanded new rules to limit the length and purposes of special-order speeches, but no action was taken, although Alexander promised to proceed with his effort to organize speeches by Democrats.

On May 10, Speaker O'Neill, who never liked televised sessions, decided that the credibility of the Republicans' dramatic special-order speeches could be undermined by requiring the cameras to use a wide-angle lens to show that no one but the member speaking and a few staff members were in the chamber. Previously, the cameras focused narrowly on the person speaking, which created the impression for unsuspecting viewers that there was an audience for special-order speeches. Republican leader Robert Michel complained to O'Neill in writing the next day. O'Neill responded on May 14 by announcing that during special orders a message would be placed on the screen that "the House has completed its scheduled legislative business and is proceeding with special orders."[43]

The television war had just begun. The COS turned to the Republican campaign committee to produce television commercials accusing O'Neill of violating House rules and obstructing House consideration of Republican

42. A 1987 COS document asserted that House Republicans must "fight constantly to expose and define the increasingly corrupt left-wing machine and to make its marginal members pay the full cost of supporting a machine which repudiates their districts values." "House GOP Majority Proposal," July 23, 1987.

43. Diane Granat, "The House's TV War: The Gloves Come Off," *Congressional Quarterly Weekly Report*, May 19, 1984, pp. 1166–67.

legislation.[44] Efforts by Republicans to prohibit the use of a wide-angle lens and panning of the chamber were easily defeated by House Democrats. In fact, the Democrats barred the consideration of one such amendment on a successful motion to rise from the Committee of the Whole during the consideration of an appropriations bill in early June.

Before the start of the next Congress, Democrats considered changes in House rules to limit special-order speeches or cease television coverage of the special-order period at the end of each day. The party's Committee on Organization, Study, and Review recommended that each day's special orders be limited to one hour for each party and controlled by the party leaders. Differences among Democrats stalled any rules change, however. Many Democrats wanted to preserve their own speaking privileges, with some preferring to combat the Republicans with a better organized and staffed Democratic effort.[45] Democrats have not raised the issue since then.

Television and Power in the House

Just as it is impossible to determine whether television stimulated more amending activity, it is not possible to determine whether television changed outcomes on floor votes that did occur. The obvious importance of many other factors, along with too few years of televised sessions, makes even a guess unwise. Nevertheless, a few speculations are in order about the implications of televised floor sessions for the role of the floor.

The most conspicuous effect was that television boosted, and some might say artificially inflated, the influence of the small group of COS Republicans within their party. Some of them, particularly Robert Walker, already had established a significant presence on the House floor by spending many hours on the floor scrutinizing the moves of the Democrats. Walker had taken over the role of minority floor watchdog from Robert Bauman after Bauman was defeated for reelection in 1980. The 1984 television war propelled Walker, Gingrich, and others into the national limelight, but Walker's floor activism already had given him influence disproportionate to his formal position in the party.[46]

44. Diane Granat, "GOP Ads Attack O'Neill in House Video War," *Congressional Quarterly Weekly Report*, June 2, 1984, p. 1300.

45. Diane Granat, "House Rules Changes Proposed: Democratic and GOP Leaders Named for 99th Congress," *Congressional Quarterly Weekly Report*, December 8, 1984, pp. 3053–54.

46. Technically, Walker became a "minority objector on the consent calendar," a position that involves reviewing the legislation to be considered on the consent calendar to make sure that it is minor and noncontroversial. Like Bauman, Walker takes an active interest in floor activity that goes far beyond his work on consent measures. See T. R. Reid, "'Minority Objector' Conscientiously Flays Foes with House Rules," *Washington Post*, March 21, 1984, p. A3.

Nevertheless, the attention the Republican "young Turks" drew as a result of their television antics gave them a voice they would not have had otherwise—despite the fact their activity irritated many senior Republicans. Walker, for example, asserted that "if you accept the fact that you won't get the title of party leader, you actually can, by default, get a central leadership role."[47] Their ability to attract attention, their persistent scrutiny of floor activity, and their willingness to challenge their own party's committee leaders have forced others to anticipate their reaction to policy and strategic decisions. Their success may have played a role in the election of four COS activists to party leadership posts in 1988 and 1989.

The activity of the COS, which, it must be remembered, was only partly stimulated by televised sessions, led Democrats to be even more cautious in crafting special rules. In the view of many Democrats, senior committee Republicans could no longer speak authoritatively for their party in discussing prospective floor action. This development forced the Rules Committee to anticipate guerrilla attacks from Walker and his comrades.[48] Thus, while television may have helped the COS group to acquire influence at the expense of Republican committee leaders, COS influence also may have contributed to a stiffening of resolve among Democrats and a contraction in floor amending opportunities for Republicans.

A more lasting effect of House television is improved awareness of floor activity and procedure among rank-and-file members.[49] In a 1980 survey of House members, 90 percent of those who saw some benefit in House television mentioned first their enhanced ability to follow the floor.[50] The ability to watch the floor from their offices reduces members' reliance on senior party and committee leaders for information about the parliamentary situation and the substantive issues being debated on the floor. One scholar has argued convincingly that "the more the system gives members the chance to follow the floor closely, the more it weakens the power of committees, fellow members, staff, and the leadership."[51] By reducing dis-

47. Interview with Robert Walker, April 22, 1987.
48. Interview with Rules Democrat Tony Beilenson, July 31, 1987.
49. The in-house television system also contributed to dwindling attendance during floor debates. Members watching the floor from their offices no longer had to be on the floor to be aware of what was going on. The decline is reflected in the numbers of members available for division votes, for which the bell system is not used. In 1979–80, for example, only 56 members, on average, were present to cast division votes on amendments, down from nearly 130 in 1971–72.
50. Garay, *Congressional Television*, p. 142.
51. Michael J. Robinson, "Three Faces of Congressional Media," in Thomas E. Mann and Norman J. Ornstein, eds., *The New Congress* (Washington: American Enterprise Institute for Public Policy Research, 1981), p. 69.

parities in information, television has reduced disparities in influence and made House decisionmaking more individualistic. The independence of rank-and-file members, in turn, enhances the potential importance of floor decisions.[52]

Innovation in Special Rules

The continuing innovation in the provisions of special rules was far more important than television in shaping a new era of floor decisionmaking in the House.[53] The conditions underlying the move to restrictive rules in 1979 remained in place in the 1980s: strong incentives to sponsor floor amendments, great uncertainty about floor amending activity, high political costs of recorded voting, intense partisan differences on major issues, declining ideological diversity among House Democrats,[54] and a membership willing to exhaust its parliamentary options on the floor.[55] The 1980s also brought new pressures. The intense conflict over budget priorities, tight deadlines for budget decisions, and politically sensitive decisions to cut spending on popular programs all reinforced the perceived need for restrictive special rules among House Democrats. A closely divided House in 1981–82 meant that procedural advantages were even more important to majority party leaders. Complicating matters on money bills, as well as

52. Of course, televised floor sessions are only one fragment of television's role in House politics. The television age also has reached into the committee and subcommittee rooms, where legislative entrepreneurs fashion hearings to raise the visibility of issues and themselves. Party and committee leaders, as I have noted, continue to top the lists of members appearing on network news and interview programs. Weighing the broader influence of television on the distribution of influence in the House is beyond the scope of this book. A good argument can be made that the ability of party and committee leaders to attract media attention more than compensates for the influence over the rank and file they lose from the in-House system.

53. Material for this section draws heavily from Stanley Bach and Steven S. Smith, *Managing Uncertainty in the House of Representatives: Adaptation and Innovation in Special Rules* (Brookings, 1988), chaps. 3, 4.

54. This trend, which began in the early 1970s, continued through the 1980s. As noted in chapter 2, 54 percent of southern Democrats in the House supported the party position on party votes 60 percent of the time in 1979–80; in 1987, 82 percent did so. See David W. Rohde, "Variations in Partisanship in the House of Representatives, 1953–1988: Southern Democrats, Realignment and Agenda Change," paper prepared for the 1988 annual meeting of the American Political Science Association, tables 1, 2, 3.

55. For example, when an immigration reform bill was sent to the floor in late 1983, opponents prepared 300 amendments to offer on the floor. And a forty-two-hour debate, stretching over two months, resulted from an open rule for a nuclear freeze resolution, leading the Democratic leadership to go back to the Rules Committee for another rule to limit debate. See Alan Ehrenhalt, "The House: Adopting Senate's Bad Habits?" *Congressional Quarterly Weekly Report*, October 15, 1983, p. 2155.

other measures, was Republican control of the Senate between 1981 and 1986. In anticipation of negotiations with the Republican Senate and White House, House Democrats often had to craft bargaining positions that floor amendments could easily upset. And unfriendly floor amendments were more dangerous when there was less certainty about the ability of House conferees to reverse the floor decisions in conference.

Intercommittee conflict also played an important role in the 1980s.[56] By their very nature, the omnibus money bills affected the jurisdictions of many House committees. Nonappropriations items in appropriations bills stirred opposition from authorization committees, eventually leading the Rules Committee to announce in 1985 that it would not waive House rules that bar legislative provisions from appropriations bills when the affected authorization committee objected to the waiver. Similarly, items in the reconciliation packages of one committee that infringed on the jurisdiction of another committee often were brought to the attention of Rules.[57]

Legislation referred to more than one committee also posed problems. Multiple referral was first authorized by the Committee Reform Amendments of 1974, which made it possible for the Speaker to send legislation to committees jointly or sequentially or by splitting it into parts.[58] Measures subject to multiple referral increased from less than 7 percent of all measures receiving a special rule in the 94th Congress (1975–76) to 14 percent in the 95th and 96th Congresses (1977–80). One of the first highly complex rules was designed for the 1977 energy bill in the 95th Congress, a bill that represented the work of many House committees. But with the restructured agenda of the 1980s, multiply referred bills increased to 19 percent of Rules' work load.[59] The problem of resolving intercommittee conflict on the floor posed special problems for the majority party leadership and the Rules Committee. For example, the Rules Committee might have to decide that one committee's bill would be brought to the floor and that the competing committee's version would be considered as an amendment, an arrangement that might advantage one of the committees. Open conflict on the floor between the committees could embarrass the majority

---

56. The Rules Committee has long played a role in resolving intercommittee disputes. See James A. Robinson, *The House Rules Committee* (Bobbs-Merrill, 1963), pp. 30–33.

57. A common Rules solution was to allow the floor to resolve the conflict by permitting a member of the aggrieved committee to offer a floor amendment that would be protected from further amendment. For example, see H. Res. 296 in the 99th Congress, providing for the consideration of H.R. 3500, the reconciliation bill for fiscal 1986.

58. On the growth of multiple referrals, see Roger H. Davidson, Walter J. Oleszek, and Thomas Kephart, "One Bill, Many Committees: Multiple Referrals in the U.S. House of Representatives," *Legislative Studies Quarterly*, vol. 13 (February 1988), pp. 3–28.

59. Calculated from Bach and Smith, *Managing Uncertainty*, p. 40, table 3-1.

party, encourage further unfriendly amendments, and reduce the probability of passing the legislation.[60]

As a result of these developments, the Democratic leadership and the Rules Committees began to employ special rules in an increasingly tactical fashion. The shift to more restrictive rules continued apace and was particularly dramatic for the top layer of key vote issues. But there was much more to it than restrictions on amendments alone. No single formula could solve the array of political problems the majority party leadership and the Rules Committee faced in the 1980s. New parliamentary contrivances for limiting amendments, ordering amendments, altering relations between amendments, and creating legislative vehicles for amending action were invented to manage floor activity on a case-by-case basis. These developments had striking effects on the character of floor decisionmaking. Most important, the innovations in special rules countered the momentum for a fully open, collegial process that appeared to develop in the 1970s.

Only the central features of the innovations in special rules can be addressed here. For convenience, the discussion is organized into three parts: (1) the legislative text to be considered on the floor; (2) methods of restricting floor amendments; and (3) the volume of amending activity under restrictive rules.

Legislative Text

Two innovations—alternative substitutes and self-executing provisions—concern a basic component of most special rules, the identification of the legislation that is to be brought to the floor. The primary function of most special rules is to specify the legislative text that will be debated and perhaps amended on the floor. Sometimes the text is a bill or resolution as originally introduced, although a rule may designate some other text to be the subject of debate and amending activity. This is accomplished by providing that the substitute text be treated "as an original bill for the purpose of amendment under the five-minute rule." Most often that substitute text is the version the reporting committee recommends. Because the committee substitute is the version that nearly everyone assumes will pass, it makes sense to direct the attention of the House to the substitute.[61]

The Rules Committee increasingly has put in order legislative text other than the introduced measure or the substitute reported by a committee. Such text might best be labeled an *alternative substitute* to distinguish it

60. For more background on multiple referral and special rules, see Bach and Smith, *Managing Uncertainty*, pp. 18–23, 41–45, 59–68.

61. Committee substitutes, technically speaking, are "amendments in the nature of a substitute" that replace the entire text of a measure as introduced.

from committee substitutes. It usually is developed after a committee has reported its version but before floor consideration—a sort of legislative twilight zone. In 1981–86, one in ten special rules provided for an alternative substitute, compared with one in fifty in 1975–80.

A major impetus for alternative substitutes is the difficulty in managing multiple-committee legislation on the floor. In fact, what makes the use of alternative substitutes so important is the significance of the multiple-committee legislation that has been so treated. Multiple-committee bills generally are relatively complex and controversial. The 1979 Alaska lands bill, a 1984 bill on the regulation of pharmaceuticals, and the 1985 Superfund bill providing for the cleanup of chemical wastes were all multiple-committee bills subject to alternative substitutes. In 1983–86, special rules for multiple-committee measures were roughly seven times more likely to provide for an alternative substitute than were those for single-committee measures. Moreover, alternative substitutes were employed for multiple-committee measures more frequently than were either original bills or committee substitutes.[62]

The Rules Committee frequently has insisted that committees sharing jurisdiction over a measure work out their differences before the Rules Committee reports a special rule. The product of the intercommittee negotiations is then treated as a substitute. Amendments, if any are allowed, are directed to the substitute.[63] This procedure greatly simplifies the Rules Committee's task of structuring floor debate. It also may improve the chances of passage for the legislation on the floor by forcing the committees to resolve their differences in advance.

Alternative substitutes are frequently accompanied by severe limits on floor amendments.[64] In fact, sometimes there is an explicit deal between Rules and the committees involved: if the committees can resolve their differences, the sensitive elements of the compromise version will be insulated from unfriendly floor amendments. Guaranteeing insulation from floor amendments that otherwise would be offered may be the only way to induce the committees to call a truce in a battle over legislative jurisdiction. And a restrictive rule may be the only way to make sure that floor amendments, sponsored by one of the committees or its allies, do not unravel a compromise represented by the alternative substitute.[65]

---

62. Bach and Smith, *Managing Uncertainty*, p. 40.

63. This has the effect, in the absence of other restrictions, of permitting both first- and second-degree amendments to the alternative text.

64. Fully one-half of the rules providing for alternative substitutes in the 1980s restricted amending activity in some way.

65. Even in the absence of restrictive rules, however, the use of substitutes, including

Relatively few members participate in crafting alternative substitutes. The negotiations usually are conducted by committee leaders. In most cases, committee leaders must consult their committee members in order to maintain good relations and to determine what opposition can be expected on the floor. But unlike formal committee markups, the informal negotiations over an alternative substitute are not governed by procedural safeguards for rank-and-file members, and no formal committee vote of approval is required. Frequently, only the majority party leaders of the committees are involved, often to the dismay of minority party members. Concessions minority party members obtained in committee may be dropped during the negotiations over an alternative substitute.

There are times when only relatively simple changes in committee recommendations are required. In such cases a large substitute is unnecessarily cumbersome and time-consuming to draft. Instead, the rule may include "self-executing" provisions. That is, the rule provides that upon the adoption of the rule some additional action is considered to have been taken by the House. For example, a self-executing rule may provide that the text of the legislation is considered amended in a specified way by the Committee of the Whole and by the House. This procedure allows the committee or the leadership to make potentially controversial modifications in legislation without separate floor votes on the changes in the Committee of the Whole or the House. Amendments subject to such treatment usually have originated in the committee of origin and often are designed to solve some last-minute problem discovered by the chairman or the party leadership. In 1987, for example, a self-executing rule for a continuing resolution provided for the adoption of three politically important amendments on the regulation of airplane maintenance, congressional pay raises, and spending cuts.[66]

While self-executing rules were used in prior decades, particularly for handling conference reports, they became much more common in the 1980s as the majority leadership and the Rules Committee found them a useful tool in other circumstances. A survey conducted by the minority staff of the Rules Committee found twenty self-executing rules in the 99th Congress (1985–86), up from just two in the 97th and five in the 98th.

---

regular committee substitutes, often inhibits floor amending activity. While the text of substitutes normally is printed in the *Congressional Record* in advance of the floor debate, the interval may be only a day or two between the time the text is printed and the floor debate. Amendment sponsors are left with little time to examine the text, prepare amendments with the appropriate citations to the text, and solicit support.

66. See Jacqueline Calmes, "The Advantage of Writing the (House) Rules," *Congressional Quarterly Weekly Report*, December 5, 1987, pp. 2972–74.

During the 100th Congress (1987–88), the tally reached twenty-six, or 16 percent of all special rules.[67] While self-executing provisions often are a convenient way to make technical corrections in a bill, major policy questions—such as contra aid, budget reconciliation, U.S. internment of Japanese-Americans during World War II, and insurance risk pools—have been decided by self-executing provisions in recent years.[68] Like alternative substitutes, self-executing provisions are usually discussed in informal settings that may involve very few people.

Both alternative substitutes and self-executing provisions, then, represent the efforts of committees, the majority party leadership, and the Rules Committee to adjust to the conditions of the postreform House. As uncertainties and dangers of floor decisionmaking multiplied, the postcommittee, prefloor stage became more important. Rapidly changing political conditions, as well as intraparty or intercommittee conflict, make prefloor adjustments to legislation vital to the majority party. But as these approaches have become more popular, more critical issues have been decided by a handful of members at a stage in the legislative process that is not governed by written rules. Informal norms have not yet developed about who may or must participate in negotiations over alternative substitutes. Thus, even though the special rules must be adopted by the House, increasing reliance on alternative substitutes and self-executing provisions is likely to further narrow the policy options on the floor in the future.

Restricting Amendments

The most obvious feature of special rules in recent Congresses is restrictions on floor amendments. By the 99th Congress (1985–86), nearly half of all special rules restricted amending activity in some way, up from just over 15 percent in the 94th (1975–76) and about 31 percent in the 96th (1979–80) (see table 3-1). For the top layer of key vote measures, over 86 percent were subject to a restrictive rule in the 99th Congress, compared with just 36 percent in the 94th and 48 percent in the 96th. By the start of the 100th Congress (1987–88), one could safely assume that the most important, controversial measures would be taken to the floor under a rule that limited and ordered floor amendments in some fashion.[69]

As the proportion of special rules that limited amendments increased in

67. *Congressional Record,* daily edition, October 21, 1988, p. E3656.
68. For example, see H. Res. 415 of the 99th Congress, a rule providing for the consideration of a contra aid resolution and a supplemental appropriation. *Congressional Record,* daily edition, April 15, 1986, pp. H1820–21.
69. Bach and Smith, *Managing Uncertainty,* p. 124. Both the "restrictive" and "closed" categories shown in table 3-1 limit amending activity.

TABLE 3-1. *Types of Special Rules Adopted by the House, by Type of Measure, 94th–99th Congresses (1975–86)*
Percent

	Congress					
Type of rule	94th (1975–76)	95th (1977–78)	96th (1979–80)	97th (1981–82)	98th (1983–84)	99th (1985–86)
All measures						
Open	84.3	83.9	68.9	71.2	64.0	55.4
Restrictive	11.3	12.4	20.0	22.1	22.4	33.7
Closed	4.4	3.8	11.1	6.7	13.6	10.9
N	248	186	180	104	125	101
Key vote measures[a]						
Open	63.6	70.6	52.0	23.5	31.8	13.6
Restrictive	31.8	23.5	40.0	64.7	63.6	72.7
Closed	4.5	5.9	8.0	11.8	4.5	13.6
N	22	17	25	17	22	22

SOURCE: Stanley Bach and Steven S. Smith, *Managing Uncertainty in the House of Representatives: Adaptation and Innovation in Special Rules* (Brookings, 1988), table 3-3.
a. Measures associated with at least one "key vote," as identified by *Congressional Quarterly*.

the 1980s, so did the degree of restrictiveness in those rules. Whereas less than a third of the few restrictive rules of the 1975–78 period permitted only one or two amendments, over 60 percent of the restrictive rules of the 1979–84 period were so restrictive.[70] Experimentation extended to the manner in which special rules limited amending activity as well. Indeed, in the 1980s, the simple categories—open, modified, and closed rules—no longer captured the rich diversity of restrictive provisions employed in special rules. But the basic thrust of Democratic strategy remained the same: to reduce majority party uncertainty about floor decisionmaking.

The degree of specificity in special rules increased in the 1980s. Between two-thirds and three-fourths of special rules stipulated the specific amendments that would be in order on the floor, up from one-third or less in the mid-1970s.[71] Until 1985, this meant that the amendments were either described in the rule itself or printed in the *Congressional Record* and cited in the rule by reference.[72] In 1985 the Rules Committee frequently re-

70. Bach and Smith, *Managing Uncertainty*, p. 67.
71. Bach and Smith, *Managing Uncertainty*, p. 62, table 3-5.
72. In the aftermath of the 1981 reconciliation fight, Rules Chairman Richard Bolling announced a new policy on preprinting requirements for amendments to "very complex matters such as budget resolutions, reconciliation bills and tax bills." In a letter (dated July 9, 1981) addressed to each member of the House, Bolling wrote: "In order to protect the right of Members to know the contents of matters under debate—not only the majority and minority Members of the committees involved but also the right of all Members—I intend to proceed as follows. I will seek to insure that not only the basic bill or resolution to be considered by the House be available in printed form but also that all amendments of any kind will

quired that the full text of amendments be printed in the committee report accompanying the rule so that there would be no doubt about the amendments to be offered.[73] When accompanied by such a committee report, the rule provides a clear statement of the way in which the House will proceed on a measure. As a senior aide to Speaker O'Neill put it, "The members appreciate having a theater program which tells them what to expect and when to expect it."[74]

Among the most important features of restrictive rules is their use to alter relations among amendments. They may limit amendments to first-degree amendments, allow only certain second-degree amendments, or even allow third-degree amendments that otherwise would not be in order under House rules. These possibilities give the majority party leadership and the Rules Committee the ability to structure carefully the choices available to the House, subject to the approval of the House, of course.

A quite fundamental alteration of the normal amendment tree is the arrangement that has been labeled "king-of-the-mountain" in the House. Initially designed for the first budget resolution of 1982, such a rule puts in order several broad substitute amendments, specifies the order in which they will be voted on, and provides that the last substitute to receive a majority vote is the winner. The last substitute to receive a vote must survive only one direct vote, while others may have to survive six or seven votes, depending on the number of substitutes that are included in the rule. Such a rule may permit amendments, sometimes even specifying which amendments, to some of the substitute versions.

As employed in 1982 and later for other measures, "king-of-the-mountain" rules have several advantages. When there are several large, complex substitutes proposed, the procedure provides a convenient way for all of the substitutes to be considered as whole alternatives to the committee version. On each vote on a substitute, the choice is narrowed to one between (1) the new substitute and (2) any substitute that obtained a majority previously, simplifying the comparisons required at one time.[75]

---

be officially printed in their final form in a timely fashion before the Rules Committee orders reported a 'rule' on the matter in question. . . . In other words, in the future I will attempt to prevent any vote on matters which Members of the House have not had the opportunity to examine and consider for a reasonable time."

73. The change was stimulated by an occasion on which Rules members believed that a member switched amendments on them. The member had printed in the *Record* several amendments, only one of which was included in the rule. The rule, however, cited the intended amendment by noting only the member's name, and the member took advantage of the ambiguity to offer one of his other amendments. Rules members and staff refer to the practice as the "Burton rule," after Dan Burton of Indiana, the alleged miscreant.

74. Interview with Jack Lew, November 3, 1986.

75. It should be noted that in the rules for the 1982 and 1984 budget resolutions, the

These rules have been applauded by minority party Republicans as an equitable way to consider the major alternatives. In fact, when the Democratic leadership concocted a complex rule in 1986, a Rules Republican complained, "Whatever happened to the king-of-the-mountain approach that we had in last year's supplemental rule? So much for fairness, decency, and civility."[76] It turns out that the standards for decency and civility are quite mercurial in Congress.

The admissibility of amendments also has been made conditional on the adoption or defeat of other amendments. In a 1986 rule, the consideration of a Democratic compromise on contra aid was contingent on the rejection of a stronger amendment that barred contra aid. Because the Democratic leadership supported the stronger amendment, it was considered first; if it was adopted, the compromise version would not be in order. The Democrats thus ensured that the full contra aid package would be adopted only if their first-choice and second-choice positions were rejected, in that order. This arrangement of contingent amendments angered Republicans.[77] Given the distribution of policy preferences in the House, the Democratic rule made it likely that the compromise version would be adopted by the House. Republicans, deciding they would rather have no bill than pass the compromise version, upset the Democratic strategy by supporting the stronger amendment, assuring its adoption but also guaranteeing the rejection of the larger measure itself. Republican leader Robert Michel claimed, "We refuse to play the role assigned to us by the directors of this farce."[78] With Republican votes, the stronger amendment was adopted, leading the Democratic leadership to pull the legislation from the floor.

The 1986 experience on contra legislation demonstrated that there often is no procedural solution to a scarcity of votes. Restrictive rules can eliminate uncertainty about what will be offered on the floor, but they cannot always eliminate all uncertainty about which alternative will win on the floor. Only if the designers of a rule have adequate information about the policy preferences of the chamber and about their opponents' parliamentary tactics can uncertainty about outcomes be eliminated.

Budget Committee's version also was treated as a substitute (identical to the resolution) so that it could be amended in the same manner as the other major substitutes.

76. *Congressional Record*, daily edition, April 15, 1986, p. H1824.

77. Minority Leader Robert Michel proposed a king-of-the-mountain rule for considering the contra aid alternatives, but Democratic cohesiveness for the Rules Committee rule prevented it from being offered.

78. See John Felton, "House Republicans Go for Broke on 'Contra' Aid," *Congressional Quarterly Weekly Report*, April 19, 1986, p. 836.

Amending Activity under Restrictive Rules

The innovations in special rules indicate that House Democrats, through their leaders' control of the Rules Committee, have managed to overcome the collective action problem presented by the surge in floor amendments during the 1970s. Rank-and-file Democrats have proven willing to give up some of their individual opportunities to offer floor amendments in order to protect their party and committees from unpredictable and politically dangerous floor amendments. No doubt the intensity of interparty conflict in the late 1970s and 1980s convinced rank-and-file Democrats that their collective interests deserved greater weight in their preferences for various types of floor procedure.

As attitudes about amending activity changed, Rules Democrats and majority party leaders developed views about how to choose among their colleagues' amendments when drafting restrictive rules. Such choices often are uncomfortable for Rules members and party leaders, although they are an important source of influence. Rules members stress the case-by-case nature of their decisions, but they have evolved a few rough-hewn guidelines for making and justifying their decisions. The products of these guidelines are rules they call "fair" and floor amendments they label "legitimate." These views have proven to be widely shared among majority party Democrats, and often among Republicans as well, as is evidenced by the great success Rules has had in garnering majority support on the floor for the resolutions embodying the rules.

Rules Committee members and staff report that several factors influence the design of special rules. The preferences of the Speaker are of primary significance. During the O'Neill years, leadership preferences were communicated through Richard Bolling, who served as Rules chairman between 1979 and 1982. Bolling assumed personal responsibility for designing most rules and demanded deference from other Rules Democrats on the basis of his relationship with O'Neill. But Bolling and his committee did not consult the leadership on most special rules. When the Speaker did take an interest, usually because of an overriding party interest in the legislation, the Speaker's wishes were translated by Bolling into the rules reported from the committee.[79]

Rules Democrats also operated fairly independently of the Speaker on most rules after Claude Pepper took over the chairmanship in 1983. Pepper explained, "Ninety-nine percent of the time, the Speaker never communi-

---

79. Interview with Richard Bolling, October 28, 1986; and interview with Ari Weiss, July 17, 1987.

cates at all."[80] The difference was that Pepper did not dominate the committee the way Bolling did. The committee's decisions usually reflected a consensus among its Democratic members. But the committee lost much of its independence during the first session of the 100th Congress, Jim Wright's first term as Speaker. As one Rules staff member put it at the time, "Wright is writing the rules now. O'Neill was very loose in his control of the committee, but Wright controls everything of any importance now."[81] And Wright sought, and received, even more restrictive rules in his first Congress as Speaker.[82]

In the absence of instructions from the Speaker, several factors play a role in shaping restrictive special rules. For individual amendments, the party or committee position of the amendment sponsor, the technical quality of the amendment, the amendment's prospects of success on the floor, and previous floor action on the same issue are the most frequently mentioned considerations. The amendments seen to be the most "legitimate" are those supported by party or committee leaders, considered in committee, and supported by a substantial number of committee members. When there are deadlines and a need to be even more selective, such factors play a more important role.

The treatment of any measure is always conditioned by the degree of controversy. Rules member Tony Beilenson noted that "when there is much controversy involved, some sort of limit on amendments is usually considered."[83] In fact, some Rules members now feel that the committee is quite generous in reporting open rules for half the measures. Rules Democrats judge a rule to be "fair" as long as important issues are subject to floor amendments and the minority party is granted an opportunity to offer a substitute version or a motion to recommit.

Republicans often do not share Democrats' view of what constitutes a fair restrictive rule. The core of the Republican criticism is that a single alternative, even one on each of the major issues, is not likely to capture the variety of policy preferences within the House. Moreover, the policy position of the Republican party leadership or its ranking committee members—the position that is most likely to be seen as legitimate—may not represent the views of many rank-and-file Republicans. Highly restrictive rules also prevent the minority from exploring, in a series of amendments,

80. Quoted in Andy Plattner, "Controlling the Floor: Rules under Chairman Pepper Looks Out for the Democrats," *Congressional Quarterly Weekly Report*, August 24, 1985, p. 1674.

81. Confidential comment, interview August 6, 1987.

82. See Janet Hook, "GOP Chafes under Restrictive House Rules," *Congressional Quarterly Weekly Report*, October 10, 1987, pp. 2499–52.

83. Interview with Tony Beilenson, July 31, 1987.

April 1, 1987

Dear Colleague:

I am writing to all Members to explain the Rules Committee guidelines for amendments to all bills for the remainder of the 100th Congress.

Under the "Newrule" policy, all future rules providing for the consideration of any measure or matter will be modified-closed or closed rules in keeping with the long-standing precedents established by the Rules Committee earlier in this session.

Of course, I do not know what kind of rule the Committee will grant for each bill, but, in case the Committee decides to grant a modified closed rule, all amendments must be submitted in advance of our meeting. Specifically, the Committee asks that all amendments to all bills which might be considered in the future be submitted no later than 6 p.m yesterday.

In the event we grant a modified closed rule, it is the intention of the Committee not to make in order any amendments submitted after yesterday's deadline. In the event we decide to grant a closed rule, you're up the proverbial creek without a paddle.

Finally, Members are asked to draft their proposed amendments to the page and line numbers of the bill which will represent their best estimate of (a) the version that will be reported by committee; (b) the substitute version that will be imposed by the Democratic leadership; or (c) the 1988 Democratic Platform. As usual, we request 35 copies of your amendment, embossed in gold-lettering on parchment, submitted to the Rules Committee office (Room Catch-22 in the Capitol), by 6 p.m. yesterday.

Always sincerely,

George Orwell
Chairman
Committee on Rules

"COMMEMORATING 200-YEARS OF CONSTITUTIONAL DEMOCRACY"

various versions of key provisions to identify the one that may gather majority support. The price of greater predictability in amending action is reduced tactical flexibility.

Republicans, like Democrats, are not always of one mind about what constitutes a fair rule (the box on page 80 shows that Republicans also have a sense of humor). Rules Republicans sometimes find themselves divided on the appropriate rule, a division that may reflect policy or tactical disagreements among House Republicans. Senior Republicans on the reporting committee sometimes support, often quietly, their chairmen's request for restrictive rules, having accomplished all they think they can in the committee bill. Their position, which generally is supported by Rules ranking Republican James Quillen, is not always appreciated by rank-and-file Republicans.[84] The age-old minority party dilemma of whether to oppose whatever the majority party proposes or to cut the best possible deal underlies these differences among Republicans.[85]

The shift to restrictive rules has radically changed the conditions under which floor amending activity occurs in the House (table 3-2). The vast majority of amending activity in the House occurs on measures subject to a special rule for their initial consideration on the floor. Unfortunately, inferences about systematic change on this score are precluded by the short time frame of available evidence. Amendments to regular appropriations bills comprise most of the amending activity on measures not subject to a rule. As privileged matters, appropriations bills do not require special rules. Appropriations bill managers usually ask for unanimous consent that the House resolve into the Committee of the Whole and that points of order against their bills be waived.

Since the late 1970s there has been an increase in the proportion of floor amendments considered under restrictive rules (see table 3-2). The trend is even more dramatic for amending activity in the top stratum of key vote issues. In the 1980s, only a small fraction of amending activity on key vote issues has occurred under open rules. Bill managers, the majority party leadership, and the Rules Committee have reduced significantly their uncertainty about what amendments will be offered on the floor on important legislation.

The 1986 contra controversy suggests that more than just the management of uncertainty is involved. A reasonable hypothesis is that restrictive

84. Quillen's Rules Committee aide explains that Quillen "is very deferential to the ranking Republicans. On most bills, he goes with the ranking member, even if that gets him in trouble with Republicans on the floor." Interview with Michael Hynes, August 6, 1987.

85. For more on Republican views of restrictive rules, see Bach and Smith, *Managing Uncertainty,* chap. 4.

TABLE 3-2. *House Floor Amendments, by Type of Measure and Rule,
94th–99th Congresses (1975–86)*
Percent

Type of measure and rule	Congress					
	94th (1975–76)	95th (1977–78)	96th (1979–80)	97th (1981–82)	98th (1983–84)	99th (1985–86)
All measures						
Open rules	86.9	86.1	86.9	75.4	74.6	35.0[a]
Restrictive rules	13.1	13.9	13.1	24.6	25.4	65.0[a]
Closed rules	0	0	0	0	0	0
Total	100.0	100.0	100.0	100.0	100.0	100.0
Number of amendments under special rules	1,088	1,316	921	631	822	868
Total number of amendments in Congress	1,366	1,695	1,377	n.a.	n.a.	1,074
Key vote measures[b]						
Open rules	71.4	64.5	65.3	11.2	55.0	13.3
Restrictive rules	18.6	35.5	34.7	88.8	45.0	86.7
Closed rules	0	0	0	0	0	0
Total	100.0	100.0	100.0	100.0	100.0	100.0
Number of amendments on key vote measures	301	293	343	269	327	548

SOURCES: Bach and Smith, *Managing Uncertainty*, table 3-8; also see appendix 2 of this book.
n.a. Not available.
a. When two measures that faced a very large number of amendments under restrictive rules are excluded, the open-rule percentage is 65.2 and the restrictive-rule percentage is 34.8.
b. Includes only key vote measures subject to a special rule.

rules have reduced the success rate of amendments. After all, the Democrats may have shaped the floor agenda so as to permit only unfriendly amendments with no chance of adoption. Furthermore, restrictive rules may have filtered out minor amendments that would be accepted with little debate and by voice vote. Indeed, both processes occur frequently, but table 3-3 indicates that it is not true in the aggregate. For both special rule measures and key vote measures, the move to more restrictive rules does not appear to be associated with lower success rates.

In summary, the Democrats have developed a large repertoire of special rules provisions. The repertoire includes a remarkable variety of ways to frame and package issues, to narrow the range of alternatives considered on the floor, and to order the consideration of the allowed alternatives. The use of alternative substitutes and self-executing provisions reflects the case-by-case, tactical approach taken by the majority party leadership and the Rules Committee. Nearly all special rules for major, controversial legislation limit floor amendments in some way and most specify the individ-

TABLE 3-3. *Percentage of Amendments Adopted in the House, by Type of Measure and Rule, 94th–99th Congresses (1975–86)*[a]

Type of measure and rule	Congress					
	94th (1975–76)	95th (1977–78)	96th (1979–80)	97th (1981–82)[b]	98th (1983–84)[b]	99th (1985–86)
All measures						
Open rule	71.2	67.6	60.9	79.4	72.9	27.7
Restrictive rule	10.0	14.5	9.1	20.6	27.1	54.0
Closed rule	. . .	. . .	. . .	. . .	. . .	. . .
No rule	18.7	17.9	30.0	n.a.	n.a.	18.2
Total	99.9	100.0	100.0	100.0	100.0	99.9
Key vote measures						
Open rule	81.8	94.9	70.4	7.3	33.9	11.6
Restrictive rule	18.2	5.1	29.6	92.7	35.6	88.4
Closed rule	. . .	. . .	. . .	. . .	. . .	. . .
No rule	0	0	0	0	30.5	0
Total	100.0	100.0	100.0	100.0	100.0	100.0

SOURCE: See appendix 2.
n.a. Not available.
a. Each cell is the percentage of amendments that were adopted, for all measures or for key vote measures, under the specified type of rule.
b. Data are not available for all measures in the 97th and 98th Congresses. The percentages shown are for measures receiving special rules for those two Congresses.

ual amendments that may be offered. Most amendments on major legislation, including those that are adopted, are considered under restrictive rules.

Interpreting Change in the House

Do the developments of the 1980s constitute a genuine counterrevolution in the character of House decisionmaking? Unfortunately, no concise answer is possible at this point. There are additional aspects of the interaction between committees, party leaders, and the floor to be explored in subsequent chapters. But a few observations are in order here.

The three styles of decisionmaking outlined in chapter 1 can each be associated with different centers of power in the House. *Decentralized* decisionmaking is associated with the appropriations and authorization committees and subcommittees of the House. *Collegial* decisionmaking is characteristic of wide-open floor activity, where the full equality of membership can be exercised by the rank and file. And *centralized* decisionmaking is associated with a strong central party leadership and its institutional arms, such as the Rules and Budget committees. The last three decades have witnessed changes in the relative importance of these decisionmaking styles.

The theme of chapter 2 was that the 1970s brought a shift from a decentralized pattern toward a more collegial pattern, one that enhanced the ability of rank-and-file members, including minority party members, to influence legislative outcomes. This chapter has described the ways in which the shift to a collegial pattern was arrested by budget politics and innovations in special rules.

Characterizing the new era of House decisionmaking is difficult. Consider the mix of features present in the 1980s. First, the vast majority of legislative decisions still are made in standing committees, and committee and subcommittee leaders remain the chief strategists for the bulk of legislation, although committees' decisions now are more likely to be constrained by budget considerations and later checked by the rank and file on the floor. Second, committees have recaptured some protection from the political hazards of floor decisionmaking through omnibus legislating and the expanded use of restrictive special rules. Third, thanks to the preeminence of highly partisan budget politics, the Speaker's role in appointing Democrats to the Rules Committee, and the leadership's role in negotiating with the administration and the Senate, the majority party leadership has a greater influence in setting general policy directions and structuring floor consideration of legislation. At times, it even appears that central leaders are making key policy decisions single-handedly and imposing rigid policy constraints on their chambers. Fourth, when given an opportunity, the rank-and-file members of the House still demonstrate a remarkable interest in sponsoring floor amendments. And finally, both parties' leaders must still employ task forces, party caucuses, and other means to respond to rank-and-file demands for an effective voice in party strategy and policy decisions, just as they did in the 1970s. In short, key elements of all three patterns of decisionmaking are present.

From a longer historical perspective, however, it is clear that the floor remains a more important and—from the point of view of committees and the majority party—potentially dangerous arena of policymaking than it was in the prereform years. This is reflected in the ways in which floor amendments are restricted. In the 1950s the power of full committee chairmen, floor procedure, and informal norms limited the floor challenges to committee recommendations. In the 1980s no one in the House has the political muscle to counter the tremendous incentives for members to pursue floor amendments. Challenges must be explicitly restricted in formal rules. One result is that a new legislative craft has blossomed in the House: the design of intricate special rules. The net effect has been the emergence of a new balance in decisionmaking styles, albeit one not susceptible to simple description.

Thus, if there has been a counterrevolution in the House, it is not simply a matter of reinstituting prereform practices for the postreform practices of the 1970s. The strategic context of House policymaking has changed dramatically, making the 1980s a quite distinctive period. Committees relate differently to the floor, and both committees and the floor relate differently to party and budget leaders. The House retains some of the collegial biases introduced in the 1970s, but appears to have halted the trend toward further decay in committee power and enhanced the power of central party leaders.

CHAPTER FOUR

Evolution in the Senate

Substantially smaller than the House of Representatives, the Senate has a far more informal, floor-oriented, and collegial decisionmaking process. In fact, the traditional characterization of political institutions in terms of their location on a continuum from centralized to decentralized has never fit the Senate very well. That was true in the 1950s and it remains true today.

The House and Senate were subject to similar pressures for change. The increasing volume, complexity, and controversy of issues created more incentives, more pressures, and more targets for floor action by individual senators, just as they did for representatives. Like representatives, senators became less dependent on local party organizations for their political well-being and more independent and assertive in building their political careers. Senators gained more personal staff, more committee and subcommittee assignments and staff, and more assistance from congressional support agencies in the 1960s and 1970s, giving them the capacity to play a more active role on the floor. As a result, the Senate floor, like the House floor, has become a more important arena of policymaking.

Evolution in the nature of floor decisionmaking in the Senate, at least since the 1950s, has occurred without dramatic changes in floor procedure. For example, acquiring a recorded vote on amendments and other motions has been relatively easy throughout the history of the Senate. All that is required, as the Constitution provides, is one-fifth of a quorum, currently eleven senators, to demand a recorded vote.[1] In practice, most senators seeking a recorded vote easily obtain the required support. The Senate has not installed an electronic voting system. Nor has the Senate employed special rules to formally manipulate the amendment process on the floor.

Nevertheless, Senate floor procedure has been the subject of great controversy and occasional reform since the 1950s. Rule XXII, which specifies

---

1. The Senate does not employ a committee of the whole for the consideration of legislation.

the procedure for ending debate and bringing an issue to a vote, has been subject to intense scrutiny throughout the post–World War II period and has been altered in modest ways several times, most recently in 1986. Germaneness and other restrictions on floor amending activity also have been debated and sometimes adopted in modest forms. And in 1986 the Senate finally followed the House in televising its floor sessions. But, compared with that in the House, the procedural arena in which floor debate is conducted in the Senate has remained remarkably stable since the 1950s.

The modest procedural reforms that were adopted in the Senate came hard. In the House, where simple majorities can alter the chamber's rules, even a sizable minority ultimately will lose a procedural war with a cohesive chamber majority. House Republicans lost such a war during the last decade. In contrast, the Senate's Rule XXII makes it possible for large minorities to block procedural change. Under the current rule, thirty-four senators can prevent any change in the Senate's rules by refusing to end debate—filibustering—on the matter.[2] Change in the Senate's formal rules comes only when a very sizable majority favors the change. The Senate's battles over procedural reform are more likely to produce stalemate and temporary truces than majority victories and reform. Procedural reform in the Senate therefore tends to come incrementally and sporadically.

The Senate's adaptations to changing conditions usually have taken the form of adjustments in informal practices. The central story in the Senate is the expansion of individual prerogatives, reflected in modifications in everyday parliamentary practice, and the institutionalization of those prerogatives in the 1970s and 1980s. No distinctive eras in floor decisionmaking stand out in the Senate as clearly as they did in the House. No sharp deviations in practice transformed the character of floor activity. Rather, the mechanics of floor decisionmaking evolved as incremental changes in informal practices accumulated over the years.

In this chapter, I explore the broad outlines of changes on the Senate floor, starting with the growth of floor amending activity. As in the House, the developments in the role of the Senate floor are much richer than amending activity alone. The evolving use of filibusters, unanimous consent agreements, and "holds" is therefore described in some detail, providing a larger context for understanding Senate floor activity. Then I survey the effects of budget politics and televised floor sessions. The chapter concludes by reviewing differences between the House and Senate in their styles of floor decisionmaking, in light of the developments of the 1980s.

2. The current rule requires a two-thirds majority of those present and voting for invoking cloture on debate for changes in the Senate rules, in contrast to the requirement of a three-fifths majority of all members for cloture on other matters.

Contrary to impressions created by the turbulent 1970s, the House and Senate remain quite distinctive legislative institutions.

Senate Amending Activity

In broad brush, the pattern of Senate amending activity is remarkably similar to the pattern for the House.[3] Between the mid-1950s and the late 1970s (figure 4-1), the number of floor amendments nearly tripled, with sharp increases in the mid-1960s when civil rights measures stimulated waves of amendments. Amending activity surged ahead again in the 1970s, peaked in the 94th and 95th Congresses (1975–78), and leveled off thereafter. During the 1980s the total number of amendments remained at levels far higher than the levels of the 1960s, but no longer showed the expansive trend of the previous two decades.[4]

The top layer of important measures shows a pattern of change somewhat different from the pattern for all measures. While the data are sketchy, Senate amending activity on key vote measures surged in the early 1960s and has maintained high levels since then (figure 4-1). Senate key vote measures faced more amendments in the 1950s than House key vote measures, and the difference between the chambers grew during the 1960s and into the early 1970s. Thus the conventional wisdom about interchamber differences is even more consistent with the pattern of amending activity on major bills than it is overall.

The proportion of measures facing floor amendments parallels the House pattern, as figure 4-2 illustrates (compare with figure 2-2). Both the proportion of measures facing at least one amendment and the proportion subject to ten or more amendments shot upward in the 1970s and declined somewhat thereafter. Nevertheless, the number of genuine

3. This view of Senate floor amending activity is limited by the fact that complete data on amending activity have been collected for only five selected Congresses. I was aided by some excellent work by Barbara Sinclair on amendments subject to recorded votes for every other Congress during the same period under investigation here. See Barbara Sinclair, "Senate Styles and Senate Decision Making, 1955–1980," *Journal of Politics*, vol. 48 (November 1986), pp. 877–908; "The Transformation of the U.S. Senate—Institutional Consequences of Behavioral Change," paper prepared for the 1987 annual meeting of the Midwest Political Science Association; and *Transformation of the U.S. Senate* (Johns Hopkins University Press, 1989).

4. In the Senate, like in the House, second-degree amendments are included in these amendment totals. The proportion of Senate amendments that are second-degree amendments tends to be lower than in the House. In the 96th and 99th Congresses combined, for example, 13.6 percent of all amendments subject to a recorded vote were second-degree amendments, about 5 percent less than the comparable House figure.

FIGURE 4-1. *Number of Senate Floor Amendments, by Type of Measure, Selected Congresses, 1955–86*

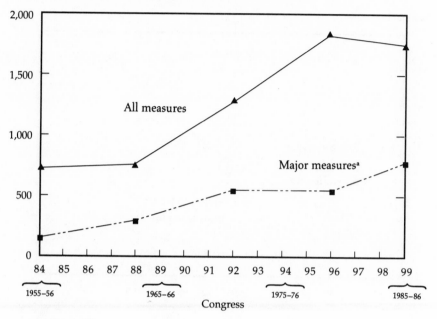

SOURCE: See appendix 2.
   a. Measures associated with at least one "key vote," as identified by *Congressional Quarterly.*

amending marathons has been greater in the Senate than in the House. The House reached its peak of fifty-five measures to which ten or more amendments were offered in 1977–78, in contrast with the Senate's peak of sixty-seven in 1979–80 (in the Congresses for which I have data). These differences are consistent with the conventional wisdom about differences between the two chambers—the Senate is more floor-oriented than the House. The differences are not so great as one might have expected, however, at least in the aggregate.

A classic Senate amending extravaganza occurred on the 1987 State Department authorization bill, traditionally one of the Senate's favorite legislative punching bags. A total of eighty-six amendments were added to the bill on the floor, many of which were nonbinding "sense of the Senate" provisions, which produced an equally traditional complaint that senators were trying to run foreign policy from the Senate floor. During the middle of the debate, Senator Daniel Evans exploded at what was happening. His views reflected those of many of his colleagues:

FIGURE 4-2. *Measures Subject to Floor Amendments in the Senate, Selected Congresses, 1955–86*

Percent of measures

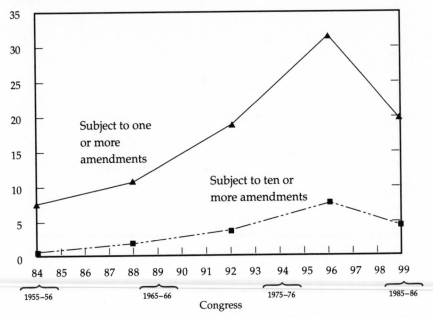

Congress

SOURCE: See appendix 2.

We seem to create amendments, Mr. President, by reading yesterday's headlines so that we can write today's amendments so that we can garner tomorrow's headlines. . . .

Mr. President, I think that it is time that there be some recognition of committee action, of a committee's report and of a committee's expertise. Not just this committee [Foreign Relations] but all committees of the Senate.[5]

His plea fell on deaf ears as the amending activity continued apace.

The expansion of floor amending activity in the Senate has been accompanied by a sharp increase in amendments' success rates. However, as table

5. *Congressional Record*, daily edition, October 8, 1987, pp. S13869–70. Evans's colleagues, David L. Boren and John C. Danforth, echoed his complaints; see their article, "Why This Country Can't Lead: Torn Between a Freebooting Executive and 535 Secretaries of State," *Washington Post*, December 1, 1987, p. A21. Also see John Felton, "Senators Load Up State Department Measure," *Congressional Quarterly Weekly Report*, October 17, 1987, pp. 2535–38.

TABLE 4-1. *Amendments Adopted and Contested in the Senate, by Type of Vote, Selected Congresses, 1955–86*[a]

	Percent adopted			Percent contested[b]	
Congress	Voice vote	Recorded vote	Overall[c]	Recorded vote	Overall[c]
84th (1955–56)	81.1	30.4	69.3	47.3	9.0
	(461)	(112)	(590)	(112)	(590)
88th (1963–64)	81.2	14.5	44.0	28.9	15.5
	(308)	(380)	(702)	(380)	(702)
92d (1971–72)	94.1	34.7	65.9	33.9	15.8
	(664)	(593)	(1,261)	(593)	(1,261)
96th (1979–80)	98.8	36.3	79.7	39.2	11.3
	(1,260)	(523)	(1,802)	(523)	(1,802)
99th (1985–86)	98.9	28.1	80.5	41.2	10.4
	(1,300)	(442)	(1,752)	(442)	(1,752)

SOURCE: See appendix 2.
 a. Number of amendments in parentheses.
 b. Amendments for which the margin of victory was 60–40 or closer.
 c. Includes amendments for which a division vote was the method of final disposition.

4-1 shows, the increase is due almost entirely to the growth in the number of amendments treated by voice vote and to their increasing rate of success. Amendments subject to recorded votes have shown no systematic change in their success rate. Moreover, nearly all of the growth in Senate amending activity since the early 1970s occurred among amendments considered solely by voice vote. It appears, therefore, that the growth in amending activity since the early 1970s has occurred in the form of noncontroversial amendments. The net effect is a slight drop in the proportion of floor amendments subject to contested votes, even though the absolute number of contested amendments remains nearly as high in the 1980s as in the early 1970s.

The increase in minor amendments during the 1970s and 1980s was supported by the expansion of a practice that might be called "proxy sponsorship." Since the mid-1970s, amendments have increasingly been brought up on the floor by a floor leader or bill manager on behalf of absent senators. In the 92d Congress (1971–72), there were less than a dozen "proxy-sponsored" amendments, but there were over 100 in the 96th Congress (1979–80) and over 250 in the 99th (1985–86).[6] Such sponsorship in absentia makes it possible for individual senators to take credit for amendments with virtually no effort on their part (the chances are good that an outside group or staff member designed the amendment). It is not uncommon for senators to issue press releases and send taped statements

6. Amendments may not be offered by proxy in the House of Representatives.

to targeted constituencies claiming credit for amendments adopted by the Senate while they were miles from the Capitol. While such amendments generally are minor and usually are cleared by all sides, the practice obviously encourages amending activity. Senate floor leaders and bill managers find, however, that the practice eases their floor scheduling problems and speeds floor consideration by avoiding speeches, which is appreciated most in late-night and end-of-the-year sessions.

Nevertheless, there can be little doubt that the volume of contested, nonsymbolic amending activity has increased in the Senate since the 1950s. By the early 1970s, nearly one in every five measures faced at least one floor amendment and one in four was successfully amended on the floor. Although amending activity fell in the 1980s, the basic pattern of important amendments on nearly every major bill remains in place. In the 99th Congress, nineteen of twenty-three key vote measures were successfully amended in some way on the Senate floor.

The Senate's pattern of change adds some perspective on what has been observed about the House. The general similarity of the chambers' patterns suggests that forces common to both chambers are responsible for most of the change in amending activity. External forces—a shifting policy agenda imposed on Congress, changes in the Washington political community, an evolving electoral environment—were propelling changes in floor activity in the 1960s. The Senate pattern also puts in sharper relief the role of procedural reform in the House. In the 1960s, procedural constraints in the House appeared to insulate the floor from many of the external forces of change, but once the shackles of suppressive rules were removed, the level of House amending activity nearly reached the levels of the Senate. Then in the 1980s, as House Democrats began to employ more restrictive special rules, the patterns of the two chambers again diverged (see top panel of figure 4-3).

Other differences are apparent as well. In most Congresses, the success rate for floor amendments has been significantly higher in the Senate than in the House, although the House has made up much ground in this respect (middle panel of figure 4-3). The proportion of amendments subject to a contested vote, in contrast, has been slightly higher in the House, particularly in the 1950s and 1960s, when fewer minor amendments were offered on the floor (bottom panel of figure 4-3). During the reform era of the mid- and late 1970s, before the growth of restrictive rules, the House faced nearly as many contested amendments, in absolute numbers, as the Senate. With the increasing use of restrictive rules in the 1980s, the House fell behind the Senate.

FIGURE 4-3. *Amending Activity in the House and Senate,*
Selected Congresses, 1955–86

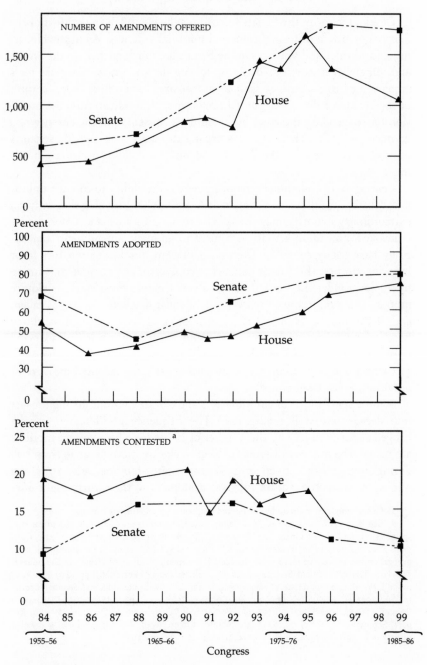

SOURCE: See appendix 2.
a. Amendments for which the margin of victory was 60-40 or closer.

Cloture and Unanimous Consent

Developments on the Senate's floor must be viewed in the context of the Senate's own web of formal rules and informal practices. As in the House, procedural rules and practices in the Senate are much more than the arcane and somewhat mysterious backdrop for legislative battles. They are tools employed by combatants to gain advantage over each other. Three features of the Senate's rules are of special importance: the cloture rule, the provision for suspending the rules by unanimous consent, and the absence of a germaneness rule. These features expand the ways rank-and-file senators can influence policy on the floor far beyond their ability to offer amendments.

Central to the individual senator's power is the ability to conduct unlimited debate—to filibuster. The Senate's Rule XXII provides that only an extraordinary majority may invoke cloture to cut off debate. Once cloture is invoked, amending activity is limited to germane amendments that already have been proposed.[7] Even if a sufficient number of senators favor invoking cloture, the rule is somewhat cumbersome and time-consuming to employ. Under the current rule, sixteen senators must sign the cloture motion, the motion must lay over one calendar day before a vote is taken, and, if the motion is approved by at least sixty senators, another thirty hours of consideration is permitted. As a result, the majority leader and most senators seek to forestall filibusters by compromising with the senators who threaten to filibuster or by setting aside the disputed measure or provision, at least temporarily.

Some essential facts about filibusters and cloture motions during the last four decades are well established.[8] The frequency of filibusters can be gauged at least crudely by the number of issues for which cloture motions are made. The number of issues subject to cloture motions grew from two during 1951–60 to sixteen in 1961–70, twenty-four between 1971 and mid-1975, when the cloture rule was changed, and then thirty-eight dur-

7. Other amendments may be considered if allowed by unanimous consent.
8. See Bruce I. Oppenheimer, "Changing Time Constraints on Congress: Historical Perspectives on the Use of Cloture," in Lawrence C. Dodd and Bruce I. Oppenheimer, eds., *Congress Reconsidered*, 3d ed. (Washington: CQ Press, 1985), pp. 393–413. For additional background on the history of cloture, see Richard R. Beeman, "Unlimited Debate in the Senate: The First Phase," *Political Science Quarterly*, vol. 83 (September 1968), pp. 419–34; Raymond E. Wolfinger, "Filibusters: Majority Rule, Presidential Leadership, and Senate Norms," in Wolfinger, ed., *Readings on Congress* (Prentice-Hall, 1971), pp. 286–305; and Jacqueline Calmes, "'Trivialized' Filibuster Is Still a Potent Tool," *Congressional Quarterly Weekly Report*, September 5, 1987, pp. 2115–20. Senator Robert Byrd also has produced a detailed history of cloture: *Congressional Record*, March 10, 1981, pp. 3879–88.

ing 1975–80.[9] Civil rights legislation was subject to the most filibusters, although a few other issues stimulated extended debate as well. In the 1970s filibusters spread to a set of issues that were increasingly varied in both content and importance. These filibusters also were led by a large number of members. By one count, twenty-seven different senators led filibusters between 1969 and 1985.[10]

The increasing number of filibusters is a part of the broader trend toward exploitation of floor opportunities by senators pursuing their political interests. More controversial issues, more pressure from constituents and organized groups, and more aggressive members encouraged amendment sponsorship and speech making, as well as filibusters. In addition, the increasing severity of time constraints on floor activity in the Senate stimulated more filibusters and threats of filibusters.[11] During the 1960s and 1970s the tremendous growth in the size of the congressional agenda and the associated expansion of floor amending activity intensified scheduling problems. The Senate moved to sessions of more than 300 days for the first time in the early 1960s and has maintained that pace since then. Under these conditions, a filibuster of even moderate length exacts a heavy price on the Senate. Senators are forced to spend time near the floor answering endless quorum calls and voting on the procedural motions of the obstructionists. Committee business, trips home, and other activities may be disrupted. A backlog of legislation awaiting floor consideration may be created. As time became a scarce commodity, the leverage gained by carrying out a filibuster or threatening to do so increased, and more senators found the filibuster a useful legislative weapon.

Responses to the growth of filibusters came in two forms. First, repeated efforts were made to modify Rule XXII, which since 1959 had required two-thirds of those present and voting to invoke cloture. These were attempts both to reduce the number of senators required to invoke cloture and to make a successful cloture vote effective in stopping debate. At first, such efforts were led by liberals seeking to break conservative filibusters on civil rights issues. But in the 1970s, frustration with filibusters broadened

9. It is difficult to determine with any precision just when debate to block action occurs. Not all filibusters produce cloture votes, and some cloture motions are aimed more at nongermane amendments than at extended debate. Nevertheless, the number of attempts to cut off filibusters with cloture motions is a good indicator of change in the relative frequency of filibusters. These numbers are taken from Oppenheimer, "Changing Time Constraints on Congress," p. 401.

10. The count is Senator Thomas Eagleton's, as he reported on the Senate floor. See *Congressional Record*, November 23, 1985, p. 33454.

11. Oppenheimer, "Changing Time Constraints on Congress."

the base of support for reform. In 1975 the Senate changed the 1959 rule to require that three-fifths of the entire membership support cloture, except on measures changing the Senate's standing rules, in which case the old requirement still applied. But the new rule allowed "postcloture filibusters" of innumerable procedural motions because it did not count procedural motions against a one-hundred-hour limit on debate following cloture. The rule was tightened in 1979 to include all activity in the one-hundred-hour limit. In 1986, as a part of the package providing for televised floor sessions, the Senate further reduced the burden of postcloture consideration by restricting it to thirty hours.

Second, floor leaders made tactical adjustments to individual filibusters.[12] Exhausting the obstructionists by around-the-clock sessions was attempted by Majority Leader Mike Mansfield in the 1960s and a few times by his successor, Robert Byrd. However, a large minority organized into shifts can withstand such an assault. At times Mansfield sought multiple cloture votes, thereby repeatedly testing the obstructionists' political strength. While such a tactic helped to demonstrate the leader's resolve, its success ultimately depended on changing votes and thus it seldom succeeded. As a third approach, Mansfield, with Byrd's help, devised a "track system" in which the Senate would set aside the measure subject to a filibuster in order to consider other legislation. The procedure requires unanimous consent, and so is not always available, but when unanimous consent could be achieved to place the filibustered measure on a separate track, scheduling difficulties for other legislation could be minimized.

These formal and informal adjustments had a necessarily limited effect. They did not reduce the size of the Senate's policy agenda, so even streamlined filibusters still imposed serious burdens on the Senate schedule. Moreover, an extraordinary majority still was required to invoke cloture. And, in some respects, the adjustments served to reduce interpersonal pressures against filibustering. For senators peripheral to the fight on a filibustered measure, separate tracking made filibusters more tolerable, made them less resentful of the filibustering senators, and even may have reduced the incentive to vote for cloture. And for the filibustering senators, tracking may have improved the chances of success and reduced the costs of filibustering. The net result appears to be greater exploitation of this procedural weapon and the further acceptance of the filibuster as a component of senators' parliamentary arsenals.[13]

The filibuster against a campaign finance reform bill in the 100th Con-

---

12. Oppenheimer, "Changing Time Constraints on Congress," pp. 405–06.
13. On these points, see Sinclair, "Transformation of the U.S. Senate."

gress is quite remarkable in light of the experience of the last two decades. After seven unsuccessful cloture votes, Majority Leader Byrd attempted to wear down the filibustering Republicans with around-the-clock sessions during the last week of February 1988. Given the size of his opposition— Byrd never had more than fifty-five votes for cloture—there was little chance that he would break the filibuster. The filibustering senators easily maintained control of the floor by taking turns carrying on the debate and by pestering the majority party leadership with repeated quorum calls. Byrd eventually gave up after fifty-three hours of debate over four days and a record eighth unsuccessful cloture vote. He succeeded in bringing media attention to the issue, an election-year ploy to raise the visibility of the campaign spending issue.[14] But the episode probably served to reinforce the perception among senators that filibusters and threatened filibusters are effective.

The continuing viability of filibustering as a parliamentary weapon also is apparent in the rather high probability of achieving policy gains. In the thirty-seven filibusters between 1981 and 1986, the targeted measure or provision was blocked in twelve cases and significant concessions were extracted in three additional cases, for a success rate of 40 percent.[15] Unfortunately, there is no practical way to assess systematically the policy concessions made to senators threatening to filibuster. The policy consequences of the filibuster therefore are grossly understated by the success rate for the fully developed filibusters.

The parliamentary arms race of amending activity, filibusters, cloture, and scheduling tactics feeds upon itself. Senators seeing colleagues reap political payoffs for employing last-resort tactics tend to follow suit. If that is not impetus enough, outsiders—the administration, interest groups, constituents—expect their legislative champions to exploit the full complement of parliamentary tools on their behalf. Innovation begets imitation; move begets countermove. By the 1980s, Senator Thomas Eagleton could report, without too much exaggeration, that his colleagues "are prepared to practice the art of gridlock at the drop of a speech or the drop of an amendment. The birds do it, the bees do it, all Senators in a breeze do it."[16]

For majority leaders, the desire to avoid filibusters, particularly unantic-

---

14. For background on the filibuster, see Helen Dewar, "Midnight Manhunt in the Senate," *Washington Post*, February 25, 1988, p. A1; Dewar, "Show of Force Ends in Senate: Campaign Finance Filibuster Vote Set," *Washington Post*, February 26, 1988, p. A11; Dewar, "Campaign Finance Bill Loses Again in Senate: GOP Blocks Vote on Spending," *Washington Post*, February 27, 1988, p. A4; and Janet Hook, "Stalemated Senate Shelves Campaign Measure," *Congressional Quarterly Weekly Report*, February 27, 1988, pp. 485–90.

15. Sinclair, "Transformation of the U.S. Senate," pp. 23–24.

16. *Congressional Record*, November 23, 1985, p. 33454.

ipated ones, and pressures to move floor business along expeditiously put a premium on getting consent to limit debate. Because Senate rules do not provide limits on debate for most matters, unanimous consent must be given to establish some constraints. This is made possible by Senate Rule V, which provides that "any rule may be suspended without notice by the unanimous consent of the Senate, except as otherwise provided by the rules."[17] Agreements to limit debate or otherwise structure floor consideration of measures and amendments have been labeled "complex unanimous consent agreements" in recent years. The majority leader assumes primary responsibility for crafting and gaining approval of such agreements.

In addition to limiting debate, unanimous consent agreements may impose a germaneness requirement on floor amendments, a requirement that is not provided in the chamber's rules except for general appropriations bills. Without a restraining agreement, senators are free to offer an amendment on any subject to most measures. The text of entire bills may be considered as amendments to other measures, giving senators a ready-made avenue for circumventing committees and raising issues on the floor. The absence of a germaneness rule greatly increases uncertainty about floor action, enhances the ability of senators to pursue their individual interests, and expands the number of possible subjects for filibusters on any measure. Therefore, gaining unanimous consent to limit or bar nongermane amendments often is a high priority of leaders and bill managers.

The expanded use of actual and threatened filibusters, along with a larger work load and more amending activity, has put an additional burden on the majority leader to gain unanimous consent to limit and structure debate. But the pressures and leverage spurring amending activity and filibusters have also prompted objections to unanimous consent requests. As a result, the process through which agreements are devised has become more complex, as has the content of the agreements achieved.[18] A brief historical review of complex unanimous consent agreements since the 1950s will show the important ways in which amending activity and fili-

17. Senate Rule XII provides the primary constraints on unanimous consent requests: a senator may not vote after the vote's outcome has been announced, even with unanimous consent, and a unanimous consent request for setting a date for a final vote on a measure must be preceded by a quorum call.

18. An excellent history of complex unanimous consent agreements is available in Robert Keith, "The Use of Unanimous Consent in the Senate," *Committees and Senate Procedures,* Senate Commission on the Operation of the Senate, 94 Cong. 2 sess. (Government Printing Office, 1977). My review of the changing character of agreements also is based on a careful examination of agreements in five Congresses. See the discussion later in this chapter and in appendix 2.

busters have interacted with new leadership tactics to shape the role of the Senate floor. After the review, the content of complex agreements is examined more systematically.

The Use of Complex Unanimous Consent Agreements

A modern turning point in the use of complex unanimous consent agreements occurred during Lyndon Johnson's service as majority leader during the 1950s. During Johnson's first two Congresses as majority leader (1955–58), Senate Democrats enjoyed only slim one- and two-member majorities. On many vital issues, such as civil rights, policy outcomes were controlled by a conservative majority or at least a sizable obstructionist conservative minority. The conservative coalition also controlled decisions on several key committees and so was in a position to block committee action on legislation important to many Democratic liberals. Norms of committee deference and apprenticeship served to reinforce the power of the conservative oligarchy.[19] For his part, Johnson attempted to avoid open intraparty splits by refusing to bring up highly divisive legislation to the floor until he had the votes, and even then he worked to avoid amendments and recorded votes on which party factionalism would surface.[20] Thus, much to the dismay of some liberal Democrats, Johnson's deliberate strategy reduced the number of controversial bills brought to the floor, the number of filibusters, and the volume of amending activity.

Time-Limitation Requests under Johnson

Johnson moved quickly to bring a measure to a vote once negotiations to obtain majority support had been completed successfully. He did so by obtaining unanimous consent to limit debate, usually after noting that he had consulted the minority leader and the chairman and ranking minority member of the committee originating the measure. Evans and Novak explain:

19. David W. Rohde, Norman J. Ornstein, and Robert L. Peabody, "Political Change and Legislative Norms in the U.S. Senate, 1957–1974," in Glenn R. Parker, ed., *Studies of Congress* (Washington: CQ Press, 1985), pp. 147–88.

20. On Johnson's approach, see Bobby Baker with Larry L. King, *Wheeling and Dealing: Confessions of a Hill Operator* (Norton, 1978), pp. 65–66; Robert Caro, *The Path to Power* (Knopf, 1982), p. 149; Rowland Evans and Robert Novak, *Lyndon B. Johnson: The Exercise of Power* (New American Library, 1966), chap. 6; Ralph K. Huitt, "Democratic Party Leadership in the Senate," *American Political Science Review*, vol. 55 (June 1961), pp. 333–44; and John G. Stewart, "Two Strategies of Leadership: Johnson and Mansfield," in Nelson W. Polsby, ed., *Congressional Behavior* (Random House, 1971), pp. 61–92.

Johnson transmogrified this occasional procedural device into a way of life. He applied it to every major bill. And so, gradually, attention and interest deserted the once stately public debate and centered on the cloakroom where Johnson, in nose-to-nose negotiations, hammered out his unanimous consent agreements.[21]

The primary difference between Johnson's time-limitation requests and those of his predecessors was their tactical timing. Like those of his predecessors, most of his time-limitation requests were made after a measure had been debated for some time. As soon as he had acquired the necessary support to pass a measure, he pressed for unanimous consent to bring the debate to a close before his opponents had an opportunity to react. But a large minority of his requests were made before the motion to proceed, that is, before the Senate agreed to consider a measure. Indeed, they often incorporated the motion to proceed, usually by specifying a certain time for the consideration of the measure. When Johnson could gain consent for such an agreement—and he often could not—it allowed him to push his agenda forward rapidly and to minimize the time his opposition had to splinter the slim majority coalitions he had pieced together.

Contrary to the impression created by Evans and Novak, the typical Johnson time-limitation request took a form that had been used for many years. One provision would limit the time available for debating any amendment, motion, or appeal to one or two hours and another provision would limit debate on the measure itself, usually to two hours. Another provision barred nongermane amendments. The time limits helped to insulate the measure from filibusters, while the germaneness clause limited the number of unanticipated amendments and preserved the substantive integrity of the legislation. With only a few exceptions, Johnson did not attempt to limit germane amendments. Complex agreements were common for measures of even modest importance, as Johnson sought to manage floor business carefully and avoid surprises. To make certain that proceedings under an agreement did not come unraveled, he personally managed major legislation on the floor.

Johnson occasionally faced situations for which a more complex arrangement of floor debate was required to gain unanimous consent. For example, a few Johnson agreements provided for the adoption of an amendment without a separate vote on the amendment itself, which had nearly the same effect as the "self-executing" amendments employed in House special rules of the 1980s. Alterations in the amendment tree, such as permitting a previously approved amendment to be amended, and proscribing amend-

21. Evans and Novak, *Lyndon B. Johnson*, p. 114.

ments not submitted by a certain time, were among the other variants that expanded or restricted options on the floor. These too had later parallels in House rules. In each case, unanimous consent was required so that senators had an opportunity to object. But as Evans and Novak described the "Johnson treatment," objectors were likely to suffer personal harassment and possible retribution from the majority leader.

Conditions changed considerably after the 1958 elections, which changed the margin of Democratic control from two to thirty, a margin that held up for the next decade. Overnight, the Senate changed from a bastion of conservative strength to one in which Democratic liberals, along with a few Republicans, had the upper hand on many domestic issues.[22] Under pressure from the liberals and with more votes to break a filibuster on those issues, Johnson became more willing to bring to the floor measures that were likely to face extended debate. Invoking cloture also was made easier by the 1959 alteration of Rule XXII that changed the threshold from two-thirds of all senators to two-thirds of senators present and voting. Just as important, the class of liberals swept into the Senate in 1958 reinforced the efforts of Senate mavericks to gain a greater voice for rank-and-file senators on the floor.

The Elaboration of Unanimous Consent Agreements under Mansfield

The demands of the liberal Democrats were heeded by the next majority leader, Mike Mansfield, who assumed his position in 1961 after Johnson became vice president. Mansfield's mild-mannered, even passive, personality was consistent with his view that each senator's full array of floor privileges should be carefully guarded.[23] Mansfield did not offer as much resistance as Johnson to bringing to the floor measures that were likely to be subject to many amendments or even a filibuster. Faced with more filibusters and increasing time pressures, Mansfield resorted more frequently to cloture motions than his predecessor did.

Unanimous consent agreements in the 1960s reflected these changing conditions and leadership styles. As rank-and-file senators became more aggressive, unanimous consent requests were subject to far more discussion

22. On the ideological trends in the Senate, see Randall B. Ripley, *Power in the Senate* (St. Martin's Press, 1969), chap. 3; and Rohde and others, "Political Change and Legislative Norms in the U.S. Senate."

23. Much of what follows on complex unanimous consent agreements and holds since the 1960s is drawn from interviews with several staff participants. For their assistance, I thank former Senate parliamentarians Floyd Riddick, Murray Zwebin, and Robert Dove; past and present leadership aides Martin Gold, Elizabeth Green, Roy Greenaway, and William Hildenbrand; and four leadership aides who wished to remain anonymous. The interpretations provided in the text should not be attributed to any one of these Senate aides.

and modification on the floor, much to the consternation of Mansfield himself. Consider the following exchange from 1964:

> MR. HICKENLOOPER. Following the pattern of the inquiry of the distinguished leader, would it be in order to ask that the amendment to which I have referred be put in the line of progression?
>
> MR. MANSFIELD. There is nothing to stop it.
>
> MR. HICKENLOOPER. May I ask that there be added to the Senator's [Mansfield's] list of developing programs the amendment relating to writing instruments to which I have referred so that it will follow the three or four amendments to which he has already referred?
>
> MR. MANSFIELD. Mr. President, I ask unanimous consent that the Dirksen-Hickenlooper amendment be considered sometime tomorrow.
>
> MR. HICKENLOOPER. Mr. President, reserving the right to object, that is not what I asked. I asked if the amendment could follow the succession of amendments which the majority leader has outlined.
>
> MR. MANSFIELD. If the Senator wishes to make such a unanimous consent request, it is satisfactory with me.
>
> MR. HICKENLOOPER. I hoped that, out of the charity of the Senator's heart, he would include the amendment in his request.
>
> MR. KEATING. Mr. President, reserving the right to object, I have an amendment—
>
> MR. MANSFIELD. I give up. . . .[24]

Assertive members seeking to protect their opportunities on the floor, a tolerant but frustrated floor leader, detailed provisions, and confusion were typical of efforts to obtain unanimous consent for time-limitation agreements in the 1960s.

Unanimous consent requests were constantly adjusted to meet individual senators' political and scheduling needs, often at the expense of efficient use of time on the floor. As Mansfield put it in a 1963 interview:

> I have bent perhaps too often to extend favors of this nature to my colleagues. I have been criticized. The criticism is justified. But I do not know how else to operate if the Members themselves do not show a sense of maturity and recognize the fact that their job is here [on the Senate floor], to represent the people and their States, and that their engagements are of secondary importance.[25]

He even suggested, to no avail, that the Senate "ought to do something about the authority which each individual Senator has to object to unani-

24. *Congressional Record*, February 4, 1964, p. 1890.
25. *Congressional Record*, November 27, 1963, p. 22864.

mous consent requests." But Mansfield proved quite willing to seek unanimous consent to modify a previous agreement if an individual senator had not been available to protect his own interests when the original agreement was reached.

Further innovation occurred in the provisions of unanimous consent agreements to meet the shifting and often competing demands of senators of the 1960s. Agreements included provisions such as consent to offer an amendment after the third reading of a bill, incorporation of final passage for two bills in a single vote, a requirement that debate be germane, a variety of time limits for different amendments, and separate treatment of second-degree amendments. Agreements often came in bits and pieces, adjusting to new developments on a day-to-day basis. Mansfield sought to bar nongermane amendments whenever possible; in fact, a germaneness requirement often was included even if it was not requested directly or indirectly.[26] Usually out of necessity, then, unanimous consent requests became an even more elastic tool for staging floor debate.

Unanimous consent agreements also took on an importance beyond their significance as a leadership tactic for limiting debate and amendments. When measures were considered under an agreement, individual senators could better plan their personal schedules and bill managers could better anticipate when the next measure would reach the floor. Agreements became a service function of the floor leadership. Even senators not particularly interested in a measure benefited from the greater predictability provided by agreements, and they came to expect the leadership to pursue agreements whenever they could be reached. Senators' scheduling needs, of course, are seldom fully compatible, so the majority leader's scheduling problems became more severe.[27]

Unanimous consent requests developed an interesting dynamic in the 1960s. As they became more necessary and varied, senators began to see the potential of objection—or at least of "reserving the right to object"—as a way to accomplish goals beyond preserving debate and amending op-

26. The "usual form" of a unanimous consent agreement includes a standard prohibition of nongermane amendments. During the 1960s, the usual form often was assumed by the parliamentarian even though the majority leader did not explicitly request the usual form or the germaneness provision.

27. As Majority Leader Byrd more recently indicated: "It is extremely difficult to deal with the wishes of 99 other senators, attempting to schedule legislation, because in almost every case, at any time it is scheduled, it inconveniences some senator, and I cannot fire any of them. . . . I often say, when I am to fill out a form and the form says 'occupation,' I should put 'slave.'" Quoted in Jacqueline Calmes, "Byrd Struggles to Lead Deeply Divided Senate," *Congressional Quarterly Weekly Report*, July 4, 1987, p. 1422.

portunities on the floor. For example, the threat of objection to a time-limitation agreement for one measure sometimes was used to gain a promise that another measure would be brought to the floor expeditiously.[28] Each unanimous consent agreement therefore was of potential interest to all senators, regardless of their interest in the issue immediately before the Senate. Senators became more suspicious of the implications of unanimous consent requests, leading them to ask more questions and insist on formal clauses that protected their prerogatives on the floor. Even more complex agreements were the result.

Senators began to demand a more institutionalized mechanism for receiving advance notice of unanimous consent requests. Because senators can afford to spend only a small part of each day on the floor, they are dependent on floor leaders to warn them when an agreement might affect their interests. In previous decades, when senators had lower expectations about floor participation and unanimous consent agreements were relatively fixed in scope, extensive consultation and advance warning were not required. But in the 1960s the burden of notification became quite severe for floor leaders and their aides. Leadership aides developed extensive records on who might want notification as it became increasingly difficult for leaders to keep all the information in mind. But as careful as floor leaders were in protecting the interests of colleagues known to be affected by an agreement, it often was difficult to touch all bases in advance. In 1969, in response to grievances about notification, several senators pressed for a new system. They offered ideas such as requiring a quorum call before all complex requests, providing for one-day advance notice before the request was approved, or employing the bell system to give fifteen-minute notice before final approval. Nothing formal came of their effort, primarily because of the inflexibility involved in any effective system.

In the absence of a formalized notification system on the part of the leadership, individual senators sought to notify the leadership of their concerns about legislation that might come up. Senators often requested only advance warning of the consideration of a measure so they could be prepared with amendments. Some senators specifically demanded protection for an amendment, particularly if it was not germane, whenever a particular measure was brought to the floor. In other cases, senators notified leaders that they objected to any unanimous consent request to provide for the consideration of a measure, thus placing a "hold" on the measure, and they sometimes indicated the conditions under which they would lift their holds. Holds quickly became a standard element of the scheduling process.

28. See *Congressional Record*, September 10, 1963, p. 16609.

Further Innovation under Byrd

Since the late 1960s, no one has been as important as Robert Byrd in shaping the role of unanimous consent agreements. Byrd assumed a role in floor scheduling after being elected as Democratic conference secretary in 1967.[29] By the time he became his party's whip in 1971, Byrd had taken primary responsibility for crafting unanimous consent requests.[30] Although he was always careful to explain that he was acting under Mansfield's supervision, Byrd was the parliamentary expert upon whom the majority leader and most other Democrats rapidly became very dependent for fashioning the details of agreements. Byrd served as the majority leader (minority leader while the Republicans controlled the Senate from 1981 to 1986) from 1977 until he gave up the post in 1988.[31]

As floor activity mushroomed in the early 1970s, Byrd sought to further reduce the inefficiency and unpredictability of floor proceedings. More confident in his knowledge of the rules than other senators, Byrd did not hesitate to devise an agreement on the floor, rapidly adjusting and complicating an agreement as senators raised additional concerns. Byrd was aggressive in seeking an agreement for most important measures coming to the floor and was far more careful than his predecessors to close loopholes in agreements that might be exploited by others. With Byrd directing traffic on the floor, senators were more likely to find their floor activity restricted if they had not made their concerns explicit. This is not to say that Byrd trampled on his colleagues' floor privileges, for he generally was very responsive to requests for protective provisions and in the end could go only as far as unanimous consent would allow. But he was less willing to leave matters to chance.[32]

29. See Robert C. Albright, "Hard Worker in Ascendancy: West Virginia's Byrd Gains Key Senate Role," *Washington Post*, October 4, 1967, p. A1.

30. See Steven S. Smith, "Senate Leaders and the Use of Complex Unanimous Consent Agreements," paper prepared for the Hendricks Symposium on the United States Senate, University of Nebraska-Lincoln, October 6–8, 1988, table 3.

31. On Byrd's role in scheduling and unanimous consent requests, see his own comments in *Congressional Record*, January 26, 1973, pp. 2300–03, as well as Keith, "The Use of Unanimous Consent in the Senate," pp. 161–62; Robert L. Peabody, *Leadership in Congress: Stability, Succession, and Change* (Little, Brown, 1976), p. 332; and Sanford J. Ungar, "The Man Who Runs the Senate: Bobby Byrd: An Upstart Comes to Power," *Atlantic Monthly*, September 1975, pp. 29–35. Hubert Humphrey, majority whip between 1961 and 1964, also played an active role on the floor under Mansfield; see Stewart, "Two Strategies of Leadership," p. 75. Byrd, however, played a far more dominant role in scheduling and drafting agreements than had Humphrey.

32. Not surprisingly, one of Byrd's critics was Senator James Allen, the Senate's premier filibusterer, who claimed that "the Senate is being destroyed as a deliberative body." Quoted in "We Need to Get Back to the Past," *National Journal*, December 25, 1976, p. 1804.

TABLE 4-2. *Motions to Table Amendments in the Senate,*
Selected Congresses, 1955–86

	Amendments subject to a motion to table	
Congress	Number	Percent of all floor amendments
84th (1955–56)	3	0.2
88th (1963–64)	20	2.8
92d (1971–72)	67	5.3
93d (1973–74)	112	n.a.
94th (1975–76)	204	n.a.
95th (1977–78)	359	n.a.
96th (1979–80)	205	11.4
99th (1985–86)	272	15.5

SOURCE: *Congressional Record.*
n.a. Not available.

Under Byrd's guidance, both the number and complexity of agreements increased.[33] Mansfield was "not too keen" about the expanded use of time-limitation agreements, but argued that time constraints made it a necessity.[34] Agreements in the 1970s were more likely to cover multiple days of floor activity, to cluster votes in order to abbreviate floor sessions, to incorporate provisions for more than one measure, to require that debate be germane, and, of course, to provide for dual tracking to manage measures subject to filibusters. The complexity of Byrd-drafted agreements is evident in their number of restrictive provisions.[35] The mean number of such provisions was 5.5 in the 93d Congress (1973–74) and 5.3 in the 96th Congress (1979–80), compared with 3.7 for Mansfield in the 88th (1963–64).

The necessity of obtaining unanimous consent to limit debate or amendments meant that there was a limit to what Mansfield and Byrd could accomplish through time-limitation agreements. Floor leaders and bill managers relied increasingly on motions to table to dispose of amendments, as table 4-2 indicates. Motions to table are not debatable and, if adopted, speed the consideration of amendments and other motions. In many cir-

33. No complete count of complex unanimous consent agreements is available. However, the Senate's *Calendar of Business* included 123 agreements in the 93d Congress, up from the 33 noted in the *Daily Digest* during the 88th. Keith's findings confirm the interpretation offered here; Keith, "The Use of Unanimous Consent in the Senate," p. 157. Participants also noted this shift. For example, William Hildenbrand, Minority Leader Hugh Scott's floor assistant during the early 1970s, reported that "Byrd began to work unanimous consent agreements on nearly everything. He did not want to take any chances"; interview, August 18, 1987.

34. Richard E. Cohen, "Marking an End to the Senate's Mansfield Era," *National Journal,* December 25, 1976, pp. 1803–04.

35. See appendix 2 for a list of the provisions coded in this count.

cumstances, senators find it easier to vote for the procedural motion to table than to vote directly against an amendment itself. This gives an edge to the opponents of the amendment. And because there is a separate vote on the amendment if the motion to table fails, opponents of the amendment can seek additional support to defeat the amendment on the subsequent vote. Byrd, not one to miss many parliamentary tricks, made motions to table a nearly standard mechanism for disposing of unfriendly amendments. As motions to table became more common in the early 1970s, however, senators occasionally began to use unanimous consent agreements to gain protection from tabling motions for their amendments.

After Byrd was elected majority leader in 1977, he moved to improve the notification system. Byrd regularly circulated among his Democratic colleagues a form that made it easy for senators to note their concerns about measures about to be considered on the floor. This mechanism gave Byrd advance warning of objections to the consideration of measures under time limitations, putting him in a better position to plan the floor schedule without fearing that he had overlooked a colleague's interests.[36] It also permitted him to demonstrate his commitment to meeting the political needs of his party colleagues. But the system made it easier for senators to object to the consideration of legislation, sometimes bringing a matter to a senator's attention for the first time, stimulating holds, and complicating floor scheduling.

Creativity and assertiveness did not ensure Byrd success in gaining unanimous consent for the agreements he sought. In 1979, for example, Byrd struggled to obtain a time-limitation agreement for debate on a measure concerning the windfall profits tax on domestic crude oil and amendments to it. He described the process and results on the Senate floor:

> Many hours have been spent in meetings that have been conducted . . . in an effort to reach an orderly means of proceeding with the bill and amendments thereto.
>
> Senators from both sides of the aisle, senators from the Finance Committee, representing a broad spectrum of opinion, have been involved in these meetings. A good-faith effort has been put forth by all concerned to reach an agreement—not necessarily an agreement that would include every detail. That was never the intention or the purpose. It is only the

36. Byrd also initiated the unanimous consent calendar in 1977. The calendar provided at least one day's notice that the listed measures had been cleared with the leadership of both parties for adoption by unanimous consent. Senators who objected to such consideration could then raise their objections with their floor leadership. The practice was discontinued after one year. It should not be confused with complex unanimous consent agreements providing for time and amendment restrictions.

hope that we might agree on some rather broad approach that would, in the end, avoid a filibuster and break what appeared to be an impasse and produce a product that would be not only fair and equitable to the oil companies, but a bill which would be fair and equitable to the American people and would result in the production of more energy.

So, it was intended, hopefully, that these meetings would produce this kind of broad consensus that would protect the rights of all Senators to offer any amendments they wished but which would expedite consideration of the bill. In other words, the final product would not be decided in offices off the floor, but would be decided by the Senate and would be modeled and hammered out and shaped by the Senate, with every Senator being able to call up his own amendment if he wishes to, or any number of amendments, have them voted on, and let the Senate work its will and get on with other business. . . .

No agreement has been reached, but the discussions have been beneficial.[37]

Byrd was helpless in the face of committed opposition and members jealously protecting their options. His persistence eventually led to a series of agreements to limit debate on most amendments.

Unanimous Consent under Baker and Dole

Byrd's Republican successor as majority leader, Howard Baker, had more difficulty in gaining unanimous consent for time-limitation requests. Although Baker chose not to use a regular notification system, the Democrats continued to do so. Byrd used the Democrats' telephone "hotline" to notify his colleagues of pending unanimous consent requests and frequently received word of a senator's objection. He then faithfully voiced the objection on that senator's behalf, preventing Baker from proceeding under the proposed agreement. And, sometimes in a manner that must have irritated Baker, Byrd critically scrutinized Baker's unanimous consent requests, often suggesting clarifications or more proper terminology. Consequently, Baker faced even more protracted floor discussions about agreements and obtained consent for time limitations at early stages of floor debate less frequently than Byrd had.

Baker was exceptionally open and accommodating to the requests of his colleagues, particularly fellow Republicans, for protective provisions in unanimous consent agreements. For example, Republicans were allowed to reserve spots for their amendments without identifying what their amendments were about. Such "blank" amendments preserved senators' amending opportunities without losing flexibility to determine their specific form,

37. *Congressional Record*, December 4, 1979, pp. 34438–39.

or even their subject matter in some cases. Baker was dependent upon his staff to prepare most agreements; they would routinely incorporate individual senators' concerns in most situations.

Robert Dole, the Republican majority leader in the 99th Congress (1985–86), tightened up several of Baker's rather loose practices.[38] He was far more willing to bring a measure to the floor, challenge his colleagues to object to proposed agreements, and, at least implicitly, threaten retaliation. He also was generally unsympathetic to colleagues seeking to reserve opportunities to offer unspecified amendments and often pressured party colleagues into concurring with unanimous consent requests that did not fully accommodate their interests. One result of Dole's style was a further increase in the number of restrictive provisions in agreements. But because of the difficulty of getting unanimous consent, Dole, too, depended on piecemeal agreements that, on average, were shorter than Byrd's agreements.[39]

Compared with agreements in the 1970s, Dole's agreements were far more likely to provide for a vote on final passage at a specified time, to place explicit restrictions on amending activity, and to prevent recommittal and other motions that might intervene between debate and a vote on an amendment or the measure. Several types of restrictions on amendments became more common, such as provisions to permit only certain specified amendments, to bar amendments on certain subjects, or to bar second-degree and nongermane amendments. These restrictions sometimes were used to avoid "time-agreement filibusters" in which debate is extended by endless amending activity.

One of the most convoluted unanimous consent agreements in Senate history was developed in 1986, Dole's second year as majority leader. At issue was a contra aid package attached to a military construction bill, which liberals threatened to filibuster, and a bill to impose sanctions against South Africa, which conservatives threatened to filibuster.[40] After many hours of negotiation, Dole managed to break a two-week standoff by proposing an agreement providing for cloture votes on both issues, along with an automatic follow-up cloture vote if one of the first cloture votes failed,

---

38. For background on Baker-Dole differences, see Andy Plattner, "Dole on the Job: Keeping the Senate Running," *Congressional Quarterly Weekly Report*, June 29, 1985, pp. 1269–73.

39. While his agreements were shorter on average than Byrd's, Dole continued the trend toward more complex agreements when he could obtain consent. The net effect was greater variance in the number of restrictive provisions in complex agreements. The standard deviation in the number of restrictive provisions per agreement was 1.65 in the 93d Congress, 1.89 in the 96th, and 2.72 in the 99th (see appendix 2 for further details).

40. See *Congressional Record*, August 9, 11, and 12, 1986.

and requiring that cloture be successfully invoked for both measures before the Senate could proceed to consider either measure. The agreement provided that 121 specified amendments on the two measures would be in order and included one-and-one-half additional pages of single-spaced text explaining how the two measures were to be handled if cloture was successfully invoked in both cases, much of which was devoted to closing procedural loopholes that might be exploited to extend debate.[41] The leverage gained by tying the cloture votes together was sufficient to produce successful cloture votes. Both measures eventually passed after being amended many times.

The developments in the use of unanimous consent since the early 1970s must be kept in perspective. The 1980s did not bring a substantial contraction of amending activity on the Senate floor, despite the use of more detailed unanimous consent agreements. The requirement of unanimous consent gives individual senators sufficient leverage to protect their amending opportunities on the floor. As a result, the "restrictiveness" of agreements barely keeps up with senators' expanding interest in floor amendments. Only in exceptional circumstances are floor leaders or bill managers in a position to browbeat their colleagues into withholding their amendments. To do so, they must threaten to hold all-night and weekend sessions or even to cut into scheduled recesses before substantial compliance with their requests is attained.[42]

Unanimous Consent and Holds

The use of holds became a central part of the process for obtaining unanimous consent agreements during the 1970s. By the late 1970s, holds became a serious impediment to moving measures to the floor.[43] As floor leaders of both parties systematized the practice of recording and observing senators' objections to proceeding with legislation, senators came to expect that floor leaders would respect their holds. Lobbyists and other outsiders seeking to block legislation or extract concessions from bill sponsors also became familiar with the practice and solicited senators to place holds on

41. See the Senate's *Calendar of Business*, August 13, 1986, pp. 2–5.

42. For example, Majority Leader Robert Byrd used such threats to move a major trade bill through the Senate during the summer of 1987. See Jonathan Fuerbringer, "In the Senate, Once More unto the Beach," *New York Times*, July 22, 1987, p. A24.

43. For example, the *Congressional Quarterly Almanac* noted Byrd's difficulties: "Even though holds could not officially keep bills off the floor, they became more effective in blocking action in 1978. With the Senate schedule so overburdened, Byrd was reluctant to bring up any bill unless all senators had agreed to a time limit on debate." *Congressional Quarterly Almanac, 1978*, vol. 34 (1979), p. 5.

their behalf. Holds even became a general tool for holding measures hostage in order to gain leverage over a committee chairman or even the administration on unrelated matters. The greater complexity in the use of holds was reflected in the hold notices sent to floor leaders. Some hold notices indicated the conditions under which the objecting senators would lift their hold. A system of advance notification was transformed into single-senator vetoes of legislation, a privilege into a right, and a leadership service into a leadership obligation.

In general, floor leaders seek to accommodate colleagues' wishes. After all, leaders need the cooperation of all senators to operate the Senate under unanimous consent agreements and may need particular senators' votes in upcoming legislative battles. Open conflict, particularly within the majority party, often delays passage of a measure and creates interpersonal friction. The confidential nature of holds puts leaders in a position to facilitate quiet negotiations before conflict between colleagues becomes more open.

The strength of a hold depends on the credibility of a senator's implied threat to object to the floor leader's request to proceed to the consideration of a measure. The floor leader may seek to bring up a measure even in the face of a senator's hold, in effect challenging the senator to object and obstruct Senate consideration of a measure. Byrd, Baker, and especially Dole called senators' bluffs on occasion, particularly on major legislation deemed essential to the party or the Senate. In such cases, the weight of opinion and the concern about retribution from alienated senators usually are great enough to suppress objections. Yet holds retain their effectiveness, even for measures of moderate importance, because of the continuing severity of time constraints in the Senate.

Baker's accommodating approach, which included the observance of holds, received rave reviews during 1981, his first year as majority leader. Holds proved to be little problem that year because Baker sought to keep the schedule clear for the few major measures of the Reagan administration. Indeed, as a Baker aide explained, holds were useful excuses not to bring to the floor measures that Baker preferred not to call up anyway. After 1981, support for the Reagan program waned, other matters resurfaced on the Senate's agenda, and Baker wanted to move legislation. But Baker experienced problems with holds that were even more debilitating than Byrd's problems. Baker's Republican colleagues, some of whom believed they had a conservative policy mandate, saw holds as a way of blocking legislation inconsistent with that mandate. Many new Republicans, those elected in 1978 and 1980, were unaware of the tortured history of unanimous consent agreements and readily adopted the view that holds were a matter of right. Senior colleagues eventually lectured them on the original purpose of holds as notification devices, but junior senators' expectations made it difficult for Baker to move legislation without alienating colleagues whose support was required to obtain consent.[44] Baker's announcement in 1982 that the leadership would no longer treat holds as binding did not change practice much at all, primarily because threatened objections to proceeding with measures still had credibility, the severity of time constraints had not changed, and the political incentives for senators to press their cases remained.[45] In 1983, two former senators, commissioned by the Senate to propose reforms, fruitlessly recommended the elimination of holds.[46]

The effectiveness of holds was strengthened by their status as confidential communications to the floor leader. In most cases, the floor leaders do not disclose the identity of the senator placing a hold, reducing the possibility of retribution from other senators against the objecting senator. Floor leaders sometimes may share the information with the bill manager, usually with the approval of the objecting senator, in order to facilitate a resolution of the conflict. When the senator's identity is divulged, the leader normally asks the receiving party not to share that information with others. Given senators' expectations about holds, publicizing the hold probably only alienates the holding senator and creates further delays in moving the legislation to the floor.

By the time Dole became majority leader in 1985, disenchantment with the use of holds was widespread, although still not universal. A group of reform-minded senators targeted holds and their secrecy in late 1985. Their recommendations were followed by a Dole announcement in early 1986 that holds would no longer constitute vetoes and that senators could learn the identity of those placing holds. In fact, Dole had already begun to call up a few measures on which holds had been placed after giving the

44. On obstructionism under Baker, see Alan Ehrenhalt, "Every Man Is an Island: In the Senate of the '80s, Team Spirit Has Given Way to the Rule of Individuals," *Congressional Quarterly Weekly Report*, September 4, 1982, pp. 2175–82; and Diane Granat, "Tuesday Through Thursday Club: Ruling Rambunctious Senate Proves to be Thorny Problem for Republican Leader Baker," *Congressional Quarterly Weekly Report*, July 16, 1983, pp. 1427–32. Also see Senator Ted Stevens's comments in Granat, "Tuesday through Thursday Club," pp. 1429–30; and Senator William Armstrong's comments, *Congressional Record*, daily edition, February 20, 1986, pp. S1464–67.

45. For Baker's announcement, see *Congressional Record*, December 6, 1982, p. 28790. As Senator David Durenburger explained a few months earlier, "If you sacrifice one day for the collective will, you do it knowing that somebody else will refuse to do the same thing the next day. So you're reluctant to make the sacrifice." Quoted in Ehrenhalt, "Every Man Is an Island," p. 2177.

46. Andy Plattner, "Cut Committees, Debate: Report Urges Major Changes in Senate Structure, Rules," *Congressional Quarterly Weekly Report*, April 9, 1983, pp. 695–96.

affected senators advance warning. Dole, however, could not speak for the Democrats, whose practice did not change noticeably. In the end, the practice of holds remained firmly established for both parties.

Senators vary widely in the frequency with which they request holds; for some, holds are a central feature of their legislative activity. Party leaders develop great facility at estimating which senators mean business when they place a hold and which senators' bluffs can be called. Liberal Democrat Howard Metzenbaum is one senator who means business and has developed an extraordinary role in the Senate with his use of holds and threatened filibusters. Nearly all legislation is scrutinized by Metzenbaum's staff, with the possibility of a hold always in mind. Metzenbaum's obstructionism became so widely anticipated but unpredictable that even Republican majority leaders of the early 1980s regularly screened measures coming to the floor with him in advance, rather than depending on the Democratic floor leader to serve as an intermediary. In the 99th Congress, Democratic leaders took official recognition of Metzenbaum's role on a form used for clearing measures for floor action: the form has check-off boxes for the floor leader, ranking committee member, and Metzenbaum. A Senate colleague noted, "When you prepare an amendment or a bill, subconsciously you're thinking about Howard Metzenbaum. Will it pass the Metzenbaum test?" [47]

In summary, the informal practice of holds became institutionalized for several reasons. The underlying necessity of obtaining unanimous consent gives rank-and-file members a source of leverage over the majority leader. That leverage is enhanced by the severe scheduling pressures recent leaders have faced. At the same time, the political incentives to place holds have multiplied as outsiders have learned how to exploit the practice. And even when the majority leader gains the cooperation of his party colleagues, he can do little about practices within the minority party, whose members generally have more incentive to be obstructionist and are less sensitive to the scheduling problems of the majority leader.

The Changing Content of Unanimous Consent Agreements

Many of the developments in the use of unanimous consent agreements are observable in the changing provisions of the agreements. I have examined all complex agreements in five selected Congresses, as well as complex agreements for key vote measures in nine Congresses. My data include each unanimous consent agreement that limited debate or structured

---

47. On Metzenbaum's role, see Ward Sinclair, "Thank God For Metzenbaum," *Washington Post*, December 12, 1982, p. C5; and Jacqueline Calmes, "Democratic Gatekeeper: Howard Metzenbaum," *Congressional Quarterly Weekly Report*, January 3, 1987, pp. 16–17.

TABLE 4-3. *Complex Unanimous Consent Agreements,*
Selected Congresses, 1955–84

Congress	Percent of measures with agreements	Number of agreements per measure	Largest number of agreements on a measure
Key vote measures			
84th (1955–56)	72.2	1.1	2
86th (1959–60)	71.4	1.5	5
88th (1963–64)	88.2	2.0	6
90th (1967–68)	90.0	3.9	16
92d (1971–72)	84.0	4.6	14
94th (1975–76)	75.0	3.4	24
96th (1979–80)	86.7	2.9	18
97th (1981–82)	92.0	3.8	15
98th (1983–84)	85.7	2.9	14
All measures[a]			
84th (1955–56)	2.2	0.03	3
88th (1959–60)	7.1	0.1	8
92d (1971–72)	18.1	0.4	23
96th (1979–80)	26.3	0.5	21
98th (1983–84)	14.2	0.2	14

SOURCE: *Senate Journal.*
    a. For the first and second columns the denominator in calculating the percentages is the number of bills and joint resolutions passing the Senate, taken from Norman J. Ornstein, Thomas E. Mann, and Michael J. Malbin, *Vital Statistics on Congress, 1987–1988* (Washington: Congressional Quarterly, 1987), p. 167.

amending activity in any way, so they reflect all unanimous consent agreements of substantive importance. While many of the agreements are not long and detailed, I have labeled them "complex" agreements so as to distinguish them from routine unanimous consent agreements that have no effect on debate or amending activity.[48]

Two important features of the changing use of complex unanimous consent agreements are documented in table 4-3. First, throughout the period since the mid-1950s, a high proportion of key vote measures has been subject to unanimous consent agreements that limited debate or structured amending activity in some way, much more so than other legislation. The proportion has varied considerably from Congress to Congress, reflecting the difficulty of obtaining agreements in some Congresses. Second, the number of separate agreements adopted has been considerably higher since the mid-1960s than previously, especially relative to the number of measures passed. Sometimes out of necessity and sometimes as a matter of convenience, recent majority leaders have used agreements in highly flexible ways to adjust to senators' scheduling needs, unexpected amendments,

    48. For a similar use of the term, see Walter J. Oleszek, *Congressional Procedures and the Policy Process,* 3d ed. (Washington: CQ Press, 1989), pp. 185–86.

and changing political circumstances. A dozen or more complex agreements on a single measure are no longer uncommon for complicated, contentious measures.

The provisions of complex agreements can be divided into two major groups: debate limitations and amendment restrictions. Although the two groups are neither fully exhaustive nor mutually exclusive, they are sufficiently distinct in form and function for purposes of this discussion.

Limitations on debate come in two basic forms. The first is a direct limitation on the number of hours or minutes that measures, amendments, or various motions can be debated. Such debate limitations can apply to whole classes of amendments or motions or can be tailored to individual amendments and motions. The second form is the specification of a certain time for a vote on a measure, amendment, or other motion. A time-certain provision has the advantage of limiting the time that is available for the consideration of amendments, second-degree amendments, and other motions, while a direct time limitation allows debate on other motions to push back the time at which a vote takes place on the measure, amendment, or motion subject to the time limitation. Therefore, time-certain provisions make floor deliberations less vulnerable to dilatory tactics and reduce uncertainty about the floor schedule, but provide a weaker guarantee that senators will have time to speak on an issue.

The tremendous change in leaders' requests affecting debate limitations is shown in table 4-4. In Johnson's first Congress as majority leader (1955–56), there was great uniformity in the requests. A time limit for debate on the measure and a separate time limit for all amendments and debatable motions were standard. No time-certain provisions were requested for votes on final passage, amendments, or other motions. In the early 1970s the pattern changed dramatically. For debate on the measure, agreements less frequently included time limits for debate and more frequently included provisions for time-certain votes on final passage. For debate on amendments, a mixture of direct and time-certain restrictions has been used since at least the 1950s, with time-certain votes becoming more common in the 1960s.

Senate leaders' tactics for managing time clearly have become more flexible and creative. The severity of their scheduling problems and their desire to reduce the number of amendments and motions that slow final approval of legislation have increasingly caused leaders to use highly detailed time-limitation agreements. Since the mid-1960s a large majority of key vote measures have had at least one unanimous consent agreement that specified debate limitations for one or more individual amendments (table 4-5). In fact, since the late 1960s, specifying debate limitations for particular

TABLE 4-4. *Debate Limitations in Complex Unanimous Consent Agreements, Selected Congresses, 1955–84*[a]

Percent

| | Type of limitation | | | | | |
| | Direct time limits | | | Time-certain votes | | |
Congress	Measure	Amendments[b]	Other[c]	Measure	Amendments[b]	Other[c]
Key vote measures						
84th (1955–56)	100.0	100.0	100.0	0	0	0
86th (1959–60)	73.3	86.7	66.7	6.7	33.3	0
88th (1963–64)	66.7	80.0	33.3	0.0	40.0	0
90th (1967–68)	57.9	94.7	52.6	5.3	31.6	5.3
92d (1971–72)	33.3	95.2	47.6	28.6	47.6	4.8
94th (1975–76)	38.1	90.5	42.9	33.3	61.9	4.8
96th (1979–80)	42.3	61.5	50.0	42.3	42.3	11.5
97th (1981–82)	17.4	87.0	17.4	17.4	39.1	4.3
98th (1983–84)	22.2	83.3	38.9	33.3	44.4	16.7
All measures[d]						
84th (1955–56)	2.2	1.5	1.4	*	0	0
88th (1963–64)	3.1	4.1	2.2	0.7	0.9	*
92d (1971–72)	13.8	14.9	10.1	2.9	2.4	0.2
96th (1979–80)	16.3	15.4	11.4	4.1	4.3	0.9
98th (1983–84)	6.9	4.5	3.1	1.9	1.3	1.3

SOURCE: *Senate Journal.*

* Less than 0.1 percent.

a. Each cell is the percentage of measures for which at least one agreement included a provision of the specified type.

b. Includes provisions that apply to all amendments or just some amendments.

c. Includes provisions that apply to motions (such as motions to recommit), appeals, and points of order.

d. The denominator in calculating the percentages is the number of bills and joint resolutions passed by the Senate, taken from Ornstein and others, *Vital Statistics,* p. 167.

TABLE 4-5. *Debate Limitations on Individual Amendments in Complex Unanimous Consent Agreements for Key Vote Measures, Selected Congresses, 1955–84*

Congress	Percent of key vote measures with agreements specifying debate limitations on individual amendments[a]	Percent of agreements on key vote measures specifying debate limitations on individual amendments, by number of amendments specified[a]			Total
		None	One	More than one	
84th (1955–56)	11.1	87.5	0.0	12.5	100.0
86th (1959–60)	28.6	64.5	22.6	12.9	100.0
88th (1963–64)	75.0	34.4	53.1	12.5	100.0
90th (1967–68)	70.0	23.1	67.9	9.0	100.0
92d (1971–72)	72.0	21.7	58.3	20.0	100.0
94th (1975–76)	64.3	23.2	53.7	23.2	100.1
96th (1979–80)	56.7	50.0	34.1	15.9	100.0
97th (1981–82)	80.0	20.0	54.7	25.3	100.0
98th (1983–84)	71.4	33.3	55.0	11.7	100.0

SOURCE: *Senate Journal.*
a. Includes agreements with either direct time limits or time-certain votes.

TABLE 4-6. *Restrictions on Amendments in Complex Unanimous Consent Agreements, Selected Congresses, 1955–84*[a]
Percent

	Type of restriction			
Congress	*Specified only certain amendments in order*	*Barred amendments for certain subjects or sections of measure*	*Barred at least some second-degree amendments*	*Barred nongermane amendments*[b]
Key vote measures				
84th (1955–56)	0	0	0	92.3
86th (1959–60)	0	0	0	67.7
88th (1963–64)	0	0	6.7	40.0
90th (1967–68)	0	0	0	21.1
92d (1971–72)	4.8	4.8	0	19.0
94th (1975–76)	0	0	4.8	19.0
96th (1979–80)	23.1	3.8	15.4	26.9
97th (1981–82)	8.7	4.3	13.0	17.4
98th (1983–84)	38.9	16.7	11.1	22.2
All measures[c]				
84th (1955–56)	0.1	0	0	1.4
88th (1963–64)	0.1	0	0	2.5
92d (1971–72)	*	*	0.4	4.2
96th (1979–80)	2.8	2.1	2.3	2.1
98th (1983–84)	5.1	2.8	2.9	0.9

SOURCE: *Senate Journal.*
*Less than 0.1 percent.
a. Each cell is the percentage of measures for which at least one agreement included a provision of the specified type.
b. Includes some provisions that only require that second-degree amendments be germane.
c. The denominator in calculating the percentages is the number of bills and joint resolutions passed by the Senate, from Ornstein and others, *Vital Statistics*, p. 167.

amendments has been the primary purpose of most unanimous consent requests on key vote measures. Leaders sometimes have found it necessary to list more than two dozen amendments, along with debate limitations on each amendment, in an agreement (see table 4-3).

Restrictions on amendments come in many forms, including the ordering of amendments and provisions barring certain types of amendments, such as amendments on certain subjects, second-degree amendments, or nongermane amendments (table 4-6). As rank-and-file senators became more assertive in preserving their options under the standing rules, leaders found it increasingly difficult to gain unanimous consent to bar all nongermane amendments. Here, too, leaders turned increasingly to more detailed unanimous consent agreements. Rather than barring all nongermane amendments, for example, recent leaders have simply listed all amendments, germane and nongermane, that will be in order. Leaders also have moved to close loopholes that would allow unanticipated amendments or motions to delay final action on legislation. The change is not limited to key vote measures, as the table confirms.

To reemphasize an important point, the greater detail in complex agreements does not necessarily mean that measures are debated under conditions that severely restrict senators' ability to participate as they see fit. To the contrary, detailed requests and loophole-closing provisions must receive unanimous consent, so leaders must accommodate senators who insist that a certain amendment or motion remain in order. Much of the detail represents an effort to make explicit that certain senators' options remain open. Accommodating individual senators' concerns, while at the same time closing loopholes that obstructionists might exploit, usually complicates the negotiations of unanimous consent requests and the content of the agreements.

The pattern of change in complex unanimous consent agreements reflects the struggle of Senate leaders to cope with the changing conditions of floor decisionmaking. Leaders have sought to streamline debate as much as possible in the face of the nearly constant resistance of individual senators seeking to protect their parliamentary prerogatives. The result has been innovation in the provisions of unanimous consent agreements but little genuine restraint on amending activity and debate.

Pressure to Elaborate the Formal Rules

The developments of the last three decades further entrenched individualism in the Senate, which enhanced the viability of filibusters. Increasing floor activity created severe pressures on the floor schedule. In combination, time constraints and the credibility of filibuster threats produced even greater dependence on unanimous consent agreements to limit and structure debate. The requirement of unanimous consent further fortified individual senators' power to obstruct the consideration of legislation and made floor scheduling more difficult for leaders. The result has been rising frustration with Senate floor activity, but continuing resistance to restraints on individual participation.

This intensifying procedural problem, solved in the House with the help of special rules adopted by simple majorities, has not been surmounted by the Senate. In the mid-1960s, just before the number of floor amendments and filibusters skyrocketed, Lewis Froman noted:

> The Senate is able to have such loose and flexible rules primarily because no senator takes advantage of them, at least not very often. It would be

possible for a senator or a small group of senators to delay and postpone action in the Senate time and time again. But such action would undoubtedly create a situation in which other senators simply could no longer tolerate the delays.[49]

Intolerance of delays, Froman believed, would lead to further elaboration of the rules and a loss of flexibility in Senate floor procedure. He was correct in predicting that perceived abuse of unanimous consent practices would lead to a search for more effective measures to overcome obstructionism and limit amending action on the floor. He did not foresee the obstructionism of the following two decades; nor did he fully anticipate the difficulty of imposing more rigid rules to limit debate and amending activity. Nearly continuous efforts since the mid-1970s have produced only the most modest reforms.[50]

The efforts to alter Rule XXII reflect the frustration about the costs of actual and threatened filibusters.[51] Recent proposals to again lower the cloture threshold, to allow a simple majority to cut off debate after a certain number of hours of debate, and to further tighten postcloture debate restrictions have only a slim chance of adoption in the near future. The other major target of recent reform proposals has been the germaneness of floor amendments. Lowering the cloture threshold would by itself make it easier to impose a germaneness requirement on amendments because the current rule requires that amendments be germane after cloture is invoked. Other proposals include Robert Byrd's suggestion that three-fifths of the senators present and voting be able to impose a germaneness restriction, and a more radical recommendation that all measures be considered on the floor by title and that amendments be required to be germane or relevant to the title under consideration.[52]

A wide range of proposals was studied in 1988. The Senate Committee

49. Lewis A. Froman, Jr., *The Congressional Process: Strategies, Rules, and Procedures* (Little, Brown, 1967), p. 118.

50. The recommendations and results of several efforts—the Culver commission of 1975–76, the Stevenson committee of 1976–77, the Pearson-Ribicoff study group of 1982–83, and the Quayle committee of 1984—are reviewed in a report of the Senate Committee on Rules and Administration, *Congressional Record*, daily edition, September 22, 1988, pp. S13055–60.

51. On the connection between decisionmaking costs and voting rules, see James M. Buchanan and Gordon Tullock, *The Calculus of Consent: The Logical Foundations of Constitutional Democracy* (University of Michigan Press, 1962), chap. 7.

52. Byrd's suggestion is in *Congressional Record*, daily edition, January 6, 1987, p. S92. Senator J. Bennett Johnston made title-by-title consideration a part of his platform during his campaign for majority leader in 1988. See Shannon Bradley, "Johnston Vows to Improve Senate's Quality of Life If He's Elected Leader," *Roll Call*, May 8, 1988, p. 1.

on Rules and Administration reported a set of recommendations for reform of Senate rules and practices, including several proposals altering floor procedure. The committee noted:

> Three principal characteristics of the Senate are among the primary sources of Senators' frustrations: (1) Senate rules, precedents, and practices governing debate, (2) the opportunity for Senators to offer nongermane amendments except under cloture and to appropriation and budget measures, and (3) perhaps most important of all, the expectation and assumption that the interests of individual Senators are to be accommodated and their prerogatives protected whenever possible.[53]

The committee proposed that debate on the motion to proceed be limited or prohibited, that the Senate be allowed to bar nongermane amendments by an extraordinary majority, that "sense of the Senate" or "sense of Congress" amendments be sponsored by at least twenty senators, and that amendments be introduced and considered on a title-by-title basis, similar to the practice of the House. But as important as the recommendations were, the committee offered them in the most tentative manner and the prospects for such reforms remain bleak.[54]

The primary obstacle to reform is that it takes an extraordinary majority to accomplish change.[55] Reformers have argued since the 1950s that the Constitution implies that simple majorities may alter the Senate's rules at the start of each Congress. They base their argument on article I, section 5 of the Constitution, which provides that "each house may determine the rules of its proceedings." This provision, the argument goes, implies that the Senate, at least at the start of each Congress, may choose its rules under standard parliamentary procedure—that is, by majority vote.[56] Three presidents of the Senate (Vice Presidents Richard Nixon, Hubert Humphrey, and Nelson Rockefeller) have concurred with this view, but complex parlia-

---

53. *Congressional Record*, daily edition, September 22, 1988, pp. S13052–68, quote on p. S13054.

54. In its executive summary, the committee noted that "while the Committee believes that each of these proposals has much to recommend it, many of them could have far-reaching consequences and will require even more thorough study and full debate than they have received to date." *Congressional Record*, daily edition, September 22, 1988, p. S13053.

55. On the stability of decisions under supramajority decision rules, see Norman Schofield, Bernard Grofman, and Scott L. Feld, "The Core and the Stability of Group Choice in Spatial Voting Games," *American Political Science Review*, vol. 82 (March 1988), pp. 195–211.

56. Under this interpretation, the reformers argue, the constitutional provision supersedes Senate Rule V(2), adopted in 1959, which provides that "the rules of the Senate shall continue from one Congress to the next Congress unless they are changed as provided in these rules."

mentary entanglements have prevented simple majorities from effectively invoking cloture on rules changes.[57]

Consequently, efforts to limit debate and restrict amendments by rule or statute have produced only piecemeal results. In each instance where some limit was adopted, the need for restrictions was seen as particularly acute. For example, nongermane and legislative amendments are barred from general appropriations bills, primarily because they would infringe on the jurisdiction of authorizing committees.[58] Nongermane and legislative amendments are often added, however, either by unanimous consent or in a vote overturning the ruling of the presiding officer. Moreover, continuing resolutions are not considered general appropriations bills and so are open to all types of amendments. Strangely enough, all amendments are barred by statute for measures implementing or approving certain international trade agreements.

In only one area, budget measures, has the contemporary Senate made a concerted effort to limit floor activity. Nongermane amendments to budget resolutions are prohibited by the 1974 budget act, which also limits debate on budget resolutions and reconciliation bills to twenty hours. The Gramm-Rudman-Hollings plan, the five-year deficit reduction scheme adopted first in 1985, bars amendments to budget resolutions and reconciliation bills that raise the projected deficit beyond specified levels and further provides that a successful point of order against an ineligible amendment may be overridden only by a three-fifths constitutional majority of the Senate.[59] These limits on amending activity, it should be noted, remain substantially weaker than is typically true of House special rules for the same measures.

The time limitations and amendment restrictions for budget measures clearly are the exception to the rule in the Senate. They were adopted at times—1974 and 1985—when institutional ineffectiveness seemed particularly acute. They also were adopted as a part of large packages of budget process reforms, in which there were many other important items that distracted the chamber's attention from the amendment-constraining provi-

57. See Senator Byrd's review of these issues in *Congressional Record*, March 10, 1981, pp. 3879–88.

58. Senate Rule XVI(4) provides that "on a point of order made by any senator, no amendment offered by any other senator which proposes general legislation shall be received to any general appropriation bill, nor shall any amendment not germane or relevant to the subject matter contained in the bill be received."

59. On the Gramm-Rudman-Hollings provisions, see Elizabeth Wehr, "Congress Enacts Far–Reaching Budget Measure," *Congressional Quarterly Weekly Report*, December 14, 1985, pp. 2604–11. The House may override points of order by a simple majority vote, as under normal procedure, but the problem of overturning rulings of the chair has not been nearly as severe in the House as in the Senate.

sions. And, of course, the restrictions were limited to a specific set of measures of special importance to Congress. These unusual circumstances made it possible to overcome resistance to limiting individual senators' opportunities to shape policy on the floor.[60]

Budget Politics and Senate Amending Activity

The budget politics of the 1980s affected the Senate's floor agenda as well as that of the House. The Senate experienced great difficulty in passing regular appropriations bills, so it was even more dependent than the House on continuing resolutions for making spending decisions. Omnibus measures, particularly continuing resolutions and reconciliation bills, became vehicles for enacting nonbudget matters. The protective time limit and germaneness rule for reconciliation measures made them very attractive to Senate committees accustomed to having their legislation twisted out of shape by floor amendments. And massive year-long continuing resolutions, usually passed in the last hours of a session and often seen as veto-proof, proved to be useful conveyances for legislative items disliked by the administration, as was the case in the House.

In other ways, though, Senate floor activity was very different from House floor action on omnibus budget measures during the 1980s. With only one exception, first budget resolutions, reconciliation bills, and year-long continuing resolutions faced more floor amendments (usually far more) in the Senate than in the House. For example, first budget resolutions had an average of nearly twenty-three floor amendments subject to recorded votes during 1981–87—reaching a peak of over three dozen in 1985—compared with an average of about three amendments to such measures in the House during the same period. Senate amending activity on reconciliation measures was somewhat more restrained, averaging only eleven or twelve recorded-vote amendments between 1981 and 1987. Year-long continuing resolutions averaged about fourteen recorded-vote

60. Electronic voting has been considered occasionally in the Senate as a way to reduce the burden of voting on amendments and other motions, most recently during the 1986 debate on whether to televise floor sessions. However, rules changes providing for a new system have never come close to adoption. As in the House, the argument in favor of electronic voting is that it would save time. Senate rules provide for a twenty-minute period for roll call votes, and recent majority leaders have received consent to abbreviate the period to fifteen minutes. However, the roll often is kept open for longer periods so senators requiring more time to make it to the floor can vote. Opponents to an electronic system cite the flexibility of current arrangements, the benefits of interaction among senators while they wait for their names to be called, and the value to the leadership of being able to explain amendments and solicit support while members mingle in the well of the Senate during roll call votes.

amendments during the same period, but were subject to dozens of amendments that were incorporated by voice vote. Many of the amendments to continuing resolutions represented attempts to attach the text of unrelated legislation to the omnibus budget bills.

The contrast between the two chambers' approaches was most obvious in late 1985, when Congress was struggling to pass a reconciliation bill to avoid the first Gramm-Rudman-Hollings cuts. In the House, more than two dozen members appeared before the Rules Committee seeking a special rule that would permit them to offer their amendments. The Rules Committee responded, in typical fashion, by reporting a rule providing for only three amendments, two of which dealt with nonbudget authorization issues.[61] In the Senate, floor consideration of the reconciliation measure quickly broke down as senators prepared to offer amendments on abortion, civil rights, school prayer, and textile trade protection. The latter faced a threatened filibuster, which forced Majority Leader Dole to pull the bill from the floor. After Dole managed to work around a filibuster, seventeen amendments were proposed and subject to a roll call vote, with many others handled by voice vote. It was at the end of this ordeal that Byrd proposed that a three-fifths majority be required to overturn a ruling of the presiding officer that an amendment is not germane.[62] In 1986 and 1987, each of the major reconciliation bills faced only six or seven amendments, still double the typical number in the House.

Beyond personal appeals, Senate leaders can do little to stifle concerted efforts to offer amendments to budget measures. Individual senators' opportunities to participate in floor decisions on budget measures have been far less severely constrained than have those of representatives. In turn, omnibus legislating has yielded less insulation from unfriendly floor amendments for Senate committees than for their House counterparts. The little additional insulation Senate committees have gained is more the product of the rush of business late in sessions, when many budget measures are brought to the floor and senators' tolerance for minor amendments is waning, than of the formal limits on floor amendments to budget measures. But, as in the House, the pressures of budget deficits have limited the fiscal policy options of both individual members and committees in the Senate.

61. See Jacqueline Calmes, "Key Elements Face Challenges: Reconciliation Bills Headed for House, Senate Passage," *Congressional Quarterly Weekly Report*, October 19, 1985, pp. 2095–96.
62. Jacqueline Calmes, "Textile Amendment Is Roadblock: House Passes, Senate Defers Major Deficit-Cutting Bills," *Congressional Quarterly Weekly Report*, October 26, 1985, pp. 2142–46.

Senators, too, have grown restless about the use of continuing resolutions, adopted at the last minute to avert a shutdown of government agencies, to package all appropriations and sundry nonspending items. Following the lead of a primarily Democratic group in the House, thirty-three Senate Republicans and one Democrat (William Proxmire) wrote Majority Leader Byrd in February 1988 that they would no longer support continuing resolutions that did more than extend funding at the previous year's level. The group wrote that current practice "damages the integrity of the authorizing committees and makes virtually impossible thoughtful analysis of appropriations bills by individual members." The teeth in their threat was their promise to vote to sustain promised presidential vetoes of massive continuing resolutions.[63] Like the House, the Senate managed to pass all thirteen regular appropriations bills in 1988.

Televising Senate Floor Sessions

The Senate finally began televising its floor sessions during the summer of 1986, seven years after the House had done so. As in the House, opponents of televised sessions predicted dire consequences for the character of floor proceedings. For example, Senator J. Bennett Johnston predicted that speech making would increase, distorting senators' priorities by taking time away from committee duties. The desire to appear on television would lead senators to protect their opportunities to give floor speeches and intensify the problem of obtaining unanimous consent for time-limitation agreements. Consequently, he argued, speech making would create an even greater backlog of legislation at the floor stage.[64] Senator John Danforth concurred:

> What is going to happen is that instead of silence being golden, there is going to be an intense desire on the part of politicians, whose very life blood is to be on television, to come over and speak or offer amendments on any subject that they can think of.[65]

63. Tom Kenworthy, "Senators Join Protest Over Catchall Spending," *Washington Post*, February 9, 1988, p. A21. It also should be noted that omnibus legislating is not limited to budget and appropriations measures, particularly in the Senate where the lack of germaneness constraints makes adding extraneous floor amendments possible. The 1987 trade bill, for example, was subject to a rash of amendments unrelated to its already complex content. See Richard E. Cohen, "Playing Games," *National Journal*, July 25, 1987, p. 1942.

64. On Senator Johnston's views, see *Congressional Record*, daily edition, February 4, 1986, p. S934, and February 20, 1986, p. S1451.

65. *Congressional Record*, daily edition, February 5, 1986, p. S1021. Senator Warren Rudman agreed with Danforth that television "is going to lead to a spawning of even more nongermane, irrelevant amendments which are going to occupy the time of the U.S. Senate

Senator Lloyd Bentsen believed that televised sessions would affect policy outcomes by forcing senators to grandstand. "Once you get the TV going here," he asserted, "you are going to find it more difficult to achieve the compromises that have to be made to make legislation work and make democracy work." [66] And several senators expressed concern that the Senate's nonmajoritarian rules and frequent quorum calls would confuse the viewing public, produce pressures for change, and ultimately alter the special role of the Senate as a sanctuary for minority rights. [67]

It is far too early to provide a systematic assessment of the effects of television on Senate floor politics. Too many other factors must be taken into account—a changing agenda, turnover in party control, changing majority leaders—for any simple review of floor activity to be of much use. A study by the Congressional Research Service of the six-week test period in 1986 showed that there was a tremendous increase (250 percent) in the number of special-order speeches, but that the time consumed by such speeches increased by less than one hour a day, thanks to shortening the period granted from fifteen minutes to five minutes a speech. [68] The study detected no change in amending activity. A study of floor activity during the early months of 1987 conducted by the Senate's journal clerk found that special-order speeches receded in their frequency and that quorum calls' frequency declined, which may have been due to the change in majority leader from Dole to Byrd. [69]

Senate television's most vitriolic opponents later agreed that television had little effect on floor activity during its first year. Senator Johnston said, "My fears did not materialize," and Senator Proxmire concluded that "TV

---

and keep us from doing our business." *Congressional Record*, daily edition, July 29, 1986, p. S9773.

66. *Congressional Record*, daily edition, February 5, 1986, p. S1024. Senator William Proxmire seconded Bentsen's view, arguing that "instead of an institution where sharp differences are ground down and compromised, this floor will become a place where they are sharpened. This change will not take place suddenly, but take place it will." *Congressional Record*, daily edition, July 29, 1986, p. S9767.

67. The Senate also debated, but failed to adopted, a proposal to televise its floor sessions in 1982. The debate was more extensive than the 1986 debate and featured particularly revealing discussions of how senators saw their institution. For a review of the 1982 discussion, see Richard F. Fenno, Jr., "The Senate Through the Looking Glass: The Debate Over Television," paper prepared for the Hendricks Symposium on the U.S. Senate, University of Nebraska-Lincoln, October 6–8, 1988.

68. The control period was a similar period in 1984. See Paul S. Rundquist and Ilona B. Nickels, "Senate Television: Its Impact on Senate Floor Proceedings," Congressional Research Service, July 21, 1986.

69. Helen Dewar, "Senate on TV: Cool Under the Lights," *Washington Post*, June 3, 1987, p. A17; and Brian Nutting, "Cameras an Accepted Feature Now: After One Year of Television, Senate Is Basically Unchanged," *Congressional Quarterly Weekly Report*, May 30, 1987, p. 1140.

has had virtually no significant effect on the Senate. . . . Most senators, including myself, go for days taking an active part in floor discussion and completely forgetting that television is in fact covering this body."[70] One reason may be that only about 9.5 million households had the C-SPAN coverage of the Senate available in mid-1987, compared with over 27 million for House coverage.[71] And network use of the floor coverage remains very limited and restricted to major issues. Continued expansion of cable television and greater use of clips of floor action by local stations may change this picture in the future.

House and Senate Differences Reconsidered

In the late 1970s, it appeared that the characteristics of House and Senate floor activity were converging in certain ways. In fact, Norman Ornstein observed in 1981 that the decade of the 1970s made "the House more like the Senate, and the Senate more like the House." He argued that the reforms of the 1970s produced a House that was less formal and hierarchical and operated under more fluid rules and procedures. The House had become "an ad hoc institution, without firm control over its own schedule or priorities—much like the Senate," and so had lost its special character as a specialized instrument for processing legislation. As for the Senate, Ornstein took notice of the new uses of complex unanimous consent agreements, which, in his view, represented a shift toward more rigid floor procedure and a loss of its special character as a deliberative body. Ornstein concluded that "neither chamber is comfortable with its contemporary role."[72]

In hindsight, it is clear that Ornstein was right about the discomfort in both chambers about the developments of the 1970s. House members had become more assertive on the floor, House amending activity approached the levels of the Senate, and the Senate was accepting unanimous consent agreements that structured floor debate in complex ways. These developments were subject to open and frequent complaints from the membership in both chambers. The inference of convergence was drawn prematurely, though. It is now necessary to extend and qualify Ornstein's interpretation in light of developments in Congress in the 1980s.

70. Quoted in Dewar, "Senate on TV"; and Nutting, "Cameras an Accepted Feature Now."

71. Dewar, "Senate on TV."

72. Norman J. Ornstein, "The House and the Senate in a New Congress," in Thomas E. Mann and Norman J. Ornstein, eds., The New Congress (Washington: American Enterprise Institute for Public Policy Research, 1981), pp. 363–83, quotes from pp. 366, 367, 371.

The 1980s demonstrated that the underlying principles of chamber rules—majoritarianism in the House and individualism in the Senate—remain powerful forces that shape each chamber's responses to external and internal pressures. In the House, the free-for-all of floor amending activity that stimulated Ornstein's observations was in the process of being restrained at the time he wrote. Since then, restrictive rules have been accepted, and even demanded, by many of the Democratic rank-and-file members who played key roles during the reform movement of the early 1970s. And budget politics and omnibus legislating have altered the nature of the floor agenda in profound ways. This is not to say that rank-and-file Democrats are now limited to the roles they played in the 1950s and 1960s. They remain far more active in committee and party settings, and, when the special rules permit, rank-and-file members still vigorously pursue floor amendments. But there is now a widely accepted view, at least within the House majority party, that unfettered floor amending activity undermines efficient decisionmaking and threatens the party's political well-being.

In the Senate, Ornstein correctly observed that floor leaders were seeking to attain through complex unanimous consent agreements what could not be obtained through the standing rules of the chamber. During the 1970s more measures were indeed considered under agreements that structured floor debate in some way. When complex agreements are used to specify the particular amendments that will be in order or even the order in which amendments will be considered, they have much the same effect as some special rules in the House.

Yet the Senate's complex unanimous consent agreements must not be viewed as rigid restrictions comparable to those found in House special rules. Complex agreements are far less effective than special rules in reducing the volume of amending activity. The need to obtain unanimous consent in the absence of cloture forces leaders to make concessions before and during floor debate on a scale that would seem quite foreign in the House. As a result, the new uses of complex unanimous consent agreements on the floor do not alter the basic principles of Senate floor politics, which remain rampant individualism and the protection of minority rights. The Senate has not yet found a general strategy for limiting amendments and reducing the dangers of floor decisionmaking for committees and party leaders. In the view of many members, the Senate's problems with floor activism are becoming more severe, with no end in sight.

As the Senate floor has become a far more important location of policymaking, the chamber continues to struggle, on a case-by-case basis, with the unpredictability and inefficiencies of floor decisionmaking. The little autonomy that House committees and the majority party regained under restrictive special rules and omnibus measures still eludes their Senate counterparts. Even the centripetal forces of budget politics have not reordered Senate floor politics to the degree they have in the House; there is no distinctive postreform period comparable to that now evident in the House. Thus change in Senate floor politics continues to have a strongly evolutionary character, one of slow and partial adjustment to changes in its political environment.

The distinctive roles of rules, election outcomes, and party in the two chambers is unmistakable in the contrasting patterns of adjustment to change. In the House, rule by simple majorities, continuity in Democratic control, and Democratic cohesiveness on procedural questions helped the chamber reach an equilibrium of sorts in the manner in which business is conducted on the floor. That is, the majoritarianism of the House allows the majority party, if it is reasonably large and cohesive, to dictate alterations in procedure. Many, if not most, of the reforms of floor and committee procedure since the early 1970s became possible only after a consensus developed among majority party Democrats. In many cases the reforms were adopted on party-line votes. As a consequence of cohesiveness among Democrats on most procedural matters, rules have proven to be quite pliable in the seemingly more rigid House.

In the Senate, the power of large minorities to block change has prevented majorities from devising rules and procedures to suit their political needs. In fact, reform proposals seldom have been sanctioned by a party conference in the Senate, even though Senate party leaders have taken the initiative in proposing reform from time to time. Rather, most reform proposals have been brought to the floor and debated at great length in open session, where the ability of sizable minorities to obstruct procedural reforms necessitates negotiations across party lines right from the start. Successful reforms therefore usually have a much less partisan cast in the Senate than in the House. But the difficulty of reforming the standing rules has made reliance on flexible informal techniques a necessity in the Senate. To the extent that there can be said to be an equilibrium in Senate floor activity, it is one infused with uncertainty, oscillating between periods of dreary routine and unproductive stalemate.

Differences in size, traditional rules and informal practices, member expectations, and the role of party continue to shape the two chambers' responses to internal and external stresses and strains. Even after four decades of tremendous change, certain essential differences remain between the House and Senate. The Senate retains its more egalitarian, collegial form of decisionmaking, while the House manages to preserve its more majoritarian and decentralized form.

CHAPTER FIVE

Why Don't We Do It on the Floor?

Embedded in the shifting tides of floor activity are changing patterns of participation among representatives and senators. A defining feature of the move to collegial decisionmaking processes in the 1960s and 1970s was more active participation by rank-and-file members in the decisions of their chambers. The percentage of representatives offering floor amendments increased from just over 40 to over 80 between 1955–56 and 1977–78, while the percentage of senators offering floor amendments has been high throughout the period, increasing from about 90 percent in 1955–56 to 100 percent in 1979–80. In the House, per capita amending activity increased from less than one amendment per Congress to nearly four between 1955 and 1978. In the same period, Senate per capita amending activity increased from just over six amendments to eighteen. Floor participation obviously remains more widespread in the Senate than in the House, but in both chambers members now look to the floor as an avenue for pursuing their legislative interests far more frequently than they did in the 1950s.

This chapter explores the patterns of individual participation that underlie the changing patterns of decisionmaking on the chamber floors. The primary focus is the demise of two norms that once limited rank-and-file participation in both houses. During the 1950s, a norm of apprenticeship restricted junior members' activity and a norm of committee deference limited challenges to committee recommendations. These norms were reinforced by the distribution of staff resources, procedural prerogatives of committee chairmen and party leaders, and floor practices. These arrangements advantaged senior members, committees, and the majority party, with the committee chairmen sitting at the intersection of these groups. Between the late 1950s and the early 1970s, Congress's political environment changed, resources were distributed more widely within the institution, procedures were altered, and the central role of committees and their chairmen came under attack. By the early 1970s, the restrictive norms seemed to have disintegrated.

Differences between representatives' and senators' patterns of participation are the second focus of the chapter. The interchamber comparison will place the effects of House procedural reform in sharper relief. It also will reinforce the argument of chapter 4 that the House and Senate floors continue to exhibit fundamental differences.

For both apprenticeship and committee deference, I highlight the evidence, sketchy as it is, of changes in members' attitudes since the 1950s and examine more systematic evidence on patterns of participation in floor amending activity. I then explore differences between the parties and the characteristics of "hyperactive" members. I conclude by taking a closer look at the cross-sectional patterns of participation in the 99th Congress (1985–86), the most recent one for which complete data have been collected.

The argument is straightforward. Apprenticeship and committee deference have completely disappeared as prescriptive norms in both the House and Senate. Nevertheless, institutional positions in the committee and party systems of Congress continue to structure patterns of floor participation in important ways, even though members holding those positions do not dominate policy outcomes as much as they did in the 1950s.

Norms and Floor Activity

Terminology is a source of confusion in the discussion of norms in both theory and practice. At least two distinctive uses of the term "norm" can be identified.[1] Where norms are nothing but labels for behavioral uniformities or average conditions, the usage has no prescriptive content. This usage is common in everyday discourse and is found increasingly in formal theories of legislative politics.[2] Where norms are treated as standards of conduct, the usage has attitudinal and prescriptive content. Prescriptive norms may or may not include a threat of sanctions for nonconformity. When they do not include explicit or implicit sanctions, prescriptive norms take on the character of strategic advice, lessons from experience, or rules of thumb, as are commonly received by newcomers from experienced members. But when norms are associated with sanctions for nonconformity, they take on the character of regulations enforced by other members, such as party and committee leaders. In practice, the boundaries between the three types of norms are quite ambiguous because the language and

1. See George C. Homans, *The Human Group* (Harcourt, Brace, 1950), p. 124.
2. For example, see Robert Axelrod, "An Evolutionary Approach to Norms," *American Political Science Review*, vol. 80 (December 1986), pp. 1095–1111; and Kenneth A. Shepsle and Barry R. Weingast, "The Institutional Foundations of Committee Power," *American Political Science Review*, vol. 81 (March 1987), pp. 85–104.

intentions of participants are ambiguous and sometimes deliberately cryptic.

For both chambers, systematic evidence on members' attitudes about appropriate floor behavior is scarce, although some evidence is available. For the Senate, Donald Matthews's discussion of "folkways" provides a glimpse of norms in the 1950s, and a study by David Rohde, Norman Ornstein, and Robert Peabody provides a look at the same set of norms as they stood in the early 1970s.[3] No similar general treatment of prescriptive norms in the House exists for either the 1950s or more recent years.[4] Fortunately, scattered evidence permits some tentative conclusions about change in House attitudes about appropriate behavior on the floor.

Matthews identified two norms that limited participation in decision-making in the Senate of the 1950s. The apprenticeship norm provided that new members were to serve an unspecified period of learning before they participated actively in decisionmaking. As Matthews put it, "The new senator is expected is keep his mouth shut, not to take the lead in floor fights, to listen and to learn." He also uncovered a norm of specialization, according to which a senator should "focus his energy and attention on the relatively few matters that come before his committees or that directly and immediately affect his state."[5] In practice, specialization means deference to the recommendations of standing committees when their measures come to the floor, at least by the senators not serving on those committees. In combination, these two norms proscribed active floor participation for junior members and members not sitting on the committee of origin for a given measure.

What was the nature of these prescriptive norms in the 1950s and how have they changed since then? Is the behavioral evidence on floor activity consistent with the evidence about the change in prescriptive norms?

Apprenticeship

A clear prescriptive norm of apprenticeship existed in both chambers during the 1950s. Its status fell somewhere between purely strategic advice

---

3. Donald R. Matthews, *U.S. Senators and Their World* (Vintage Books, 1960), chap. 5; and David W. Rohde, Norman J. Ornstein, and Robert L. Peabody, "Political Change and Legislative Norms in the U.S. Senate, 1957–1974," in Glenn R. Parker, ed., *Studies of Congress* (Washington: CQ Press, 1985), pp. 147–88.

4. The only discussion of norms in the House of the 1950s is Fenno's discussion of the Appropriations Committee, for which only one norm, specialization, is attributed to the full chamber as well as to the committee. See Richard F. Fenno, Jr., "The House Appropriations Committee as a Political System: The Problem of Integration," *American Political Science Review*, vol. 56 (June 1962), pp. 310–24.

5. Matthews, *U.S. Senators and Their World*, pp. 93, 95.

and enforced regulation. For the Senate, Matthews implied that apprenticeship was a norm with sanctions attached, although no examples of specific sanctions were offered. Instead, premature participation was reported to breed resentment, tarnish a reputation, and undermine respect. As Matthews emphasized, "The freshman who does not accept his lot as a temporary but very real second-class senator is met with thinly veiled hostility." But, like other Senate norms, apprenticeship was not observed universally. Matthews was careful to qualify his discussion of norms by noting that they were "no more perfectly obeyed than the nation's traffic laws," and he concluded that senators who had previous political experience and close ties to outside groups and who arrived in the Senate late in life were the most likely to be nonconformist. Yet, after observing that some senators believed the norm was not as strong as it once was, Matthews stressed that "the period of apprenticeship is very real and very confining" for the freshmen he interviewed.[6]

By the time Matthews's words were published in 1960, the norm of apprenticeship was under severe, and apparently successful, challenge. The class of nine northern Democratic liberals elected in 1958 refused to be restrained by such norms and demonstrated a willingness to suffer the consequences. In a review of the legislative activity of this class, one scholar argues that "by the end of 1960 the liberal freshmen felt that they had fully justified their premature activism. . . . Like the class of 1958, the senators elected in 1960 and 1962 arrived on Capitol Hill firmly resolved to develop their interests, but unlike the 1958 newcomers, they never really encountered any serious suggestions that they should do anything to the contrary."[7]

Clear threats of reprisal for nonconforming junior members are very hard to find in the House of the 1950s as well. The few instances of tit-for-tat retribution against active junior members involved senior members directly affected by the nonconforming behavior; a general norm need not be invoked to explain such retribution. But the reputational costs of nonconforming behavior should not be minimized. A period of learning and acclimation was expected of new members; certainly new representatives recognized the possible consequences of not meeting their seniors' expectations.

In the House, as in the Senate, signs of decay in the apprenticeship norm already were visible in the late 1950s. Former Speaker and Minority Leader Joe Martin, writing at about the same time as Matthews, commented:

6. Matthews, U.S. Senators and Their World, pp. 93, 94, 116.
7. Michael Foley, The New Senate: Liberal Influence on a Conservative Institution, 1959–1972 (Yale University Press, 1980), p. 129.

The men who were loaded with the coin of seniority were rather more aloof in those days [when Martin first came to Congress] than they are now. They were less reticent about letting a newcomer know that they were running the show. The large round table which is still an important meeting place in the House restaurant was reserved for the Speaker, the chairmen of the various committees, and perhaps a few senior members of the Rules Committee. Anyone serving his first term would have been completely out of place. I had been in Congress three years before I dared pull up a chair.[8]

A former congressional staff member came to an even stronger conclusion in summarizing his discussions with a group of representatives in 1963:

The old admonition that new members should observe but not participate in debate was swept aside long ago. Apprenticeship may still precede full partnership, but the increased volume and complexity of the problems with which the Congress is compelled to cope dictate more efficient use of the membership. Freshmen are now advised to defer speaking only until the moment arrives when they have something significant to say— indeed, colleagues counsel them not to wait too long—although they are cautioned to be sure they are well informed about their topic.[9]

Thus, even in the era of strong committee chairmen, apprenticeship was not a very strong regulatory norm.

By the mid-1960s, the persisting fragments of the House apprenticeship norm appeared to be advisory at best. The freshmen representatives of 1965 were told by orientation session leaders to "be in attendance on the floor," "don't speak till you know what you are talking about," "if you want to get along, go along," and "learn parliamentary procedure," but the consequences for not doing these things were expressed entirely in terms of reputation and trust.[10] An observer who interviewed many of the freshmen elected in 1964 and 1966 commented that they "rejected the idea that freshmen should be seen and not heard. Keeping quiet, they argued, is not the way to be reelected."[11] In 1969, far fewer than half of a cross section of freshmen and nonfreshmen answered in the affirmative to the question: "Do you think that freshmen congressmen should serve a period of ap-

8. Joe W. Martin, Jr., as told to Robert J. Donovan, *My First Fifty Years in Politics* (McGraw-Hill, 1960), p. 47.

9. Charles L. Clapp, *The Congressman: His Work as He Sees It* (Brookings, 1963), p. 11.

10. Richard F. Fenno, Jr., "The Freshman Congressman: His View of the House," in Aaron Wildavsky and Nelson W. Polsby, eds., *American Governmental Institutions: A Reader in the Political Process* (Rand McNally, 1968), p. 25.

11. Thomas P. Murphy, *The New Politics Congress* (Lexington Books, 1974), p. 65.

prenticeship, that is, be more an observer than an active participant in the legislative process?"[12]

In the Senate of the mid-1960s, not only was the apprenticeship norm weak, but a *Wall Street Journal* article could be subtitled, without much exaggeration, "Young Recent Arrivals Bid for Control of Upper House." It concluded that "the willingness, even eagerness, of these neophytes to take on their elders is a distinguishing mark of the Senate's young generation."[13] In 1973 only two of over forty senators interviewed by a group of scholars believed that a period of apprenticeship was expected of new members.[14]

The timing of the demise of the prescriptive apprenticeship norm is particularly interesting. While the Senate appeared to lead the way in the late 1950s, the House followed closely, suggesting that changing attitudes in the two chambers were shaped by common forces. In fact, in both chambers the charge was led by new liberal members eager to challenge the power and policies of the conservative establishment entrenched in the committee systems. Furthermore, even though the norm may have retained somewhat greater strength in the House than in the Senate during the late 1960s, the House norm was weak well before the reforms of the early 1970s. Therefore, the floor behavior of junior members in both chambers should show substantial change in the 1960s, perhaps with the House lagging behind the Senate because of lingering commitments to some period of apprenticeship and the restraining effects of House floor procedures.

Assessing the behavioral implications of the disintegrating apprenticeship norm is not as straightforward as it may seem. The problem is that very few members, junior or senior, were very active in floor amending activity in the 1950s. Only nineteen senators sponsored ten or more amendments during the 84th Congress; only one representative did so in the same Congress. As a result, even a strong norm of apprenticeship is unlikely to have produced a level of floor activity among junior members that was substantially different from that of more senior members. The action was elsewhere, primarily in the standing committees, so the full implications of the apprenticeship norm cannot be evaluated by examining the floor alone. Indeed, the generally low level of floor participation raises

12. Herbert B. Asher, "The Learning of Legislative Norms," *American Political Science Review*, vol. 67 (June 1973), pp. 508–09.

13. Dan Cordtz, "The Senate Revolution: Young Recent Arrivals Bid for Control of Upper House," *Wall Street Journal*, August 6, 1965, p. 8. Also see Robert C. Albright, "Senate Youngsters Asserting Themselves as Never Before," *Washington Post*, January 15, 1968, p. A2.

14. Rohde and others, "Political Change and Legislative Norms," p. 175.

TABLE 5-1. *Per Capita Amendment Sponsorship in the House and Senate, by Seniority, Selected Congresses, 1955–86*

Congress	Years of service			
	1–2	3–4	5–6	7 or more
House				
84th (1955–56)	0.6	0.6	0.6	1.2
86th (1959–60)	0.7	1.1	1.3	1.1
88th (1963–64)	0.8	1.4	1.2	1.7
90th (1967–68)	1.1	1.4	1.9	2.3
91st (1969–70)	1.0	1.8	1.9	2.3
92d (1971–72)	1.3	1.3	1.3	2.1
93d (1973–74)	2.0	3.5	2.8	3.6
94th (1975–76)	2.9	2.2	3.5	3.4
95th (1977–78)	3.0	4.0	4.1	4.1
96th (1979–80)	2.0	3.4	3.1	3.5
99th (1985–86)	1.9	1.6	2.4	2.9
Senate				
84th (1955–56)	2.5	3.6	3.8	8.3
88th (1963–64)	2.7	3.7	6.4	10.6
92d (1971–72)	16.1	14.7	11.3	11.6
96th (1979–80)	13.7	14.6	17.0	21.0
99th (1985–86)	12.7	16.1	19.2	17.7

SOURCE: See appendix 2.

the possibility that what was read as an apprenticeship norm was often instruction in the normal behavior of all members.

Nevertheless, junior members—defined arbitrarily as representatives and senators in their first six years of service—were considerably less likely than more senior members to sponsor floor amendments in the 1950s and 1960s, as table 5-1 indicates. In the five prereform Congresses for which data are available for the House, freshmen were half as active as more senior members, while second-term members were three-fourths as active and third-term members were four-fifths as active. Junior senators were more active than their House counterparts, but they too were considerably less active than their more senior colleagues. In fact, the disparity between first-term members and senior members was proportionately greater in the Senate than in the House during the 1950s and early 1960s.

The pattern of behavioral change in the House is consistent with the pattern of attitudinal change. During the 1950s and 1960s, junior members' rate of participation increased, although increases for the most junior members were roughly proportional to the overall increase in amending activity. In the Congresses of the early 1970s, junior members, as a group, continued to offer fewer amendments than senior members, but they became more active more quickly as they gained seniority than did junior members in the 1950s and 1960s. The greatest surges in junior members' amending activity occurred in the 93d and 94th Congresses (1973–76), the Congresses immediately following the implementation of electronic recorded voting in the Committee of the Whole. Junior members experienced a greater proportionate increase than senior members in these two Congresses. For example, the freshmen of the 94th Congress, those elected in the immediate aftermath of the Watergate affair, were 50 percent more active than the previous freshmen class, yet total House amending activity dipped slightly in the 94th Congress.

In the 1980s House freshmen became less active as the volume of amending activity declined. To read this as the reemergence of a prescriptive apprenticeship norm would be incorrect. After all, junior members' amending activity remains substantially higher than in the prereform House, and even in the 99th Congress (1985–86) was in about the same proportion to senior members' amending as in the mid-1970s. Furthermore, junior members were not proportionately disadvantaged by the move to restrictive rules. In the 99th Congress, junior members offered nearly the same percentage of amendments to restrictive-rule measures as to all other measures (24 percent versus 23 percent, respectively).

With less complete data, less precision is possible in determining the pattern of change in the Senate. One notable feature of the early and mid-1960s is the activism of the class elected in 1958. By the time this class reached the end of their first term of office in 1963–64, they were considerably more active than their predecessors at a similar stage in their careers. The general pattern in the Senate indicates that junior members gained ground on senior colleagues before their House counterparts did so: while junior senators' amending activity increased incrementally during the 1960s, they already had outpaced their senior colleagues by 1971–72, a Congress before the surge in junior activism in the House.[15] Freshmen senators elected in Nixon's 1970 mid-term election offered more amendments per capita than did senators with seven or more years of service behind them. Freshmen senators are still five or six times as active on the floor as freshmen representatives, consonant with overall chamber differences in per capita amending activity.

Differences between the chambers also are obvious in junior members' success rates. Junior representatives of the 1950s and 1960s were distinctly less successful than their senior colleagues, as table 5-2 shows, and they

15. The interpretation of changing patterns of participation among junior and senior senators is supported by Sinclair's findings for amendments subject to roll call votes for every other Congress since the mid-1950s. See Barbara Sinclair, "Senate Styles and Senate Decision Making, 1955–1980," *Journal of Politics*, vol. 48 (November 1986), p. 893, table 8.

TABLE 5-2. *Amendments Adopted in the House and Senate, by Seniority of Sponsors, Selected Congresses, 1955–86*
Percent adopted

Congress	Years of service			
	1–2	3–4	5–6	7 or more
House				
84th (1955–56)	33	55	53	54
86th (1959–60)	22	23	24	45
88th (1963–64)	26	29	23	50
90th (1967–68)	30	35	46	54
91st (1969–70)	14	33	25	55
92d (1971–72)	23	25	44	53
93d (1973–74)	49	44	47	55
94th (1975–76)	47	52	53	58
95th (1977–78)	62	52	63	63
96th (1979–80)	65	60	67	73
99th (1985–86)	69	73	80	77
Senate				
84th (1955–56)	70	82	70	68
88th (1963–64)	54	27	51	43
92d (1971–72)	58	63	65	69
96th (1979–80)	76	81	78	81
99th (1985–86)	71	79	85	80

SOURCE: See appendix 2.

did not become as successful as senior members until after recorded electronic voting was in place in the 93d Congress. Of course, they were becoming more active during the 1960s, so their frequency of success was increasing, but their success rate was roughly half that of senior members before the 1970s. The small difference between junior and senior members that remains in recent Congresses is easily explained by the remaining differences in experience, staff support, political connections, and other factors having nothing to do with a restraining prescriptive norm. The timing of the surge in junior representatives' success rates suggests that voting procedures played a role in undermining the advantages of senior members in the amending process.

In contrast, junior senators have not been at a significant disadvantage to senior senators since the 1950s. While first-term senators were less active than other senators in the 1950s and 1960s, they fared about as well as the senior senators when they did offer amendments. In fact, freshmen senators did better than senior senators during the 84th and 88th Congresses. In the 1970s, junior senators retained strong success rates as they became more active.[16]

16. In neither chamber has the proportion of amendments subject to a contested vote (60–40 split or closer) varied systematically with seniority, indicating that junior members' amending activity has not become more trivial as these members have become more active.

In sum, the apprenticeship norm, at least when judged by participation and success rates, has disappeared in both chambers. In both chambers, manifest differences in rates of participation eroded during the 1960s and virtually evaporated in the early 1970s. The behavioral change paralleled the attitudinal change detected by contemporary observers. The distinctive feature of the behavioral change was the delayed increase in junior members' success rates in the House. They were becoming more active, but their probability of success was not changing. A reasonable speculation is that the frustration associated with low success rates helped motivate junior members to seek reform of House floor procedures in the early 1970s.

Committee Deference

Apprenticeship is strongly related to specialization and deference to committees. By serving apprenticeships in the work of their committees, members developed expertise, earned the respect of their colleagues for their judgment about matters under their committees' jurisdictions and presumably gained special influence in the policy fields in which they specialized. Apprenticeship, specialization, and committee deference were inseparable, permitting overburdened members to set their priorities wisely and endowing the institution with a division of labor essential to managing a large work load.[17] Taken together, the norms appear to be reasonable strategic advice for members. Viewed in this way, the constraints on participation served the general benefit of the two chambers.[18]

Matthews implied that the pressure to specialize and respect committee recommendations also had a distinctly regulatory cast in the Senate of the 1950s, limiting senators' floor participation to areas falling within the jurisdiction of their assigned committees even if they could credibly claim expertise on other subjects. Statements about the importance of deference to committees are sprinkled throughout members' and observers' comments on the functioning of Congress in the 1950s and 1960s. For example, a House member writing to his constituents said that "the traditional deference to the authority of one of its committees overwhelms the main body. The whole fabric of Congress is based on committee expertness, and the practice of 'rewriting a bill on the floor' is thought of as a bad business."[19] But in both chambers, the price of nonconformity was largely reputational.[20]

17. See Matthews, *U.S. Senators and Their World*, pp. 95–97.
18. Rohde and others, "Political Change and Legislative Norms," pp. 151–54.
19. Clem Miller, *Member of the House: Letters of a Congressman*, ed. John W. Baker (Scribner's, 1962), p. 51.
20. Ralph K. Huitt, "The Outsider in the Senate: An Alternative Role," *American Political Science Review*, vol. 55 (September 1961), pp. 566–75. Huitt's comment on the price of

Despite the apparent strength of specialization and committee deference in the 1950s, significant differences between the two chambers were evident. Even in the 1950s, senators had more than twice as many committee and subcommittee assignments as representatives, meaning that committee specialization was much less restrictive for senators than for representatives.[21] And with larger, more heterogeneous constituencies, senators were more likely to have a compelling constituency interest in matters falling outside the jurisdictions of their own committees. In neither chamber was committee deference universal, however. There is evidence that deference was contingent on the perceived extremity of committee positions relative to the policy preferences of the full chamber.[22] Deference appeared to be something earned, rather than merely inherited, by congressional committees.

Not surprisingly, the breakdown of deference to committees as a regulatory norm appeared to track with the decline of apprenticeship. In the early 1960s, senators, particularly young liberal senators seeking federal action on a range of social problems, had low tolerance for apprenticeship and exhibited little patience with the niceties of committee jurisdictions. Indeed, senators who may have felt slighted on committee assignments because of their premature activism had even more reason to disregard a norm of deference to committee recommendations. The norm of committee deference retained substantial vitality, though, as a form of strategic advice. Even liberals found the burden of committee work and constituency relations heavy enough to warrant economizing by seeking assignment to committees with jurisdiction over constituents' primary policy interests.[23] But by 1973, Rohde and his colleagues found that "all of the senators with whom we discussed the matter said there was no bar to members being active in areas outside their committees if (as many offered the caveat) they know what they're talking about."[24]

Specialization and committee deference were no longer inseparable in the Senate. Specialization remained sound advice for senators seeking to make their mark quickly but was no longer strictly tied to committee du-

---

nonconformity in the late 1950s is worth noting: "What happens inside the Senate to the Outsider? Not much; as [William S.] White observed, the Senate is not a body disposed to impose sanctions on any behavior but the most outrageous" (p. 573).

21. See Norman J. Ornstein and others, eds., *Vital Statistics on Congress, 1982* (Washington: American Enterprise Institute for Public Policy Research, 1982), p. 100.

22. For example, the House Committees on Education and Labor and on Foreign Affairs received little deference on the floor during the 1950s and 1960s. See Richard F. Fenno, Jr., *Congressmen in Committees* (Little, Brown, 1973), chap. 6.

23. Foley, *The New Senate*, pp. 150–60.

24. Rohde and others, "Political Change and Legislative Norms," p. 177.

ties. Moreover, committee-based specialization could no longer be expected to produce deference from colleagues as a matter of privilege. This was especially true for the highly charged, divisive issues that came before the Senate in the 1960s and early 1970s, on which all senators faced difficult choices and had to inform themselves of the important considerations. Committee deference, even as an advisory norm, disintegrated in the Senate of the 1960s, closely following the demise of the apprenticeship norm.

Like apprenticeship, specialization and committee deference appeared to have greater resilience in the House. Writing about the late 1950s and early 1960s, one scholar concluded that "Senate committees are less important as a source of chamber influence, less preoccupied with success on the chamber floor, less autonomous within the chamber, less personally expert, less strongly led, and more individualistic in decision making than are House committees." [25] House committees, particularly the more prestigious ones, continued to make concerted efforts to justify deference to their recommendations by developing genuine policy expertise. In a 1973 survey, nearly four out of five representatives indicated that members should specialize. [26] Unfortunately, a direct question about deference to committees was not asked in systematic surveys of representatives during the 1960s.

Since the studies conducted in the late 1960s and mid-1970s, no systematic study of congressional attitudes about specialization and committee deference has been reported. The undisputed conventional wisdom is that, even for the House, committee deference had disappeared by the mid-1970s. [27] Because the timing of its demise is less certain in the House, the pattern of behavioral change in the House is less predictable than in the Senate. A good guess, based on the connection between the apprenticeship and deference norms, is that committee deference remained somewhat stronger in the House than in the Senate during the late 1960s, but that it too disappeared, at least as a regulatory norm, during the 1970s.

On the surface, the behavioral evidence for the demise of committee deference as a prescriptive norm is overwhelming. While only one in twenty measures making it to the House floor was subject to at least one floor amendment in 1955–56, nearly one in five measures faced amendments in 1969-70 and almost one in four in 1979–80. In the Senate, one

25. Fenno, *Congressmen in Committees*, pp. 190–91.
26. Asher, "The Learning of Legislative Norms," p. 503.
27. See John F. Bibby, ed., *Congress Off the Record: The Candid Analysis of Seven Members* (Washington: American Enterprise Institute for Public Policy Research, 1983), pp. 23–24; and Norman J. Ornstein, "The Open Congress Meets the President," in Anthony King, ed., *Both Ends of the Avenue: The Presidency, the Executive Branch and Congress in the 1980s* (Washington: American Enterprise Institute for Public Policy Research, 1983), pp. 198–99.

in ten measures faced floor amendments in 1955–56, compared with nearly one in three in 1979–80. Thus the House became more like the Senate, and both chambers witnessed more frequent challenges to the legislative products of their committees in the 1970s. A more direct assessment of the effects of expanding floor activity on committees is reserved for the next chapter. The concern here is the pattern of amending activity among committee members and noncommittee members.[28]

Discerning the effects of declining committee deference on patterns of floor participation is a little complicated. For example, if declining deference to committees by outsiders is accompanied by declining cohesiveness among committee members, floor participation rates for both committee members and noncommittee members will increase. And even if committee cohesiveness remains stable, committee members' responses to outsiders' challenges may come in the form of amending activity—such as second-degree amendments and amendments to forestall others' amendments—designed to dilute the content of and support for unfriendly amendments. Unfortunately, available data do not distinguish between first- and second-degree amendments for most of the Congresses that I have examined. So the case is stacked against finding increasing proportionate amending activity by noncommittee members.

Furthermore, participation rates for committee members and nonmembers must be judged against the changing sizes of congressional committees. Since the 1950s House and Senate committees have grown in size as members have acquired more committee assignments.[29] Thus, if the difference between the proportion of floor amendments sponsored by committee members and that sponsored by noncommittee members remains constant or shrinks over time, the activity of noncommittee members on the floor is showing a proportionate increase.

As figure 5-1 indicates, the disparity between committee members and noncommittee members has remained very stable in both chambers, im-

28. The somewhat awkward term "noncommittee members" is specific to an individual measure. Noncommittee members are all members who do not sit on the committee or committees to which a measure was referred. If a measure was not referred to a committee, the committee of origin usually can be determined by examining who manages the legislation on the floor.

29. The mean size of Senate standing committees increased from 14.2 in the 84th Congress to 17.6 in the 99th. In the House, mean standing committee size increased from 29.1 in the 84th Congress to 35.5 in the 99th. At the same time, the net number of Senate standing committees increased by one and the net number of House standing committees increased by three. For background on the House, see Bruce A. Ray and Steven S. Smith, "Committee Size in the U.S. Congress," *Legislative Studies Quarterly*, vol. 9 (November 1984), pp. 679–95.

FIGURE 5-1. *Percentage of Floor Amendments Sponsored by a Member Not Sitting on the Committee of Origin, by Chamber, Selected Congresses, 1955–86*

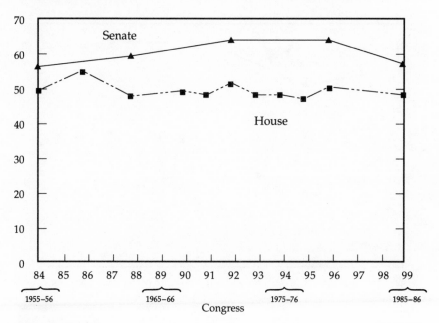

SOURCE: See appendix 2.

plying that noncommittee members have indeed become relatively more active. The pattern also shows that Senate noncommittee members are more active than their House counterparts. Just under 60 percent of Senate amendments are sponsored by senators not sitting on the committee of origin, compared with about 50 percent in the House, despite the fact that most Senate committees are larger in proportion to their parent chamber than are their House counterparts.

The demise of committee deference also is visible in the percentage of members who have offered amendments to measures originating in committees other than their own (see figure 5-2). Even in the 1950s, the vast majority of senators offered amendments to measures from committees other than their own, and nearly all senators did so in the 1970s and 1980s. Proportionately far fewer representatives sponsored such amendments in the 1950s—only one in four—but the number increased to two in five by the time the House was considering procedural reform. After

FIGURE 5-2. *Percentage of Members Sponsoring Floor Amendments to Measures from Committees Other than Their Own, by Chamber, Selected Congresses, 1955–86*

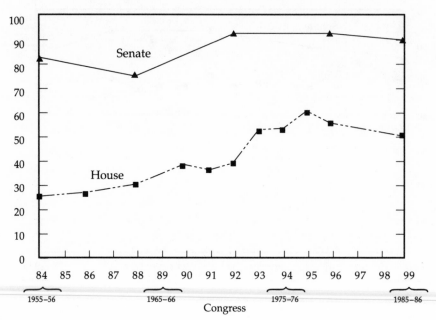

SOURCE: See appendix 2.

recorded electronic voting was in place, over half the House members were sponsoring floor amendments as outsiders; this peaked at 62 percent in the 95th Congress (1977–78). The differences between chambers are stark, but are not surprising once chamber size relative to the number of floor amendments is taken into account.

The success rate of House noncommittee members' amendments also improved relative to committee members' rates. The disparity between committee members and noncommittee members narrowed after the procedural reforms (see figure 5-3). The pattern is consistent with the view that the old procedures of the Committee of the Whole advantaged committees and their chairmen. The introduction of convenient recorded voting on amendments may have allowed opponents of committee recommendations to counter more effectively the pressure committees could bring to bear on members. The Senate pattern, in contrast, exhibits a smaller difference between committee members and noncommittee members in the

FIGURE 5-3. *Percentage of Floor Amendments Adopted, by Sponsors' Committee Membership and Chamber, Selected Congresses, 1955–86*

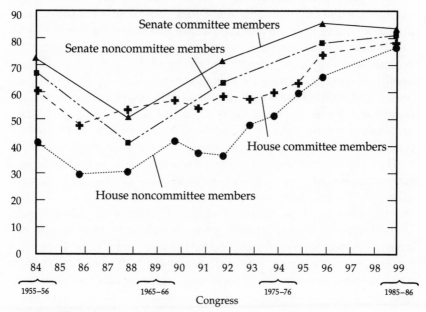

SOURCE: See appendix 2.

1950s and 1960s and, with one exception, shows higher success rates for both committee members and noncommittee members than for House committee members. (The one exception, the 88th Congress [1963-64], is due to the extremely high level of unsuccessful amending activity by just a few senators on the Civil Rights Act of 1964.) Even in the Senate, the gap between committee members and noncommittee members has narrowed somewhat in more recent Congresses.[30]

The behavioral pattern, in short, supports the attitudinal evidence for declining deference to committees in both chambers, for the traditionally greater deference in the House than in the Senate, and for more narrow but not yet disappearing differences between the two chambers.

30. In neither chamber is there systematic change in the relative contestedness of committee members' and noncommittee members' amendments that might suggest that noncommittee members' recent success is due to the trivial nature of their amendments. It is important to keep in mind that committee amendments are excluded from all tables and figures. Therefore the higher rate of success for committee members is not due to noncontroversial committee amendments.

Party, Apprenticeship, and Committee Deference

Other than noting that liberal Democrats took the lead in challenging the traditional norms, most accounts of congressional attitudes about floor participation give little attention to possible differences between the parties. Implicitly, at least, commentators have included the minority party in generalizations about the strength and change of the participation norms, usually by quoting or citing Republican statements as well as Democratic ones.[31] And yet there are several reasons to expect that the commitment to apprenticeship and committee deference differs between the parties, and furthermore that the difference between the parties' attitudes and behavior is greater in the House than in the Senate.

The most obvious reason to expect party differences is that minority party members are more likely than majority party members to be dissatisfied with the legislative products of committees. In both chambers, the majority party assumes a numerical edge in all legislative committees, and in the House the Democrats have given themselves an extra margin of safety on Appropriations, Budget, Rules, and Ways and Means. The committee systems also grant certain procedural and staff advantages to the majority party. Consequently, disadvantaged minority party members are more likely to be motivated to ignore apprenticeship and committee deference norms and to appeal committee decisions, particularly contested decisions, to the floor.

Policy dissatisfaction is not simply a function of party status, of course. Among other things, it is related to the control of committees by particular factions within the majority party. For example, the disproportionate share of House and Senate chairmanships held by conservative Democrats in the 1950s and 1960s created greater dissatisfaction in several policy areas among liberal Democrats than among Republicans. Liberal Democrats' successful challenges to conservative control increased Republican policy dissatisfaction and probably reduced Republican tolerance of constraining norms.

Motivations other than short-term policy concerns also play a role in the decisions to offer amendments. Embarrassing one's opponents, estab-

---

31. Asher's 1969 House interviews uncovered greater recognition of an apprenticeship norm among freshmen Republicans than among freshmen Democrats. See "The Learning of Legislative Norms," pp. 509–12. In addition, two studies indicate greater frustration with their role in the chamber among junior Republicans than among junior Democrats of the 1960s. See Irwin Gertzog, "Frustration and Adaptation: The Adjustment of Minority Freshmen to the Congressional Experience," paper prepared for the 1966 annual meeting of the American Political Science Association; and Jeff Fishel, *Party and Opposition: Congressional Challengers in American Politics* (David McKay, 1973), chap. 6.

lishing a public record for or against certain policies, and judging support and opposition for future efforts are among the objectives members may have for going to the floor. Such motivations are likely to be relatively more important for minority party members, for whom policy victories may be sporadic at best.

Nonetheless, the political value of most floor efforts surely is conditioned by the probability of success. For minority party members, the size and cohesiveness of their party are likely to shape floor prospects, although minority party strength does not change the fundamental fact of minority status. The ability to overcome the disadvantages of minority status depends on attracting majority party support, perhaps by bringing pressures external to Congress to bear on voting decisions. In this respect, the absence of recorded voting in the House Committee of the Whole probably discouraged minority party amendments before the 1970s; the move to recorded voting may have improved the probability of success for minority party members. Indeed, House Republicans increased their amending activity disproportionately in the 1970s, as noted in chapter 2.

Differences between the chambers in levels of amending activity, expectedly, are much larger than party differences, so patterns within each chamber must be judged on their own scale. Figure 5-4 reconfirms the presence of a surge in House Republican activism in the mid- to late 1970s. The asymmetric partisan effect of change in House floor procedures is made even more visible against the backdrop of the Senate pattern, in which there have been very small differences between majority and minority party members in recent Congresses. Minority party status per se does not appear to underlie the escalation of House Republican amending activity in the mid-1970s. Better explanations appear to be the House minority party's uniquely disadvantaged position under prereform amending procedures and frustration with the assertion of liberal control of the standing committees in the immediate postreform period.

The Republican edge in amending activity in the House vanished in the 99th Congress (1985–86). This suggests that restrictive rules may have suppressed Republican amending activity. Other evidence is consistent with such an interpretation. In the 99th Congress, Republicans retained a slightly higher per capita amending rate than Democrats (1.2 versus 1.1, respectively) for measures considered without a special rule or an open rule, but they had a slightly lower rate than Democrats (1.2 versus 1.4) for measures subject to a restrictive rule. The identical Republican rates for measures with and without restrictive rules is particularly notable because measures considered under restrictive rules, which tend to be more controversial than other measures, would be expected to attract the most Republican amendments.

FIGURE 5-4. *Per Capita Amendment Sponsorship, by Party and Chamber, Selected Congresses, 1955–86*

Number of amendments sponsored

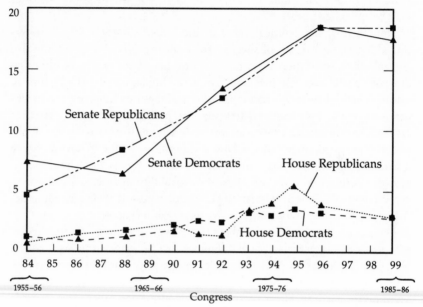

SOURCE: See appendix 2.

The success rates and contestedness of minority party amending activity show little that is surprising, but the patterns are important nevertheless. In general, minority party amendments are disproportionately contested and unsuccessful (see figure 5-5). In only one of the Congresses examined does the minority party in either chamber have a higher success rate than the majority party (see the 92d Congress for the Senate). In the House, Democrats appeared to benefit the most from the move to recorded voting in the Committee of the Whole, although Republicans' success rate also improved and the Democratic advantage was short-lived. The minority party, including the Senate Democrats in the 99th Congress, sponsored a disproportionate share of contested amendments in both chambers in each of the Congresses examined.[32]

Beyond these broad differences, majority and minority party behavioral patterns with respect to seniority and committee membership are roughly

32. The mean minority party advantage in contested amendments is 8.9 percent for the eleven Congresses for the House and 6.4 percent for the five Congresses for the Senate.

FIGURE 5-5. *Percentage of Amendments Adopted, by Sponsors' Party and Chamber, Selected Congresses, 1955–86*

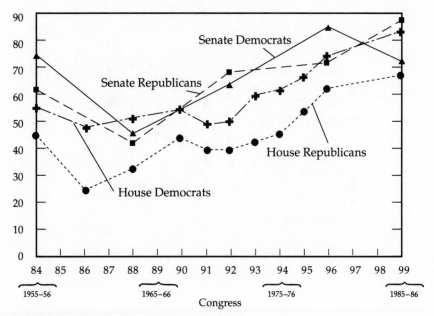

parallel. In both parties and chambers, junior members and committee outsiders have become considerably more active in floor amending activity. The pattern of change for the two parties will not be reviewed in detail here.[33]

One distinctive feature is worth special attention. The disparity in success rates between junior and senior House Democrats was much greater than the disparity between junior and senior House Republicans (see figure 5-6).[34] The reason for the extraordinary disparity for House Democrats is the very high success rates of senior Democrats in the prereform era. With the shift to recorded voting, junior Democrats' rate of success on the floor shot upward, actually surpassing that of their senior party colleagues in the 99th Congress (1985–86). Thus, despite the fact that Republicans became

33. With respect to both seniority and committee membership, no systematic differences exist between the parties in either chamber in their pattern of per capita amendments or proportion of amendments that were contested.

34. For neither Senate party was the junior-senior disparity in success rates nearly as large as was common for House Democrats in the 1950s and 1960s.

FIGURE 5-6. *Percentage of Amendments Adopted in House, by Sponsors' Seniority and Party, Selected Congresses, 1955–86*

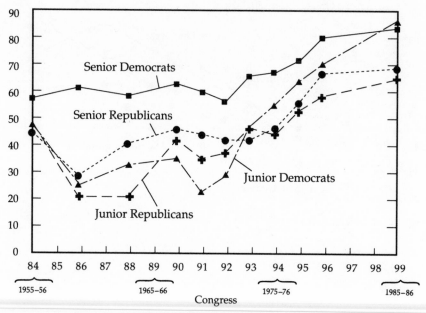

SOURCE: See appendix 2.

much more active in the aftermath of the procedural reforms, it was the rank-and-file Democrats who benefited disproportionately in floor amending victories.

This interpretation is reinforced by the pattern of success among committee members and noncommittee members for the two parties (see figure 5-7). Democratic noncommittee members were not much more successful than Republicans during the 1950s and 1960s and lagged far behind their party colleagues from the committees originating the legislation. Like junior Democrats, Democratic outsiders improved their success rates markedly after the procedural reforms. In fact, since 1973 Democratic outsiders have had a higher success rate than Republican committee members. In short, the Democratic rank and file—junior members and committee outsiders—gained the most dramatic increase in floor success rates in the postreform House.

It is in the House, then, that party membership made the most difference in shaping the pattern of decline in apprenticeship and committee

FIGURE 5-7. *Percentage of Amendments Adopted in House, by Sponsors' Committee Membership and Party, Selected Congresses, 1955–86*

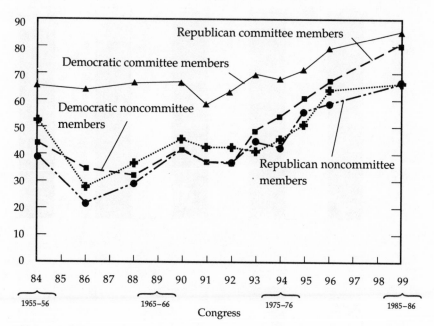

SOURCE: See appendix 2.

deference. More highly structured rules in a more highly majoritarian context produced more distinctive partisan patterns in the House. Reforms of floor procedure stimulated Republican amending activity disproportionately, perhaps to the surprise of Democrats, but the reforms also were associated with increased success rates among rank-and-file Democrats, just as many Democratic reformers had in mind. No similar partisan effects are evident in the Senate, where less restrictive rules, and perhaps less confining participatory norms, allowed members of both parties to respond in very similar ways to internal and external pressures for floor participation.[35]

35. It is worth recalling Charles Jones's observation that "a minority party senator may well be able to satisfy his personal goals as easily as a majority party senator," a proposition he contrasted sharply with his description of minority party representatives. See Charles O. Jones, *The Minority Party in Congress* (Little, Brown, 1970), chap. 8, quote from p. 172.

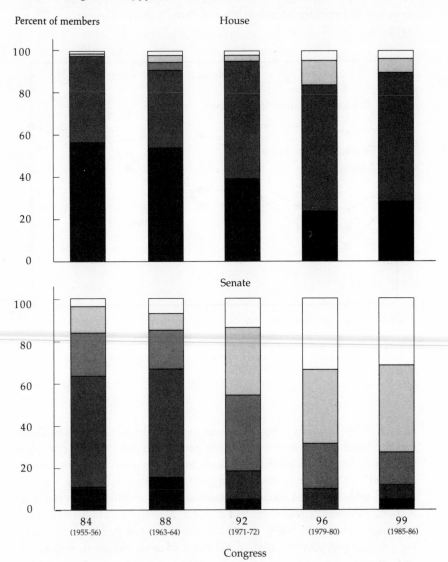

FIGURE 5-8. *Members' Amending Activity, by Chamber,
Selected Congresses, 1955–86*

Percent of members   House

Senate

Congress

Number of amendments sponsored:

21 or more   11-20   6-10   1-5   none

SOURCE: See appendix 2.

The Hyperactives

Even with norms restraining participation, a few members in both chambers always seemed willing to buck the system in the 1950s. Senators such as Wayne Morse and William Proxmire were then labeled "mavericks" (and worse) for their intrepidity on the floor. For Proxmire, Ralph Huitt wrote, "the life of the Senate is the debate on the floor. Not to be there and participate is to deny himself equal membership in the Senate." [36] Representative H. R. Gross was similarly recognized for his forays into spending and foreign aid bills on the House floor. The level of activism of such members is no longer unusual, but a handful of members in both chambers are still distinguished by their floor activism. The institutional position of House and Senate hyperactives reveals important features of floor activity in the modern Congress.

Hyperactivity, of course, must be judged against the pattern of participation in each chamber (see figure 5-8). The number of wholly inactive members has been very low in the Senate throughout the period, and has declined from over half the House in the 1950s and early 1960s to between a quarter and a third in the late 1970s and 1980s. The largest, or modal, category in the Senate changed from one to five amendments in 1955–56 to more than twenty-one amendments in 1979–80; in the House, the modal level of activity changed from no amendments in 1955–56 to one to five amendments in 1971–72 and thereafter. At the extreme, the number of senators offering twenty-one or more amendments grew from just a handful to more than thirty between the mid-1950s and the late 1970s, while the number of representatives offering such a large number of amendments remained very small (just one or two) throughout the period. The Senate has moved from "restrained activism" to "unrestrained activism," and the House has moved from "little activism" to "restrained activism." [37] Hyperactivity is very common in the Senate and remains the exception to the rule in the House. [38]

In the Senate of the 1950s and early 1960s the hyperactive senators

36. Huitt, "The Outsider in the Senate," p. 569.

37. These terms are borrowed from Sinclair, "Senate Styles and Senate Decision Making, 1955–1980," pp. 902–06.

38. Quite obviously, chamber size directly affects the opportunity and the necessity of amendment sponsorship. On many issues, there is a limited number of feasible alternatives. If those alternatives are reflected in amendments offered by a few members, other members have no need to offer amendments of their own. Because the number of feasible alternatives is roughly the same in the aggregate for the two chambers, higher levels of amending activity would be expected among senators than among representatives even if both chambers operated under the same procedures.

seemed quite distinctive—for both their personalities and their deliberate rejection of traditional norms limiting floor participation. Wayne Morse, who offered far more floor amendments in the 84th Congress (1955–56) than any other senator, switched from Republican to Democratic party affiliation after failing two years earlier to force the Senate to grant him committee assignments as an independent.[39] Proxmire became one of the most active senators on the floor soon after arriving in the Senate in late 1957 and soon became the definitive maverick.[40] In 1963–64, even with southerners actively proposing amendments to civil rights measures, Proxmire had the second highest number of floor amendments. These two senators' "outsider" roles were reflected in their dependence on the floor as their arena for influencing public policy.

In the 1970s and 1980s, Senators James Allen, Jesse Helms, Edward Kennedy, and Howard Metzenbaum continued the traditions of Morse and Proxmire. Helms, for example, set the record for the five Congresses examined with eighty-four floor amendments in 1978–80. That is a rate of more than one amendment for every four days the Senate was in session. Metzenbaum nearly reached that level in 1985–86, when he sponsored seventy-two floor amendments, also nearly one amendment for every four session days. These hyperactive senators, including Morse and Proxmire, held relatively extreme policy views. Indeed, very conservative and very liberal senators are overrepresented in the group of senators with more than twenty floor amendments. Yet it would not be fair to conclude that ideological extremism is either a necessary or sufficient condition for floor activism. Many equally liberal or conservative senators display low levels of floor activity, and some moderates display levels of activity nearly as high as the champion amenders.[41]

Hyperactive senators have been quite individualistic. They sometimes represented a faction on particular issues, but most of their causes were their own, and their extraordinary aggressiveness was difficult for even their ideological bedfellows to understand. They also held a variety of for-

39. Ralph K. Huitt, "The Morse Committee Assignment Controversy: A Study in Senate Norms," *American Political Science Review*, vol. 51 (June 1957), pp. 313–29.

40. In addition to Huitt, "The Outsider in the Senate," see Norman C. Miller, "Senate Maverick: Wisconsin's Proxmire Is Adding Substance to Showmanship," *Wall Street Journal*, June 30, 1967, p. 10; Martin Tolchin, "The Perplexing Mr. Proxmire," *New York Times Magazine*, May 28, 1978, p. 8; and Alan Ehrenhalt, "Sen. Proxmire: Iconoclast and Trailblazer," *Congressional Quarterly Weekly Report*, September 5, 1987, p. 2155.

41. Generally, the correlation between amending activity and either extremism or conservatism, as measured by *Congressional Quarterly* 's conservative coalition score, is very small and statistically insignificant. This holds for both the House and Senate. Only for the most extreme members, those least likely to be included in or satisfied with committee compromises, does the level of amending activity seem to be noticeably higher.

mal institutional positions: Proxmire was a freshman with no committee or subcommittee chairmanships and Helms was a full-committee ranking minority member and a chairman during much of his hyperactive period. When hyperactive senators left the Senate, no one immediately or self-consciously seized their role. Personality, no doubt, plays an important role in distinguishing the hyperactive senators, but this is not the place to speculate about the psychological attributes of senators.[42]

In contrast, a strain of hyperactivism in the House—the minority party watchdog—is more institutionalized, and in the last few decades the role has been passed on quite consciously from one generation to the next. The modern progenitor of the minority party watchdog was H. R. Gross, an Iowa Republican elected in 1948.[43] Gross spent as much time as possible on the floor perched at the end of the Republican leadership table, scrutinizing measures, looking for wasteful small projects in appropriations bills, challenging frivolous legislation, and pursuing his many pet legislative interests. Like other floor activists, Gross frequently objected to, or at least questioned, majority party unanimous consent requests in order to check the content of the motions and measures involved. During the 1950s, Gross is reputed to have read every major bill sent to the floor in preparation for the debate and amending stage. In the context of the 1950s and early 1960s, his floor amending activity was quite exceptional. In the four Congresses from 1955 to 1962, the period in which he made a real name for himself, Gross sponsored 135 amendments—nearly 34 per Congress—at a time when the chamber mean was about 2 amendments per member. He focused primarily on appropriations and foreign aid bills, but by the mid-1960s he was dipping regularly into subjects falling under the jurisdiction of ten or more committees in each Congress.

Upon the announcement of Gross's retirement from the House in 1974, several conservative Republican activists in the House—John Ashbrook,

42. Sponsoring amendments is not the only floor activity of such hyperactive senators, of course. Many of them were renowned for their filibusters, threats of filibusters, and, more recently, for their aggressive use of holds.

43. Gross, too, inherited his role, particularly with respect to his scrutiny of appropriations decisions. His immediate predecessor seems to have been Clare Hoffman. See Neil MacNeil, *The Forge of Democracy: The House of Representatives* (David McKay, 1963), pp. 131–33, who discusses "watchdogs of the treasury" and the "great objectors." MacNeil points out that "by special arrangement, Gross for years sponsored a bill numbered H. R. 144—one of the rarest of parliamentary phenomena, a legislative pun on the numbering of a bill." Unfortunately, there is no definitive biography of Gross, even with respect to his legislative role. But newspaper stories are numerous and often were printed in the *Congressional Record*. For example, see the *Record* for September 13, 1951, p. A5581; July 13, 1961, p. A5255; and July 18, 1973, p. 24737. For a review of his role written at the time of his retirement, see Richard L. Madden, "Iowa's H. R. Gross to Quit Congress," *New York Times*, January 18, 1974.

Robert Bauman, John Rousselot, and Steven Symms—met to consider how to fill the vacuum in floor coverage created by Gross's departure.[44] Only Bauman was able and willing to spend enough time on the floor to take over Gross's role as the "great objector," although Ashbrook and Rousselot also became very active in floor amending activity.[45] Bauman had the background for the role even though he had been in the House only since late 1973, after he won a special election. He served as a House page and committee staff member in the 1950s and worked for four years as a Republican floor aide during the 1960s. Bauman learned floor procedure from years of close personal observation that only a few members could match and, in the process, came to know Gross very well. Like Gross, Bauman relished his floor activity, soon confessing to a reporter, "I love the House. I spent most of my life here. I really feel uncomfortable not being on the floor every day."[46]

Bauman took Gross's place at the end of the Republican leadership table on the House floor and rapidly expanded the role of minority party watchdog. Bauman was far more aggressive and wide-ranging in his challenges to Democratic procedural and policy moves on the floor. He also seemed to develop a love-hate relationship with Republican party and committee leaders. At times he upset delicate compromises that his party's leaders had negotiated with the majority party, and at other times he did the dirty work for formal leaders, as he explains:

> [Minority Leader] John Rhodes, quite often, particularly to Ashbrook and I, would appeal to us "not to do this," "don't say anything," "we're trying to get this through." Of course, that was the red light for us to nail him. And sometimes he would come over to say, "Block this one because I don't want to do it."[47]

Bauman chose his amending targets carefully and had a very high success rate, reaching 70 percent in 1979–80, when he sponsored forty amendments, very few of which would be considered truly trivial. He was eventually rewarded for his role with an appointment to the Rules Committee in 1979, but was defeated for reelection in 1980 after a personal scandal.[48]

---

44. Interview with Robert Bauman, July 16, 1987. Also see Donald P. Baker, "Maryland Conservative Is Watchdog of the House," *Washington Post*, December 18, 1977, pp. B1.

45. Bauman had committee assignments with relatively light schedules, Interior and Insular Affairs and Merchant Marine and Fisheries, which he inherited from his predecessor.

46. Richard L. Madden, "A New Gadfly Keeps Eye on House," *New York Times*, April 4, 1976, p. 33.

47. Bauman interview.

48. See Bauman's autobiography, *The Gentleman from Maryland: The Conscience of a Gay Conservative* (New York: Arbor House, 1986).

Robert Walker assumed the Republican watchdog role in the 1980s.[49] Also a former congressional staff member, Walker joined the House in 1977 and spent much of his time on the floor at the side of Bauman. When the Conservative Opportunity Society, the group of conservative and mainly junior House Republicans that were dissatisfied with the lack of aggressiveness on the part of the party's formal leadership, organized in 1983, its leaders concluded that Walker could best serve the group by continuing what he was already doing on the House floor.[50] Like Bauman, Walker believes that Republican party and committee leaders cannot be trusted to challenge majority party proposals, as he wrote in a self-conscious newspaper editorial:

> The [watchdog] job exists because it is not good enough to just rely on the minority members of particular committee[s] to keep an eye on things. Committee members are, by the nature of their role, captives of the wheeling and dealing within the committee and may not be the best judge of the interests of the whole minority membership. . . .
>
> The fact is a watchdog must operate pretty much on his own. House Republican Leader Bob Michel once told me, "Walker, if you didn't do what you do, we'd have to invent someone like you." But that does not mean he knows in advance about everything I do, or that he wants to know all about my activities. As in "Mission Impossible," my leadership reserves the right to disavow my work, largely because they must show loyalty to minority committee leaders who, at times, may not be in concert with some action of mine. All of this is done in an atmosphere of mutual respect, but it can make things rather lonely in the midst of controversy.[51]

Even committee chairmen sometimes slipped Walker a clue about something they would like to see amended in their bills but which they personally could not touch because of prior commitments or the desire to appear supportive of committee decisions.[52] Walker's unique position was reflected in his amending activity. In 1985–86 Walker sponsored thirty-two floor amendments, more than any other member of the House.

49. For background on Walker, see Irwin B. Arieff, "House Floor Watchdog Role Made Famous by H.R. Gross Has Fallen on Hard Times," *Congressional Quarterly Weekly Report*, July 24, 1982, pp. 1775–76; and T.R. Reid, "'Minority Objector' Conscientiously Flays Foes with House Rules," *Washington Post*, March 21, 1984, p. A3. Reid noted that "other members may enjoy committee hearings or the give-and-take of a markup session, but Walker is transfixed by the action, even inaction, on the floor," a comment strikingly similar to Huitt's conclusion about Senator Proxmire.

50. On the Conservative Opportunity Society, see chapter 3 and citations provided there.

51. Robert Walker, "Why House Republicans Need a Watchdog," *Roll Call*, January 19, 1987, p. 10.

52. Interview with Robert Walker, April 22, 1987.

The persistence of the Republicans playing the watchdog role makes them a unique feature of congressional floor politics. At least one of the Gross-Ashbrook-Bauman-Rousselot-Walker group has been among the top three amendment sponsors in each Congress since the late 1960s. No other member appears in the top three more than once. And, as figure 5-8 suggests, few other House members appear in the top group of members sponsoring more than twenty amendments in any Congress.

The longevity of the watchdog role is a product of the weak institutional position of House minority party members, particularly those with relatively extreme policy preferences. They are the group most likely to be dissatisfied with committee recommendations and to challenge those recommendations on the floor. They also have relatively few avenues for pursuing their own policy interests because of the difficulty they experience in getting hearings and media attention for their legislation. The watchdogs themselves, of course, usually do not hold leadership positions on important legislative committees; thus they are free of burdensome committee duties that would take them away from the floor. And unlike their Senate counterparts, such House members do not have nongermane amendments and the filibuster as sources of leverage with standing committees.

The watchdog role represents a particular position on the "minority party dilemma"—whether to cooperate and compromise with the majority party whenever possible or to simply oppose and obstruct the majority party at every turn.[53] The dilemma is faced by the Senate minority party as well, of course, but the special power of House committees and the constraints placed on floor amending activity by House rules intensify differences of opinion within the minority party about floor tactics. As the Bauman and Walker comments indicate, the watchdog role symbolizes a sometimes dogmatic position on the minority party dilemma. They often are dissatisfied with the willingness of party colleagues to negotiate with the majority party and accept compromise positions and so, as a general rule, prefer to take a principled stance in opposition to committee measures. Their views on the minority party dilemma, and the role they assume on the floor as a result, tend to be respected, even if not always appreciated, by most minority party members.

A Closer Look at the 99th Congress

Several patterns of change have emerged since the 1950s. In both chambers, the expansion of amending activity and floor success has involved

---

53. These alternatives, and others, are discussed in Jones, *Minority Party in Congress.*

nearly every category of members. In both chambers, the expansion was proportionately greater for junior members and committee outsiders as the norms of apprenticeship and committee deference weakened and eventually disintegrated. But important differences between the chambers persist. The average senator continues to offer more amendments than the average representative, and a larger share of amendments is sponsored by Senate committee outsiders than by House outsiders. In several respects, the Senate pattern of change has a more individualistic flavor while the House pattern has a more partisan cast, reflecting long-standing differences between the chambers.

The responsibilities and advantages of seniority, committee position, and majority party status have not disappeared, of course. Even when the influence of these factors is not represented in different rates of amending activity or success, it is likely to be exhibited in the content of the measures brought to the House and Senate floors. Nevertheless, the importance of institutional position continues to be manifest in floor amending activity, particularly in the House. In the 99th Congress (1985–86), for example, representatives serving as formal committee or subcommittee leaders were 20 percent more likely than others to sponsor at least one floor amendment and about 20 percent more likely to sponsor at least one successful amendment. The historical changes and the continuing influence of institutional position can be put into perspective by examining the independent effects of committee position, seniority, and party on members' floor amending activity in the 99th Congress.

The importance of seniority, committee position, and party in shaping floor participation can be explored in several ways. One way is to isolate the amending activity for each committee's measures and estimate the effects of committee membership, leadership position, and other factors. This would present problems of generalizing across committees, and for many committees it would be difficult to assess the significance of the relationships because of the paucity of amendments offered to measures from those committees. I pursue an alternative strategy. Using the individual member as the unit of analysis, I divide members' amending activity into two sets—amendments to measures originating from their own committees and amendments to measures from other committees—in order to determine how committee membership structures amending opportunities on the floor.

Linear equations for three aspects of amending activity are estimated: the total number of amendments sponsored, the number of successful amendments sponsored, and the percentage of amendments sponsored that were successful. Equations are estimated for measures from the member's

TABLE 5-3. *Estimates of the Effects of Committee Activity, Committee Position, Seniority, and Party on Amending Activity in the House, by Committee Membership, 99th Congress*[a]

	Dependent variables					
	Committee measures[b]			Other measures[c]		
Independent variable	Number of amendments	Number of successful amendments	Percent of successful amendments	Number of amendments	Number of successful amendments	Percent of successful amendments
Committee activity[d]	0.38*	0.40*	0.29*	-0.03	-0.03	-0.02
Full committee chair[e]	0.19*	0.23*	0.17*	0.02	0.04	0.10
Subcommittee chair[e]	0.25*	0.25*	0.21*	0.07	0.05	0.06
Full committee ranking minority[e]	0.08	0.07	0.13*	0.04	-0.001	-0.06
Subcommittee ranking minority[e]	0.16*	0.11	0.18*	0.10	0.12	0.14*
Seniority[f]	-0.04	-0.02	-0.02	0.03	0.001	0.03
Party[g]	-0.07	-0.04	0.06	0.04	0.11	0.10
R^2	0.21*	0.23*	0.15*	0.01	0.02	0.10

* Significant at $p < 0.05$.

a. Standardized regression coefficients are reported to ease comparison across equations and to facilitate interpretation for readers not familiar with regression results. Tables with unstandardized coefficients are available from the author upon request.

b. Amending activity on measures originating in one of the member's own committees.

c. Amending activity on measures not originating in any of the member's own committees.

d. Committee activity = (number of amendments to the measures originating in the member's own committees) − (number of amendments sponsored by the member to measures originating in his own committees).

e. Committee leadership posts; = 1 if holds the post; = 0 if does not hold the post.

f. Seniority: = 1 if in fourth or greater term; = 0 if in first to third term.

g. Party: = 1 if Democrat; = 0 if Republican.

own committees and for other measures.[54] The equations include indicators for committee leadership, seniority, and party. In addition, a variable is included that represents the volume of amending activity on measures from a member's own committees. In the equations for committee members' amending activity, this variable helps to capture differences between committees in the volume of business they bring to the floor and thus in the number of opportunities they create for their members to offer floor amendments.[55] Since conditions in the two chambers are quite distinct, the chambers are considered separately.

The House

There are several expectations about House patterns of participation in the 99th Congress. First, committee position should count the most for measures originating in a member's own committees. While committee position may provide resources and political leverage that carry over into other issues, the relevance of position for the level of activity and success is likely to be limited to the measures from a member's own committees. It is on such measures that second-degree amendments designed to counter unfriendly amendments may boost committee leaders' level of amending activity. Second, with the demise of apprenticeship, junior members should not be disadvantaged in amending activity, especially once the effect of committee position is controlled.[56] Third, majority party members are not expected to have disproportionately high levels of activity, although their success in amending activity should be greater than that of minority party members. Fourth, as just noted, committee members' amending activity should be positively related to their committees' activity on the floor. If members from active committees are active generally, their own committees' activity may be related to their amending activity on other committees' measures as well. Finally, the influence of committee membership, and perhaps even seniority, should be stronger in the House than in the more egalitarian, individualistic Senate.

The first thing to note about the results shown in table 5-3 is that com-

54. Note that committee membership cannot be modeled directly for these dependent variables because all members serve as committee members on some measures reaching the floor. Separate equations must be estimated for committee member and nonmember cases.

55. Another possible indicator of committee floor activity is the number of measures a committee reports to the floor. Unfortunately, the great variance in the size and political significance of measures coming from committees makes the number of bills a very poor indicator of committees' floor agendas. For the measure used here, mathematical dependence is avoided by subtracting the number of amendments each member offers to measures from his own committees from the total number of amendments to measures from his committees.

56. Junior members are somewhat arbitrarily defined as those in their first six years of service, consistent with the definition used earlier in this chapter.

mittee activity, committee position, seniority, and party explain very little of the variation in floor participation, whether for committee measures or other measures. Including indicators of ideology, policy extremism, and region (estimates not shown here) does not change this result. Personality probably plays a major role.

Expectations for levels of amending activity are borne out for committee position and seniority. With respect to measures from a member's own committees, majority committee leadership positions are associated with greater than average amending activity and success. On the minority side, committee leaders also show greater than average amending activity and success, but not to a uniformly significant degree. Seniority and party make no significant difference net of the influence of committee position. The floor activity on members' own committees' measures also shapes their amending activity. In sum, representatives holding leadership positions and those on active committees sponsor a disproportionate number of amendments and are disproportionately successful.[57] When it comes to measures from other committees, the activity of one's own committees has an insignificant effect on amending activity, contrary to the hypothesis of the generally active member. Committee position and seniority do not produce distinctive floor activity, individually or collectively, except that subcommittee ranking members tend to show more activity and success than average. Again, seniority has little effect. Committee position—a seat on an active committee, a committee leadership post—matters for House amending activity when the position is connected with the measures on the floor.

The results for success rates also are interesting. Members holding relevant committee leadership positions are considerably more likely to be successful in their amending activity than other committee members. This is true of committee leaders in both parties, so it is not limited to the success of majority party bill managers on second-degree amendments. In fact, Democrats are only marginally more successful than Republicans, once the effect of committee leadership positions is taken into account.

A distinctive feature of the House, the use of special rules, raises a question about the robustness of these patterns. When amending activity for measures from members' own committees is split into two groups—measures considered under restrictive special rules and measures considered

57. It is important to keep in mind that committee amendments are excluded here, as elsewhere. Thus, the effect of being a committee or subcommittee chairman shown in table 5–3 is not due to routine committee amendments, although it does reflect second-degree amendments that chairmen, as bill managers, often sponsor in response to the amendments of other members.

with no rule or an open rule—two important patterns stand out (see table 5-4).[58] First, minority party committee leaders, particularly subcommittee leaders, appear to fare better under open rules than under restrictive rules, in both their level of activity and their success rates. Even under restrictive rules, minority committee leaders show greater activity than nonleaders, although the difference is very small, but under open rules they show distinctly more activity than nonleaders. Thus, while committee position still makes a difference in the House, there is evidence that restrictive rules have neutralized some of the advantages associated with minority committee leadership posts.

Second, one's committees' floor activity is not nearly as powerful a predictor of individual participation for open rule measures as it is for restrictive rule measures. One reason for this is that major bills generate both significant amending activity—including that of committee members, who are more likely to sponsor amendments—and restrictive rules. Another reason is that the Rules Committee, when considering a restrictive rule, generally gives more favorable treatment to committee members' requests for opportunities to offer amendments than to noncommittee members' requests.[59] In short, and not surprisingly, committee membership shapes floor behavior most for those committees handling the most important and controversial legislation, where resources are most likely to be mobilized and resource advantages are most likely to make a difference.

The Senate

Expectations for the Senate are similar to those for the House. That is, in the case of measures from members' own committees, committee activity and committee position should play a role in shaping floor participation, but seniority should have little independent effect. For other measures, committee position and seniority should have little effect.

A unique feature of the Senate makes it impossible to estimate equations identical to those estimated for the House. Nearly all senators have held committee leadership positions in recent Congresses, so holding a committee leadership position is not, by itself, a distinguishing characteristic of individual senators. As a result, I have dropped one of the committee leadership positions (subcommittee ranking minority member) from the Senate equations in order to use it as a baseline from which the effects of committee position can be assessed.[60]

58. See Stanley Bach and Steven S. Smith, *Managing Uncertainty in the House of Representatives: Adaptation and Innovation in Special Rules* (Brookings, 1988), chap. 3.

59. Bach and Smith, *Managing Uncertainty*, p. 94.

60. The best strategy here is to estimate a separate equation for each committee, exam-

TABLE 5-4. *Estimates of the Effects of Committee Activity, Committee Position, Seniority, and Party on Amending Activity in the House, by Type of Rule, 99th Congress*[a]

| | Dependent variables | | | | | |
| | Restrictive rule | | | Open rule or no rule | | |
Independent variable[b]	Number of amendments	Number of successful amendments	Percent of successful amendments	Number of amendments	Number of successful amendments	Percent of successful amendments
Committee activity	0.43*	0.44*	0.38*	0.10*	0.11*	0.12*
Full committee chair	0.12*	0.15*	0.05	0.17*	0.20*	0.24*
Subcommittee chair	0.16*	0.15*	0.10	0.22*	0.22*	0.21*
Full committee ranking minority	0.07	0.05	0.05	0.05	0.06	0.13*
Subcommittee ranking minority	0.06	0.03	0.15*	0.19*	0.14*	0.16*
Seniority	-0.001	-0.01	0.001	-0.07	-0.02	-0.04
Party	-0.08	-0.06	0.02	-0.02	-0.001	0.07
R^2	0.21*	0.21*	0.17*	0.06*	0.08*	0.10*

* Significant at $p < 0.05$.

a. Standardized regression coefficients are reported to ease comparison across equations and to facilitate interpretation for readers not familiar with regression results. Tables with unstandardized coefficients are available from the author upon request.

b. See table 5-3 for definition of independent variables.

TABLE 5-5. *Estimates of the Effects of Committee Activity, Committee Position, Seniority, and Party on Amending Activity in the Senate, by Committee Membership, 99th Congress*[a]

| | Dependent variables | | | | | |
| | Committee measures[b] | | | Other measures[c] | | |
Independent variable[d]	Number of amendments	Number of successful amendments	Percent of successful amendments	Number of amendments	Number of successful amendments	Percent of successful amendments
Committee activity	0.31*	0.33*	0.17	-0.03	-0.02	-0.13
Full committee chair	0.52*	0.57*	-0.16	-0.08	-0.04	0.28
Subcommittee chair	0.11	0.11	-0.24	-0.07	-0.03	0.06
Full committee ranking minority	-0.12	-0.03	0.03	-0.15	-0.10	0.13
Seniority	0.04	0.01	0.05	-0.05	-0.05	-0.18
Party	0.25	0.08	-0.64*	-0.03	-0.09	-0.08
R^2	0.29*	0.36*	0.19*	0.03	0.03	0.12

* Significant at $p < 0.05$.

a. Standardized regression coefficients are reported to ease comparison across equations and to facilitate interpretation for readers not familiar with regression results. Tables with unstandardized coefficients are available from the author upon request.

b. Amending activity on measures originating in one of the member's own committees.

c. Amending activity on measures not originating in any of the member's own committees.

d. See table 5-3 for definition of independent variables.

For committee measures, committee activity is associated with member activity in the Senate, as in the House (see table 5-5). Only full committee chairmen are clearly distinctive in their high rate of amending activity. Subcommittee chairmen are only marginally more active and full committee ranking members are only marginally less active than the base group of subcommittee ranking minority members. Thus, with the exception of full committee chairmanships, committee positions do not yield very distinctive patterns of amending activity on the floor. Seniority counts for little as well.

In contrast to those in the House, Senate success rates during the 99th Congress appear to be strongly influenced by party status but not by committee position. However, the effects of party and committee position cannot be separated in this analysis. Because nearly all senators hold committee leadership positions, the committee position variables collectively overlap nearly completely with the party variable. When party is removed from the equation for success rates, the majority committee position variables switch signs from negative to positive and are significant and large. Thus, while it is clear the majority party Republicans are more successful than Democrats, the independent effects of party and position cannot be apportioned. Interestingly, excluding the party variable from the House success rate equation does not affect the committee position coefficients. This strongly suggests, but does not demonstrate conclusively, that committee position, relative to party status, counts for more in the House.

As is true in the model for the House, the simple model is not very helpful in explaining differences between members' amending activity for measures not originating in their committees. A reasonable (even if not testable) proposition is that, overall, amending activity *not* associated with committee membership is best explained by idiosyncratic factors, such as personal interest and personality. At the same time, institutional positions—leadership posts and membership in active committees—remain important in shaping members' roles on the floor on those measures directly related to the institutional positions.

Conclusion

The patterns of floor participation in the 99th Congress caution against exaggerated inferences from the observation that the prescriptive partici-

---

ining the effect of formal position and other factors on amending activity for each committee. This strategy, however, makes it difficult to generalize over all committees, and, for the committees with little floor activity, little variance in the dependent variables makes useful estimates quite difficult.

pation norms have virtually disappeared. The primary lesson is that the committee and party systems of both chambers continue to lend some order to patterns of floor participation.[61] Prescriptive norms may no longer influence floor behavior, but the committee and party systems still structure opportunities, responsibilities, and resources in ways that shape members' roles on the floor. And, as the roles of the committee and party systems differ between the chambers, floor participation is patterned differently as well.

I have not attempted to offer a definitive explanation for the demise of participatory norms. In chapters 1–4 I outlined many of the forces inside and outside Congress that altered the incentives and disincentives, the opportunities and constraints, for floor participation. Some of these forces were transparent to Matthews as he was writing about the Senate of the 1950s:

> The trend in American politics seems to be toward more competitive two-party politics; a greater political role for the mass media of communications and those skilled in their use; larger, more urban constituencies. All these are factors which presently encourage departure from the norms of Senate behavior. In all likelihood, therefore, nonconformity to the folkways will increase in the future if the folkways remain as they are today.[62]

Perhaps even Matthews has been surprised at the rapidity with which the political context of floor decisionmaking has changed and the traditional norms have disintegrated. Institutional position still matters, of course, because procedural advantages and resource disparities remain, although the regulatory norms imposing participatory constraints have disappeared. Seniority alone plays little role in shaping participation levels, and even committee position has little effect on participation in policy areas outside the relevant committee's jurisdiction. In both the House and Senate, regulatory and advisory norms restraining floor participation have disappeared, and a substantially more collegial process has emerged.

---

61. Other studies have documented the structuring effects of formal leadership positions within committees as well. See C. Lawrence Evans, *Influence in Senate Committees* (Ph.D. dissertation, University of Rochester, 1987), chap. 4; and Richard L. Hall, "Participation and Purpose in Committee Decision Making," *American Political Science Review*, vol. 81 (March 1987), pp. 105–27.

62. Matthews, *U.S. Senators and Their World*, p. 117.

CHAPTER SIX

Floor Power, Committee Power

ALTHOUGH deference to committee recommendations gave way to an avalanche of floor amendments during the last three decades, hasty conclusions about the demise of committee power must be avoided. No detailed analysis of legislative outcomes and the origins of key provisions has been conducted. Furthermore, I have noted that omnibus legislating, restrictive special rules, suspension of the rules, and other features of congressional procedure and politics probably have limited the loss of autonomy that committees otherwise would have experienced. Committees improved their resources with expanded professional staffs and special access to new and expanded congressional support agencies at the same time the legislative capacities of individual members were upgraded. Moreover, many procedures that advantage committees' proposals on the floor and at the postpassage stages remain in place.

In principle, the issue of committee power in Congress is very simple: committees are nothing but agents of their parent chambers. All congressional committees are creations of, and may be restructured or abolished by, their parent chambers.[1] Committees exist because they are performing valued services for the chambers and individual members. Remodeling of the committee systems, and even reform targeted at particular committees, has occurred on several occasions in response to changing demands inside and outside Congress.[2] In this light, committees are never truly autonomous decisionmaking units, but rather they normally must operate in a procedural fashion and with a substantive effect that is consistent with the interests of their parent chamber.

1. The charter for most standing committees is found in the standing rules of the two chambers, although certain committees (Budget, Small Business) are created by statute.

2. For recent histories of the congressional committee systems, see Roger H. Davidson and Walter J. Oleszek, *Congress Against Itself* (Indiana University Press, 1977), chaps. 1, 2; Walter Kravitz, "Evolution of the Senate's Committee System," *Annals of the American Academy of Political and Social Science* vol. 411 (January 1974), pp. 27–38; and Steven S. Smith and Christopher J. Deering, *Committees in Congress* (Washington: CQ Press, 1984), chap. 1.

In practice, most threats to a committee's charter are not credible. Altering committee charters is difficult, if for no other reason than it sets a precedent that members of other committees would not like to see observed in the future.[3] Other tools of the parent chambers—such as control over committee budgets—and of the parties—such as committee assignments—are more viable, but they too are difficult to bring to bear in particular legislative fights.[4] The most immediate means of chamber control is rejection of committee measures reported to the floor.

Assessing the relative strength of chamber and committee power is an enterprise with many hazards, even in the context of a single policy in a single Congress. A fully developed assessment involves, at a minimum, a comparison of policy outcomes, committee policy preferences, and floor policy preferences, as I suggested in chapter 1. In most circumstances, information on members' preferences is not available independent of their observed behavior; this makes it impossible to determine whether their public behavior reflects their sincere preferences, anticipation of likely outcomes, or strategic position taking. Furthermore, because both committees and parent chambers are multimember legislative bodies, the question of committee and floor power translates into a problem of judging the degree to which the preferences of particular committee and floor majorities are reflected in the final outcome. Unfortunately, when the policy disputes involved are complex and multidimensional, as they often are, different majorities may favor different possible combinations of policy positions. No single majority can be said to represent a committee or chamber. Instead, partial winners and losers are likely to exist, which often yields no satisfactory inferences about committee and floor power. Aggregating judgments about winners and losers over the many bills and committees makes the assessment of committee and floor power even more nebulous.

And even if such a complex analysis were feasible, its conclusions still could be quite misleading. Floor and committee power exist within a larger bicameral and separation-of-powers system. While a legislative outcome may appear to favor the position of a chamber majority over that of a committee majority, for example, the larger and more important story for the participants might be that the outcome was closer to both the commit-

3. In the 100th Congress, the Senate Budget Committee's charter was under serious threat. Many senators believed the committee should be supplanted by a committee composed of the leaders of the other standing committees, and at least one candidate for majority leader supported the proposal. See David Rapp, "Budget Breaks Up in Acrimony," *Congressional Quarterly Weekly Report*, April 30, 1988, pp. 1165–66.

4. On the efforts of the House Democratic Caucus to order standing committees to act, see James L. Sundquist, *The Decline and Resurgence of Congress* (Brookings, 1981), pp. 383–87.

tee and floor positions of that chamber than to the positions of the other chamber or of the executive branch. In the wider strategic context, what might appear to be a loss for the committee is interpreted by the committee as a victory for itself and its parent chamber.

Of necessity, then, sweeping assessments of committee and floor power in Congress must necessarily rest on very crude indicators of the nature of committee-chamber interaction, such as tallies of floor amending activity. With such indicators, judgments about the distribution of power between the chambers and their committees are meaningful only in a comparative context—across committees, across the two chambers, across Congresses. This chapter focuses on such sources of variance at one stage of committee-chamber interaction, the initial consideration of legislation on the floor, and reserves for chapter 7 the subject of change at the postpassage stage.

The chapter has four arguments. The first is that House and Senate committees did indeed lose substantial autonomy by virtue of the developments on the House and Senate floors during the 1960s and 1970s. A second argument is that committees vary greatly in the degree to which floor developments affected them. A third argument is that committees retain important advantages at the floor stage. One advantage is the ability to offer counteramendments to minimize the damage of unfriendly amendments. The other, already explored in some detail, is that House committees benefit from restrictive special rules that offer some protection from the dangers of floor decisionmaking. A final argument is that pattern of lost power among committees differs greatly between the two chambers. These propositions serve to temper interpretations about the importance of floor decisionmaking in the House and Senate.

Sources of Committee Power

Committee power is observable and important only when the policy preferences of a committee and the chamber differ.[5] When committee and

5. For the most part, floor power and committee power are treated in this chapter as complementary quantities, as if more of one means that there is less of the other. While such a view is a convenience when assessing the distribution of power within each chamber, it often produces a distorted view. The policy preferences of committees and the floors often are not far apart. In fact, it is reasonable to suppose that the most common state of affairs is general concurrence between committee and floor majorities. The same party retains majority control of both the floor and all standing committees, and committee appointments are controlled by functionaries of the two parties. In recent Congresses, the best evidence is that on either standard ideological ratings or on policy-specific ratings issued by interest groups, few House committees have medians significantly different from the overall median for the House. See Keith Krehbiel, "Are Congressional Committees Composed of Preference Outliers?" Working

chamber preferences do differ, committee power can be viewed as having two forms.[6] *Negative* committee power is the ability to successfully defend the status quo in the face of a parent-chamber majority in favor of change. Negative power rests on the institutional capacity of a committee to restrict the choices available to the chamber. *Positive* committee power is the ability of a committee to change a policy in the face of a parent-chamber majority opposed to change. Positive power rests on the capacity of a committee to circumvent the floor or to convince some members to vote for the committee position and against their true policy preferences. The ability of committees to exercise each form of power rests, in part, on the rules and procedures of Congress, but it also involves other resources that committees can bring to bear in a legislative battle. Understanding these sources of committee power helps to isolate the roots of change in committees' floor experiences and yields important qualifications about the magnitude of the decline in committee power.

First consider negative committee power, which has many sources in Congress. The most obvious is the ability to obstruct legislation by refusing to report it to the floor. This "gatekeeping" power is considerably stronger in the House than in the Senate, primarily because the House germaneness rule is so stringent that it is difficult to circumvent a committee by offering floor amendments. But even in the House, the gatekeeping power is not perfect because there are mechanisms for floor majorities to bring matters to the floor, such as suspension of the rules, discharge petitions, and special rules. In both chambers, then, effective gatekeeping power relies, in part, on factors other than committees' right not to act on legislation referred to them.

Negative committee power is reinforced by other features of floor procedure. In both chambers, there are "amendment trees" that limit the number and type of amendments to amendments that may be pending at one time in the absence of a special rule or unanimous consent agreement that provides otherwise (see appendix 1). In addition, committee bill managers are recognized before other members to offer amendments on behalf of the committee before the consideration of other amendments, and, during the consideration of other amendments, they usually are recognized before others to offer second-degree amendments. In combination, amend-

---

Papers in Economics E-88-44, Stanford University, Hoover Institution, October 1988. Generally, the range of issues over which committees and the floors experience deep conflict is small, at least relative to the volume of legislation passed, leaving only a narrow range within which the power of committees and the floor can be judged.

6. See Keith Krehbiel, "Spatial Models of Legislative Choice," *Legislative Studies Quarterly,* vol. 13 (August 1988), pp. 259–319.

ment trees and recognition privileges order the consideration of alternatives to ensure that bill managers have an opportunity to offer alternatives to unfriendly amendments. The procedures permit bill managers to anticipate and short-circuit others' amendments or to dilute their effect once the unfriendly amendments are offered.[7] Such techniques make it possible for bill managers to preclude certain outcomes when they can muster majorities for their own alternatives.

On the House floor, the gatekeeping power of committees is strengthened because measures are considered for amendment title by title or section by section in the Committee of the Whole. Amendment sponsors may offer their amendments only when the appropriate section is on the floor, and amendments must be germane to that section. In some situations, these procedures effectively exclude certain kinds of unfriendly amendments.

Negative power is further fortified by restraints of a more tactical nature, such as provisions in House special rules and Senate unanimous consent agreements. House closed rules radically limit options on the floor to acceptance, rejection, recommittal, or recommittal with instructions. Most special rules are not so restrictive, however, and the Senate's unanimous consent agreements are virtually never so restrictive.

Domination of conference committees by the members of the committee of origin also reinforces that committee's ability to block certain outcomes and obtain compromises for others. Because committee members dominate conference delegations and because conference reports cannot be amended on the floor, committee members are in a position to reverse decisions made through floor amendments as long as the other chamber's conferees agree and the final product is acceptable to House and Senate majorities.[8] Reversals of floor decisions, or ex post vetoes, may abate the damage done on the floor to the committee's original plan.

The ex post veto, however, is an imperfect tool for committees. Its success is contingent on the willingness of the other chamber's conferees to agree to the change and of floor majorities in both chambers to support the conference report. For example, the floor may reject a conference report, send the report back to conference, reconstitute the conference delegation,

7. A formal treatment of these advantages in the House is provided in Barry R. Weingast, "Floor Behavior in Congress: Committee Power under the Open Rule," paper prepared for the 1987 annual meeting of the American Political Science Association. Of course, second-degree amendments also may be employed by rank-and-file senators seeking to limit the options of others. If committee leaders do not anticipate such developments, they may discover that their opponents have gained a procedural edge.

8. That is, if they are not concerned about long-term effects on their reputations for trustworthiness.

bypass the conference through an exchange of amendments with the other chamber, discharge the conference, or use other means to limit the discretion of conferees. And the preferences of the other chamber, its committee, and its conferees may severely restrict a chamber's conferees from repealing the decisions of its own floor.[9]

Taken together, these elements of congressional procedure—gatekeeping, amendment trees, conferences—confer upon committees considerable, though far from complete, power to restrict the policy options of the parent chamber. Judicious use of negative powers gives committees important bargaining advantages that may be used to buy support for their legislation; that is, negative power sometimes yields positive results. For example, a committee may threaten to drop a provision in conference if a member or faction fails to support the committee's position on other issues. In 1987 a member of the House Appropriations Committee, complaining about members who voted against a continuing appropriations resolution even though their districts benefited from projects in it, asserted, "We're going to take some hits on people who didn't vote with us."[10] There are limits on the ability of committees to translate negative power into positive power in this way. Among other things, sustained, heavy-handed uses of such leverage might be expected to produce a backlash, perhaps in the form of challenges to the procedures granting the negative powers in the first place.

Now consider positive committee power. Its direct sources are weak in Congress, at least when compared with the sources of negative power. Committees may propose and report legislation at will, of course, and their recognition privileges on the floor enhance their proposal power with respect to making adjustments while their measures are considered on the floor.[11] But the proposal power does not guarantee floor consideration of committee-reported measures. Major party leaders may refuse to schedule the legislation, and floor majorities may oppose motions to take up legislation on the floor. Avenues for circumventing the floor are very limited. Packaging legislation into omnibus bills has proven to be a useful technique, but control over the decision to devise omnibus bills usually does

9. For background on the ex post veto, see Kenneth A. Shepsle and Barry R. Weingast, "The Institutional Foundations of Committee Power," *American Political Science Review*, vol. 81 (March 1987), pp. 85–104; Keith Krehbiel, Kenneth A. Shepsle, and Barry R. Weingast, "Why are Congressional Committees Powerful?" *American Political Science Review*, vol. 81 (September 1987), pp. 929–45; and Steven S. Smith, "An Essay on Sequence, Position, Goals, and Committee Power," *Legislative Studies Quarterly*, vol. 13 (May 1988), pp. 151–76.

10. Quoted in Tom Kenworthy, "Austerity? Lawmakers Are Still at the Trough," *Washington Post*, December 5, 1987, p. A25.

11. For a formal treatment of the proposal power, see David P. Baron and John A. Ferejohn, "The Power to Propose," Working Papers in Political Science P-88-3, Stanford University, Hoover Institution, March 1988.

not lie with individual committees, and the value of packaging normally is contingent on a committee's ability to obtain restrictions on floor amendments. Committee members sometimes manage to introduce new items at the conference stage, particularly when one of the chambers has adopted an amendment in the nature of a substitute, but even then a majority of both houses must approve the conference report.

In Congress, positive committee power must rely on more than formal procedure, and many extraprocedural resources advantage committees. Committees' special role in gathering political and policy information, and perhaps their ability to reveal that information selectively to their chambers, endows them with tactical advantages on the floor.[12] Committee leaders usually are better informed about the politics and policy substance of matters under their committees' jurisdictions, which often allows them to make more persuasive arguments than their opponents. They are more likely to know the location of support and opposition, the sources of unfriendly floor amendments, and what it might take to forestall amendments or win necessary support. Committees' specialized professional staffs put committee leaders in a better position than noncommittee members to strategically frame issues, rapidly draft defensive amendments, and monitor activity in the other chamber that will affect conference negotiations. Personal relationships, developed over years of service in Congress, help committee leaders to cement deals and attract the support of indifferent colleagues. Committee leaders often are in a position to orchestrate external pressure on their colleagues. In the past, committees benefited from informal norms, such as committee deference and intercommittee reciprocity, which may have been grounded in members' assumptions about the political and informational advantages of committees. And committee leaders' relationships with party leaders aids them in gaining timely floor consideration for their bills.

Committee success on the floor is the product of an amalgam of procedural and extraprocedural resources. Negative committee power stems primarily from the particular sequence and procedures of congressional legislating. In fact, the multiple procedural advantages of committees are often sufficient to block changes in policy, particularly in the House. In contrast, parliamentary procedures cannot, by themselves, produce floor majorities in both chambers and so are not sufficient to produce positive committee power. Positive power must be developed from extraprocedural sources.

12. For a recent discussion of the long-appreciated importance of information advantages, see David Austen-Smith and William H. Riker, "Asymmetric Information and the Coherence of Legislation," *American Political Science Review*, vol. 81 (September 1987), pp. 897–918.

In practice, it is difficult to separate the negative and positive effects of many of the procedural and nonprocedural resources of committees. For example, the actions of committees to reverse some floor decisions in conference may be designed to block or to endorse policy change. Similarly, committees' expertise encourages deference to their recommendations among outsiders, which sometimes bolsters committees' gatekeeping power and enhances their ability to set the floor agenda to their liking. These mixed effects make it very difficult to evaluate empirically the relative importance of the various sources of committee power.

Nevertheless, the deterioration in committees' ability to avoid or defeat challenges on the floor over the past three decades appears to be due more to declining positive power than to declining negative power. Few sources of negative committee power have been undermined since the 1950s. Formal procedures affecting gatekeeping capacity, floor amending procedures and recognition privileges, and basic procedures at the conference stage remain largely intact. It remains true, for example, that very few measures are considered on the House and Senate floors without committee approval. In contrast, the sources of positive committee power have degenerated. Committees' informational edge over outsiders has diminished. Open meetings, larger personal staffs, the availability of experts in the congressional support agencies, assistance from more interest groups, and other factors have multiplied the sources of information, both political and substantive, to which rank-and-file members have access. In both chambers, technological and organizational developments—television, the party whip systems, notification practices—have made it easier for rank-and-file members and their staff to follow floor activity. Committees retain special advantages in information and expertise, of course, but the advantages are not nearly as great as they were in the 1950s and 1960s. Moreover, developments in the internal operations of committees—subcommittee decentralization, growth of subcommittee and minority staff, greater external pressures—subverted committee cohesiveness and further undermined the credibility of committee claims to special expertise. There is little doubt that these developments contributed to the demise of the apprenticeship and deference norms that had once reinforced positive committee power.

The sources of negative committee power have not gone unscathed. In the House, where negative committee power remains the strongest, multiple referral of legislation may be used to circumvent or dilute the recommendations of particular committees. In both chambers, the reconciliation instructions of budget resolutions may order committees to report legislation providing spending cuts that the committees normally would oppose. And as the next chapter will detail, the stranglehold of committees over the conference stage was weakened considerably during the 1970s. But these developments on the negative side of committee power cannot account for the growth of floor amendments in the 1960s and early 1970s: they occurred in the mid- or late 1970s, after the surge in floor amendments had taken place. If anything, multiple referral, the use of reconciliation, and challenges to committee conference domination were a product of attitudes and behavior that already had changed in fundamental ways.

Nevertheless, committees retain a capacity—via negative committee power—to limit, dilute, and at least partially compensate for unfriendly floor amendments, particularly in the House. Committees are still powerful, and the preponderance of their recommendations go unchallenged on the House and Senate floors.

Committees and Floor Amending Activity

Although nearly all standing committees in both chambers have experienced a significant increase in floor amending activity on their measures, committees vary in many ways that affect their floor experiences.[13] The variation is grounded in differences in the jurisdictions and active policy agendas of committees. Committees whose agendas are large, salient, and controversial attract more floor amendments than committees with small, inconspicuous, and noncontroversial agendas. This truism suggests that committees should have experienced differing patterns of change in floor amending activity. Committees with the largest, most salient, and most controversial policy agendas should have experienced the greatest change in floor experience since the 1950s. Such committees are likely to have been affected disproportionately by the disintegration of norms that limited floor participation and other changes that affected the positive power of committees. Changes in the character of committees' agendas magnify or counteract the effects of changes on the floor. Increases in the size, salience, and controversy of a committee's policy agenda should enhance the effects of the expansion of floor amending activity, and decreases should reduce them.

I use a primitive index of floor amending activity on committees' measures to characterize committee floor experiences. Because no single indi-

---

13. Lawrence C. Dodd, "Committee Integration in the Senate: A Comparative Analysis," *Journal of Politics*, vol. 34 (November 1972), pp. 1135–71; James W. Dyson and John W. Soule, "Congressional Committee Behavior on Roll Call Votes: The U.S. House of Representatives, 1955–1964," *Midwest Journal of Political Science*, vol. 14 (November 1970), pp. 626–47; Richard F. Fenno, Jr., *Congressmen in Committees* (Little, Brown, 1973), chap. 6; and Smith and Deering, *Committees in Congress*, chaps. 2, 3, 4.

cator can capture a committee's floor experience, I use a composite index of five indicators: the number of amendments, the number of amendments per measure, the proportion of measures subject to at least one amendment, the number of successful amendments, and the number of contested amendments. The index is the mean ordinal ranking for the five indicators. It has been calculated for each committee in five selected Congresses.[14] Unfortunately, good indicators of agenda size, salience, and controversy are not available, at least not independently of the patterns of floor activity to which they are related. As result, some seat-of-the-pants evaluations must be made, with the aid of some informed judgment from previous studies.[15]

With an important exception, committees with the largest and most controversial agendas do indeed face the highest levels of amending activity, as tables 6-1 and 6-2 indicate. In both chambers, the Appropriations committees stand out for their consistently high rankings. The Appropriations committees' jurisdiction over spending decisions for most federal programs and the continuous conflict over federal expenditures made their bills frequent targets on the floor. In addition, those committees with broad jurisdictions over nationally important policy areas—the foreign policy and money committees, particularly—also rank high. Most of these committees are attractive to members because of their substantive policy importance, which also stimulates interest in their legislation when it reaches the floor.[16] At the other end of the spectrum, committees with relatively small constituencies and narrow jurisdictions—the District of Columbia, Small Business, and Veterans' Affairs committees—regularly rank low in floor amending action.

The important exception is the House Committee on Ways and Means. Until the mid-1970s, Ways and Means benefited from closed or highly restrictive special rules for floor debate on its legislation, shielding it from the number of floor amendments that its Senate counterpart, the Committee on Finance, suffered routinely. The contrast was particularly stark in the 92d Congress (1971–72), the last Congress before electronic voting was installed in the House and two Congresses before the Democratic Cau-

---

14. Amendments are counted in the same way they were for previous chapters (see appendix 2). The number of measures taken to the floor for each committee was counted from the *Final Calendar* of the House for each of the five Congresses, which includes the record for Senate committees as well. Complete tables for the five indicators are available from the author.

15. Smith and Deering, *Committees in Congress*, chap. 3.

16. On members' goals for seeking committee assignments, see Fenno, *Congressmen in Committees*; Charles S. Bullock III, "Motivations for U.S. Congressional Committee Preferences: Freshmen of the 92d Congress," *Legislative Studies Quarterly*, vol. 1 (February 1976), pp. 201–12; and Smith and Deering, *Committees in Congress*, chap. 4.

TABLE 6-1. Index of Floor Amending Activity for House Committees, Selected Congresses, 1955–86[a]

84th (1955–56)	88th (1963–64)	92d (1971–72)	96th (1979–80)	99th (1985–86)
Appropriations (1.0)	Education and Labor (2.4)	Appropriations (1.4)	Appropriations (1.4)	Armed Services (1.6)
Education and Labor (4.0)	Appropriations (2.8)	Education and Labor (1.8)	Foreign Affairs (2.8)	Appropriations (2.4)
Agriculture (4.4)	Foreign Affairs (4.0)	Banking (4.6)	*Energy and Commerce (3.2)*[b]	Banking (3.0)
Armed Services (5.0)	Agriculture (4.2)	Public Works (5.0)	Judiciary (5.4)	Foreign Affairs (3.0)
Banking (5.6)	Judiciary (4.6)	Commerce (6.0)	Banking (5.6)	Agriculture (6.2)
Post Office (6.8)	Interior (7.0)	Agriculture (6.6)	Budget (6.0)	Education and Labor (6.4)
Judiciary (7.0)	Commerce (7.6)	Judiciary (7.2)	Science (8.4)	Public Works (6.8)
Interior (7.2)	Banking (7.8)	Interior (8.8)	Interior (8.6)	Ways and Means (8.4)
Public Works (8.6)	Government Operations (9.0)	Armed Services (9.2)	Agriculture (9.8)	*Energy and Commerce (10.0)*[b]
Commerce (8.8)	Post Office (9.0)	*Foreign Affairs (9.4)*	Public Works (10.4)	Government Operations (10.0)
Veterans' Affairs (9.8)	Armed Services (10.6)	District of Columbia (10.2)	Armed Services (10.6)	Judiciary (10.4)
District of Columbia (11.0)	Science (11.0)	Merchant Marine (10.6)	Education and Labor (11.0)	Interior (12.0)
Foreign Affairs (12.0)	District of Columbia (12.0)	Government Operations (11.4)	Ways and Means (13.0)	Merchant Marine (12.8)
Government Operations (13.8)	Public Works (12.2)	Post Office (13.0)	Merchant Marine (13.8)	Post Office (13.0)
Merchant Marine (13.8)	Rules (13.2)	Science (13.8)	Post Office (14.6)	Science (13.2)
Ways and Means (14.0)	Ways and Means (15.6)	Ways and Means (13.8)	Small Business (15.8)	Budget (15.2)
Rules (14.8)	Veterans' Affairs (16.4)	Rules (14.4)	District of Columbia (17.6)	Rules (16.8)
	Merchant Marine (17.8)	Veterans' Affairs (16.6)	Rules (17.6)	Veterans' Affairs (17.0)
			Veterans' Affairs (19.6)	Small Business (18.2)
				District of Columbia (18.4)

SOURCE: See appendix 2.

a. Index value (indicated in parentheses) is mean ordinal value for five indicators (see text). Committees in italics had levels of amending activity that exceeded the median values for the 96th Congress on at least three of the five indicators of amending activity.

b. The Committee on Interstate and Foreign Commerce was renamed the Committee on Energy and Commerce in 1979.

TABLE 6-2. *Index of Floor Amending Activity for Senate Committees, Selected Congresses, 1955–86*[a]

84th (1955–56)	88th (1963–64)	92d (1971–72)	96th (1979–80)	99th (1985–86)
Appropriations (1.6)	Appropriations (2.4)	Finance (1.2)	Appropriations (1.2)	Appropriations (1.6)
Agriculture (2.6)	Foreign Relations (2.8)	Labor (2.0)	Banking (3.2)	Budget (3.6)
Foreign Relations (4.4)	Labor (3.6)	Appropriations (3.2)	Finance (5.0)	Finance (3.6)
Banking (4.8)	Finance (4.0)	Foreign Relations (3.8)	Budget (5.2)	Armed Services (4.0)
Finance (4.8)	Agriculture (5.4)	Banking (6.4)	Foreign Relations (6.0)	Foreign Relations (5.0)
Public Works (7.0)	Banking (5.6)	Armed Services (6.8)	Labor (6.0)	Agriculture (5.2)
Rules (7.4)	Judiciary (6.4)	Commerce (6.8)	Energy (7.2)[b]	Public Works (8.0)
Commerce (8.4)	Commerce (8.2)	Public Works (7.4)	Public Works (8.2)	Commerce (9.2)
Judiciary (8.4)	Interior (8.6)	Agriculture (10.2)	Veterans' Affairs (8.8)	Small Business (10.2)
Veterans' Affairs (8.6)	Public Works (9.4)	Rules (10.8)	Armed Services (9.2)	Veterans' Affairs (10.2)
Armed Services (10.2)	Armed Services (9.6)	Judiciary (11.0)	Commerce (9.6)	Labor (10.4)
Government Operations (10.4)	Rules (9.8)	Interior (11.0)	Agriculture (10.6)	Judiciary (11.0)
Interior (10.6)	Government Operations (12.0)	Government Operations (11.2)	Small Business (11.4)	Energy (11.8)[b]
Labor (11.4)	Veterans' Affairs (13.4)	Veterans' Affairs (11.8)	Judiciary (12.4)	Rules (12.4)
			Rules (12.6)	Banking (12.8)
			Governmental Affairs (13.6)[c]	Governmental Affairs (13.0)[c]

SOURCE: See appendix 2.

a. Index value (indicated in parentheses) is mean ordinal value for five indicators (see text). Committees in italics had levels of amending activity that exceeded the median values for the 96th Congress on at least three of the five indicators of amending activity.

b. The Committee on Interior and Insular Affairs was renamed the Committee on Energy and Natural Resources in 1977.

c. The Committee on Government Operations was renamed the Committee on Governmental Affairs in 1977. At that time, the committee gained the jurisdiction of the Committee on the District of Columbia and the Committee on Post Office and Civil Service, which were disbanded and are not shown in the table.

cus moved to control closed rules. In that Congress, Ways and Means ranked near the bottom in the House while Finance faced more amendments, and more contested amendments, than any other Senate committee. The number of floor amendments on Ways and Means measures increased from less than a dozen in the 92d and 93d Congresses (1971–74) to more than sixty in the 94th (1975–76), when the insulation of closed rules was removed. Starting in the 96th Congress (1979–80), however, Ways and Means again benefited from restrictive rules, allowing only mid-ranking amending activity on its measures while Finance remained near the top of the Senate scale.

The proposition that committees with the largest, most salient, and most controversial agendas experienced the greatest increases in floor amending activity also is supported by the evidence. The Senate's four exclusive committees—Appropriations, Armed Services, Finance, and Foreign Relations—collectively experienced a 483 percent increase in the number of amendments per Congress between 1955 and 1986, compared with a 180 percent increase for all other committees that existed throughout the period.[17] In the House, where differences among committees were dampened in the 1980s by restrictive rules, the parallel committees—Appropriations, Armed Services, Ways and Means, and Foreign Affairs—witnessed a 445 percent increase in the number of amendments between 1955 and 1986, compared with a 304 percent increase for other committees.[18]

The rankings shown in tables 6-1 and 6-2 also suggest that committee agendas and floor amending activity are closely associated with members' motivations for seeking committee assignments. Committees that previous studies identify as particularly attractive to power- and policy-oriented members—the money, labor, judiciary, commerce, and foreign policy committees, for example—tend to be above the median in floor amending activity in each Congress. Their large, controversial agendas lure members attracted to the special importance of the issues under their jurisdictions and to the fast-paced activity and excitement surrounding their agendas. The major exception to the relationship between committee type and amending activity is again House Ways and Means, which was shielded from many floor amendments by protective special rules. In contrast, the

17. The four top Senate committees often are labeled "exclusive" because senators generally are limited by their parties to a seat on just one of them. The difference between the exclusive committees and other Senate committees is even greater in terms of successful amendments than in total amendments. The four exclusive committees experienced a 595 percent increase in the number of successful amendments, compared with 219 percent for other committees.

18. The four committees experienced a 723 percent increase in the number of successful amendments, compared with 416 percent for other committees.

committees with narrow, more parochial agendas are attractive primarily because of their constituency appeal. They tend to bring fewer bills to the floor, and those bills tend to attract little attention and fewer challenges on the floor.

These differences also are manifest in the patterns of change in committee rankings over time. Several committees whose agendas lost much of their salience and controversy, and whose attractiveness to members declined, also fell in the amending activity rankings. The prime cases are the House Committee on Education and Labor and the Senate Committee on Labor and Human Resources. Both committees were attractive to many members and ranked very high in amending activity during the 1960s and early 1970s, when they were reporting hotly contested measures on labor-management relations and expanding the federal role in education, nutrition, and job training. By the late 1970s, after the major legislative battles on labor-management relations had subsided and a broad consensus was established for federal education programs, member interest in the two committees and their legislation ebbed as well. In the 96th Congress (1979–80), both committees faced less than half as many floor amendments as they did in the 92d (1971–72). In the case of Education and Labor, the changing nature of the committee agenda counteracted the effects of floor procedural reforms, although the committee probably continued to face more floor amendments than it would have in the absence of the reforms.

Conversely, some committees experienced far greater than average increases in amending activity because of dramatic changes in their policy agendas. For example, the House Committee on Energy and Commerce moved steadily upward in rank from the 1950s to the late 1970s. During the 1950s fourteen House committees sent more legislation to the floor than did Commerce, and ten faced more amendments. During the 1960s and 1970s, though, new issues such as consumer protection, environmental protection, health care, and energy came under its jurisdiction. After facing about a dozen floor amendments in 1955–56 and two dozen in 1964–65, Energy and Commerce measures were subject to about 250 amendments in 1979–80, which was more than 1 out of every 6 floor amendments in the House. In recent years, the House and Senate Armed Services committees also have experienced tremendous increases in floor amendments, with the House committee even exceeding the levels of House Appropriations during 1985–86.

The size, salience, and controversy of committees' agendas are not the only factors that mold floor experiences. Committees' strategies vary, for example. Some committees, such as House Education and Labor during the

1950s and 1960s, seem more willing than others to report legislation that would suffer unfriendly amendments or even defeat.[19] In other cases, committee leaders, sometimes in coordination with the party leadership, may withhold controversial legislation from the floor just because they expect that many unfriendly amendments will be offered and adopted. In yet other cases, special circumstances make it possible for committee leaders to convince their chamber colleagues to exercise self-restraint in offering tempting amendments to major legislation.[20] Self-restraint may result from a successful argument that a bill represents a delicate compromise that might be upset by floor amendments. In 1988, such an argument worked when the Senate Banking Committee, chaired by Wisconsin Democrat William Proxmire, brought a major bill that would have repealed much of the Glass-Steagall Act of 1933, which restricted the types of financial activities in which banks can engage. Senators Bob Graham, Howard Metzenbaum, and John Heinz sponsored amendments that they withdrew (in the latter two cases after the chairman promised hearings on their concerns) as it became clear that others would not abide by their commitment to support the compromise if these amendments were considered and adopted. In the end, only two amendments were adopted, one minor and one jointly sponsored by Proxmire and Jake Garn, the ranking committee Republican, both by voice vote.[21]

Despite these exceptions to the rule that controversy breeds floor amendments, the general pattern is clear. Not only do committees' floor experiences differ, but they differ far more now than they did in the 1950s and 1960s. For the number of amendments faced by House committees, the standard deviation increased from 22.1 in the 84th Congress to 35.6

19. See Fenno, *Congressmen in Committees,* pp. 226–42.

20. In 1985, for example, the House Committee on Public Works and Transportation reported legislation authorizing over $20 billion for water projects of various kinds—dams, harbor and river dredging, shoreline protection, and flood control. Such legislation is potentially vulnerable to dozens of amendments to add, drop, or modify projects. Water Resources Subcommittee Chairman Robert A. Roe and ranking Republican Arlan Stangeland were united in their support for the water projects bill and in their opposition to most amendments. When an amendment was offered to delete a provision granting Mississippi River flood control projects an exemption from local cost-sharing requirements, Roe argued successfully that such an amendment, if adopted, would encourage attacks on other projects in the bill. As it became obvious that Roe and Stangeland had crafted a bill with widespread support, several members decided not to offer amendments they had prepared. Most members used the floor to applaud the efforts of Roe and Stangeland to be responsive to the interests of members of House. See Joseph A. Davis, "Vote Reflects Support from All Regions: Water Projects Authorization Wins House Passage with Ease," *Congressional Quarterly Weekly Report,* November 16, 1985, pp. 2384–85.

21. John R. Cranford, "Senate Easily Approves Bank-Deregulation Bill," *Congressional Quarterly Weekly Report,* April 2, 1988, pp. 843–49.

in the 88th, 43.5 in the 92d, 85.2 in the 96th, and 75.9 in the 99th. Senate variance increased even more: the corresponding Senate values were 30.5, 40.7, 82.4, 102.9, and 127.1. Committees with the largest, most controversial agendas now experience challenges on the floor that committees at the other end of the spectrum almost never see.

Counteramendments

Seldom do committees, subcommittees, and their chairmen sit idly by while unfriendly amendments are offered and debated. In both the House and Senate, bill managers and their allies often propose amendments in an attempt to dilute or even emasculate unfriendly amendments offered by others. In fact, a count of amendments subject to a recorded vote in the 96th Congress (1979–80) and the 99th Congress (1985–86) shows that 15 to 20 percent of such amendments are secondary amendments, which often are sponsored by the bill manager.[22] Secondary amendments do not represent a new defensive capacity on the part of committee bill managers, of course, although their defensive role may have been more important in the period since the surge in floor amendments in the early 1970s. But the trends explored in previous chapters must be understood in terms of the ability of committees to minimize the damage of unfriendly amendments by offering counteramendments.

Bill managers have an advantage over most other members in offering secondary amendments. This advantage is more clearly defined in the House. In the House, it is the long-standing custom that a bill manager be recognized for the purpose of offering a secondary amendment before others are recognized to do so, ensuring that the bill manager has the first opportunity to counter an unfriendly primary amendment.[23] In the Senate, traditional practice grants the majority leader, the minority leader, and

22. In this section, the terms "primary" and "secondary" amendments are used in place of "first-degree" and "second-degree." This helps to avoid some confusion about what constitutes a first-degree and a second-degree amendment. A primary amendment is an amendment to the bill (or to any text that is treated as an original bill for the purpose of amendment). A secondary amendment is any amendment to a primary amendment or another secondary amendment, and so may be a substitute amendment to the primary amendment.

23. See Stanley Bach, "The Amending Process in the House of Representatives," report 87-778 GOV, Congressional Research Service, September 22, 1987. Also see Lewis Deschler and William Holmes Brown, *Procedure in the United States House of Representatives*, 4th ed. (Government Printing Office, 1982), chap. 29, secs. 5.1–5.5. It should be noted that the chair's decision to recognize a certain member cannot be appealed in the House, leaving open the possibility that the chair could recognize members in a manner inconsistent with customary practice.

then bill managers, in that order, recognition privileges over others.[24] Thus the minority leader may offer amendments before the majority bill manager has an opportunity to do so. However, the majority leader usually is willing to offer amendments on behalf of a majority bill manager if it is critical that the bill manager's amendments be offered before those of the minority leader. In both chambers, other members normally have an opportunity to offer secondary amendments as well, perhaps to amend the secondary amendments sponsored by the bill manager.

It is possible that most of the potential damage of unfriendly primary amendments is avoided by careful counteramendment tactics on the part of bill managers and their allies. Consider this hypothetical pattern of primary and secondary amendments that appears to favor bill managers: most primary amendments are supported by the bill manager and are adopted, primary amendments opposed by the bill manager generally fail, and most of the few successful primary amendments opposed by the bill manager are amended in a way favored by the bill manager. If this pattern was found to be prevalent in the late 1970s or 1980s, one could infer that floor amending activity is not nearly as damaging to committee interests as the aggregate number of floor amendments and their high success rate might suggest. In fact, it might be tempting to conclude that the surge in amending activity was inconsequential for committee power in Congress.

The hypothetical pattern, it turns out, fits well what happened in recent Congresses in both chambers. A recent study of eighty measures considered in the House under an open rule during the 98th Congress (1983–84) found that the bill manager accepted 68 percent of the 548 primary amendments that were offered.[25] Of the 32 percent that bill managers opposed, only 23 percent were adopted and 77 percent were defeated. Of those amendments that were adopted despite the opposition of the bill manager, 58 percent were amended by a secondary amendment favored by the bill manager. Overall, 40 primary amendments opposed by bill managers, or 1 for every 2 bills, were adopted by the House, but only 17 primary amendments, or 3 percent of all primary amendments offered, were adopted over the objections of the bill manager without a successful counteramendment supported by the bill manager.

Additional perspective can be gained by considering a somewhat different cross-section of floor action. Table 6-3 reports the history of House and

---

24. Floyd M. Riddick, *Senate Procedure: Precedents and Practices* (GPO, 1981), pp. 878–83.

25. Barry R. Weingast, "Fighting Fire with Fire: Amending Activity and Institutional Change in the Post-Reform Congress," paper prepared for the 1989 annual meeting of the Midwest Political Science Association.

TABLE 6-3. *Secondary Amendments Subject to a Recorded Vote, House and Senate, Combined 96th and 99th Congresses, 1979–80, 1985–86*[a]
Percent

Bill manager's position[b]		Primary amendment adopted		Primary amendment defeated	
		Secondary amendment adopted	Secondary amendment defeated	Secondary amendment adopted	Secondary amendment defeated
House					
Supported primary amendment	Supported secondary amendment	23.4 (29)	9.7 (12)	1.6 (2)	2.4 (3)
	Opposed secondary amendment	9.7 (12)	24.2 (30)	0 (0)	6.5 (8)
Opposed primary amendment	Supported secondary amendment	1.6 (2)	4.8 (6)	1.6 (2)	0.8 (1)
	Opposed secondary amendment	1.6 (2)	4.8 (6)	0 (0)	7.3 (9)
	Total	36.3	43.5	3.2	17.0
Senate					
Supported primary amendment	Supported secondary amendment	30.8 (36)	6.8 (8)	0 (0)	0.9 (1)
	Opposed secondary amendment	9.4 (11)	41.0 (48)	0 (0)	0.9 (1)
Opposed primary amendment	Supported secondary amendment	1.7 (2)	1.7 (2)	0 (0)	0 (0)
	Opposed secondary amendment	1.7 (2)	2.6 (3)	0.9 (1)	1.7 (2)
	Total	43.6	52.1	0.9	3.5

SOURCE: *U.S. House of Representatives and U.S. Senate Recorded Votes* (Washington: Congressional Quarterly, various issues); and various issues of the *Congressional Record*.

a. Each entry is a percentage of all secondary amendments subject to a recorded vote. Numbers in parentheses are the number of secondary amendments in that category. Primary amendments are included more than once if there is more than one secondary amendment subject to a recorded vote for the primary amendment.

b. Determined by bill manager's recorded vote or, for a few primary amendments, assumed to be consistent with the outcome if the decision was made by voice vote.

Senate amending activity when there were secondary amendments subject to recorded votes during the 96th and 99th Congresses (1979–80, 1985–86). The focus on recorded-vote secondary amendments narrows the view to a more important set of secondary amendments and allows an unambiguous determination of bill managers' position on secondary amendments.

A relatively small proportion of House and Senate primary amendments is subject to recorded-vote secondary amendments: there were only eighty-eight in the House and seventy-eight in the Senate in the two Congresses considered here. Of these primary amendments, 81 percent were adopted by the House and 92 percent were adopted by the Senate. So the amending activity reported in table 6-3 involves primary amendments that had a higher rate of success than other amendments (see chapters 2 and 4) and engaged the chambers in relatively significant secondary amending activity. Several aspects of the pattern of secondary activity deserve notice.

First, nearly 80 percent of the House secondary amendments and nearly 96 percent of the Senate secondary amendments were offered to primary amendments that were adopted. This is not too surprising. From a bill manager's point of view, a secondary-amendment response is not necessary to an unfriendly primary amendment that is likely to fail. And other members would not find such a primary amendment a very useful vehicle for attaching provisions to a bill.

Second, secondary amendments are employed frequently by members who do not share bill managers' views. This can be seen in the large number of secondary amendments opposed by bill managers. In fact, as many or more secondary amendments unfriendly to managers' interests are offered as friendly secondary amendments. Secondary amendments opposed by the bill manager have a low success rate in both chambers, however.

Third, secondary amendments favored by the bill manager have a high but far from perfect success rate. Of the manager-supported secondary amendments to successful primary amendments, 63 percent were adopted in the House and 79 percent were adopted in the Senate.

Finally, successful secondary amendments are associated with primary amendments that bill managers eventually support. In the House, 86 percent of the primary amendments subject to a successful secondary amendment were supported by the bill manager; in the Senate, 90 percent were supported by the bill manager (data not shown in table).

On balance, bill managers appear to do very well in secondary amending activity, consistent with the hypothetical pattern. The tempting conclusion, therefore, is that committee power has been preserved in both chambers by the advantages bill managers gain in secondary amending activity. Committees seem to have retained a remarkable ability to respond effectively to the surge in amending activity in the 1970s.

Such a conclusion, however, dismisses the ambiguities of interpretation in favor of committee power. Many of the complications in interpreting the pattern have been noted in other contexts. First, it is difficult to infer the policy preferences of bill managers and others from their roll call votes on amendments. There are many tactical reasons for a bill manager to support others' amendments, such as buying support for final passage, repelling other amendments, trying to avoid open floor fights, and gaining bargaining chips for conference. Second, anticipation surely takes place. There is no way to tell how many unfriendly amendments were avoided by modifying committee bills before they were opened to amendment on the floor.[26] Similarly, bill managers failed to offer an unknown number of secondary amendments because they did not expect to gain majority support. Finally, many secondary amendments favored by bill managers may represent "damage control" amendments that do not render harmless the primary amendment. Stronger counteramendments often are not acceptable to a majority.

Furthermore, the agitation about the volume of amending activity in the 1970s suggests that committees and the majority party did not see the counteramendments as sufficient protection from unfriendly amendments. Secondary amendments are not always successful, they usually do not protect members from politically embarrassing votes, they seldom reduce uncertainty about floor outcomes, they probably compound scheduling problems and increase the frequency of obstructionism in the Senate, and they do little to preserve a special status for committee recommendations. Efforts to expand the use of suspension motions and restrictive special rules in the House and the continuing interest in some germaneness and debate restrictions in the Senate reflect the limits of secondary amendments as a means for preserving committee power. Thus, for a variety of reasons, no conclusive interpretation of the observed pattern of secondary amending activity is possible.

What is most important, the observed pattern of secondary amending activity still is consistent with the basic conclusions of previous chapters. Committee outsiders are far more important than they once were, more issues are raised and decided on the chamber floor, deference to committee recommendations has deteriorated, and committee autonomy in shaping policy outcomes has weakened. The success rate of bill managers in secondary amending activity does not by itself alter conclusions about the fundamental changes in the character of floor decisionmaking. A fair and very important qualification of earlier arguments is that much amending activity may not have a contentious character: primary and secondary amendment sponsors often find their contributions acceptable to bill managers.[27]

26. This could be done at the committee stage, through a special rule, or even in committee amendments at the floor stage.

27. The positive-sum character of much amending activity is not surprising. In the first place, while many committees represent narrow constituency interests or have an ideological slant that make their policy preferences somewhat unrepresentative of their parent chambers, most committees' preferences probably are not too far from those of the parent chamber most of the time. New policy ideas suggested by many noncommittee members are quite acceptable to the committee. In addition, the fact that members represent separate constituencies (there are two-member constituencies in the Senate, of course) means that it is often possible to incorporate parochial amendments in a bill without impinging on the interests of committee members.

Restrictive Rules and House Committees

The formal ways the House moved to limit and manage floor amending activity in the 1970s and early 1980s had important implications for individual House committees. Those ways included expanding the use of suspension motions, increasing the number of members required to call for a recorded vote in the Committee of the Whole, making it easy to block legislative riders on appropriations bills by allowing the bill manager to call for the previous question before riders are offered, and granting debate privileges to majority party bill managers on motions to recommit with instructions. And, perhaps most importantly, moving to more innovative and restrictive special rules provided a new tactical parliamentary weapon. Innovations such as advance notice requirements, self-executing provisions, and king-of-the-mountain arrangements have aided committees as well.

Assessing the importance of these developments for individual committees of the House is a difficult task because there is no way of knowing how many floor amendments were avoided by employing techniques such as suspension motions and restrictive special rules. The crackdown on appropriations riders clearly has been effective, but the move to more suspension motions and the increase in the number of members required to support a recorded vote were not accompanied by sharp breaks in the number of floor amendments. The focus here is the move to restrictive special rules, which involves, as chapter 3 demonstrated, most major legislation and thus most potential amending activity.[28]

Committees facing the most severe challenges on the floor—those prestigious and policy-oriented committees with large, controversial agendas—have the most compelling arguments for acquiring restrictive rules. A large part of the Rules Committee's work load in recent Congresses was generated by Ways and Means and by Energy and Commerce, as well as by three or four other committees (see table 6-4). It is their legislation that is most likely to provoke numerous amendments, generate protracted debate, and be subject to close floor votes. In the 1980s, all budget resolutions from the Budget Committee and continuing resolutions from Appropriations have received highly restrictive special rules even though, as privileged legislation, they could reach the floor without a special rule. For such controversial legislation, the most obvious alternative to seeking a protective special rule—suspending the rules to pass the legislation without amend-

---

28. For details on the classification of special rules, see Stanley Bach and Steven S. Smith, *Managing Uncertainty in the House of Representatives: Adaptation and Innovation in Special Rules* (Brookings, 1988), chap. 3.

TABLE 6-4. *Percentage of House Special Rules that Were Restrictive or Closed, by Committee, Selected Congresses, 1975–80, 1981–86*[a]

	Congress	
Committee	94th–96th (1975–80)	97th–99th (1981–86)
Prestige committees		
Appropriations	69.2	85.7
	(26)	(21)
Budget	100.0	100.0
	(4)	(11)
Rules	57.1	70.0
	(14)	(10)
Ways and Means	80.6	92.9
	(67)	(42)
Policy committees		
Banking, Finance, and	4.4	25.0
Urban Affairs	(45)	(20)
Education and Labor	8.1	14.7
	(37)	(34)
Energy and Commerce	14.3	26.5
	(91)	(49)
Foreign Affairs	1.9	55.2
	(54)	(29)
Government Operations	14.3	25.0
	(14)	(4)
Judiciary	10.9	39.1
	(46)	(23)
Constituency committees		
Agriculture	5.0	35.7
	(40)	(28)
Armed Services	0	19.0
	(32)	(21)
Interior and Insular	8.7	23.3
Affairs	(46)	(30)
Merchant Marine and	8.0	13.0
Fisheries	(25)	(23)
Post Office and Civil	3.2	60.0
Service	(31)	(5)
Public Works and	21.4	25.9
Transportation	(28)	(27)
Science, Space, and	2.6	0
Technology	(39)	(23)
Small Business	0	33.3
	(2)	(3)
Veterans' Affairs	. . .[b]	100.0
	(0)	(1)

SOURCE: See appendix 2; Final *Calendars* of the Committee on Rules; and various issues of the *Congressional Record*.

a. Numbers in parentheses are total number of measures subject to special rules for each committee. Multiple-committee measures are included in the count for all committees sharing jurisdiction.

b. No rules were adopted during these Congresses for initial floor consideration of measures reported by this committee.

ment—is seldom feasible because the two-thirds majority required for suspension motions usually cannot be achieved.

In addition to the large numbers of restrictive rules certain committees' measures received, the proportion of their measures receiving such rules was also high. For example, 81 percent of Ways and Means measures received restrictive rules in the last three Congresses of the 1970s, compared with 14 percent for Energy and Commerce and 2 percent for Foreign Affairs. By the 1980s Energy and Commerce, Foreign Affairs, and Judiciary were receiving restrictive special rules for much larger shares of the legislation they sent to the floor. Nine out of ten special rules for the major money committees—Appropriations, Budget, and Ways and Means—limited amendments in some way in the first three Congresses of the 1980s. About a third of special rules involving the other major policy committees and a little less than a third involving constituency-oriented committees were restrictive.

Nearly all committees are now seeking and receiving, at least on occasion, restrictive special rules. Rules Committee members even find themselves turning down many requests for restrictive rules that they consider to be frivolous or unnecessary. But care must be taken not to exaggerate the magnitude of the shift to restrictive special rules. Only for the top money committees are restrictive rules nearly universal. Other major policy committees such as Banking, Energy and Commerce, and Education and Labor continue to receive open rules on more than half of their measures subject to special rules. Although nearly all committees have benefited from restrictive rules, the use of restrictive provisions still is not universal or automatic.

Committee differences are even more transparent once the *types* of restrictions on amendments that have been employed are considered. Few special rules are highly restrictive, and those that are very restrictive are concentrated on the measures of just a few committees with jurisdiction over the most important and controversial legislation. During 1981–86 only one of ten special rules—a total of thirty-five—barred all amendments. Nineteen of those closed rules involved just one House committee, Ways and Means, and four involved continuing or supplemental appropriations from Appropriations. The other twelve closed rules affected five different committees. Furthermore, in the same period, thirty-eight rules for single-committee measures provided explicitly for ten or fewer specified amendments, twenty-three of which involved Appropriations, Budget, and Ways and Means measures. The other fifteen were spread among nine different committees, most policy-oriented.[29]

29. The nine committees are Agriculture, Banking, Energy and Commerce, Education and Labor, Foreign Affairs, Judiciary, Intelligence, Post Office and Civil Service, and Rules.

Committee differences are also visible in the pattern of amending activity under restrictive rules (see table 6-5). In the 1980s the four prestige committees and Judiciary and Agriculture had a majority of the floor amending activity related to their measures structured in some way by a restrictive rule. This was true for both single-committee and multiple-committee measures. At the other extreme, four minor House committees—Government Operations, Interior, Merchant Marine and Fisheries, and Post Office and Civil Service—had no amending activity structured by restrictive rules for measures over which they had sole jurisdiction. Only on more complex measures on which they shared jurisdiction did these four committees witness amending activity under restrictive rules.

Again, it is plain that the top prestige committees, particularly Appropriations, have benefited greatly from restrictive rules. The proportion of Appropriations amending activity occurring under restrictive rules, of those measures requiring a special rule, nearly doubled between 1975–80 and 1981–86. The use of massive continuing resolutions in the 1980s contributed to this shift, but many other regular and supplemental appropriations bills have also received restrictive rules. For the top four committees, all of which are vital to the policy interests of the majority party, restrictive rules have greatly reduced uncertainty about what amendments are expected on the floor. Nearly all of the other committees show an overall increase in the percentage of amending activity conducted under restrictive rules.

In short, those House committees with the largest, most salient, and most controversial agendas—those handling legislation that is vital to the majority party and its leadership—have received the greatest protection from the dangers of floor decisionmaking. The pattern reflects the tactical use to which House Democrats now put special rules in response to expected floor amending activity. It also represents a substantial strategic shift in the use of special rules from the immediate postreform years of the 1970s, when the restriction of amending opportunities ran contrary to Democrats' preferences, to the 1980s, when the necessity of firm majority party control of the amending stage was widely accepted by House Democrats.[30]

30. An additional gauge of the effect of restrictive rules in the House is the experience of the parallel committees in the Senate, which have not operated with the protective cover of restrictive rules. The comparisons are not easy because jurisdictions do not match perfectly, committee and party tactics other than restrictive rules affect floor activity, and many other differences in floor procedure exist. Nevertheless, the comparisons are particularly informative for three pairs of committees. With fairly comparable jurisdictions, House Ways and Means and Senate Finance face radically different levels of floor amending activity. Ways and Means, despite the fact that it sent a few more bills to the floor than Finance, faced a third as many floor amendments as Finance in the 99th Congress. For House Appropriations, which also

TABLE 6-5. *House Amending Activity Conducted under Restrictive Special Rules, by Committee, Selected Congresses, 1975–80, 1981–86*[a]
Percent

	Congress			
	94th–96th (1975–80)		97th–99th (1981–86)	
Committee	Multiple-committee measures	Single-committee measures	Multiple-committee measures	Single-committee measures
Prestige committees				
Appropriations	35.7	37.7	67.5	70.3
Budget	100.0	100.0	100.0	100.0
Rules	26.4	56.3	75.0	75.0
Ways and Means	81.0	86.7	95.9	75.0
Policy committees				
Banking, Finance, and Urban Affairs	0	0	20.1	5.6
Education and Labor	11.1	10.9	31.8	5.2
Energy and Commerce	13.5	8.9	54.8	36.9
Foreign Affairs	0	0	46.1	42.8
Government Operations	16.3	16.3	92.6	0
Judiciary	18.6	20.7	61.5	53.9
Constituency committees				
Agriculture	0	0	55.6	56.5
Armed Services	0	0	48.2	48.1
Interior and Insular Affairs	12.2	15.0	51.8	0
Merchant Marine and Fisheries	15.2	7.4	72.3	0
Post Office and Civil Service	2.4	0	76.5	0
Public Works and Transportation	44.0	42.9	63.5	46.3
Science, Space, and Technology	0	0	0	0
Small Business	0	0	4.8	0
Veterans' Affairs	. . .[b]	0	100.0	100.0

SOURCE: See appendix 2; Final *Calendars* of the Committee on Rules; and various issues of the *Congressional Record*.

a. Each committee's amending activity conducted under restrictive rules as a percentage of all amending activity on the committee's measures conducted under special rules.

b. No rules were adopted during these Congresses for initial floor consideration of measures reported by this committee.

The move to restrictive special rules, particularly for the most important legislation, represents an effort to substitute a source of negative committee power (avoiding unfriendly floor amendments) for the sources of positive power that were weakened in the early 1970s. This substitution also suggests that House committee and party leaders found the other sources of negative power wanting. The ability to avoid the damage of unfriendly amendments by holding other legislation hostage, by diluting their effects with second-degree amendments, or by peeling them away in conference has not been viewed by committee and party leaders as an adequate substitute for avoiding unlimited floor amending activity in the first place. There are several mutually reinforcing reasons for this.[31]

The most obvious reason is that the alternative sources of negative power are imperfect tools for blocking, diverting, or forestalling unfriendly amendments. For example, there often is little leverage for committees to gain by threatening to block legislation important to potential amendment sponsors. Subcommittee chairmen serving as bill managers often do not control the fate of such legislation because their subcommittees' jurisdictions are very narrow. Moreover, amendment sponsors, particularly minority party members, may care little about what offering amendments does to the prospects of other legislation. Bill managers may turn to defensive second-degree amendments, but such amendments may not modify unfriendly primary amendments enough to make them acceptable. And floor amendments may weaken committee bargaining positions in conference by giving opponents an opportunity to put the House on record against the committee's preferred policy positions. In some cases, successful floor amendments even can make conferences unnecessary on certain issues by allowing the House to endorse the Senate position.

Beyond their immediate effects on policy outcomes, restrictive special rules have advantages for committee and party leaders that other sources of negative power cannot replicate. The use of restrictive rules compels prospective amendment sponsors to disclose their intentions well in advance of the floor debate, thus reducing floor scheduling problems for the party leadership. And much of the time and effort required to be on the lookout for unfriendly amendments can be saved when amendments must be printed in the *Congressional Record* or presented to the Rules Commit-

---

benefited from omnibus legislating and the crackdown on riders, the number of floor amendments fell by more than one-half between the 96th and 99th Congresses, while Senate Appropriations' amendments increased. Similarly, starting from comparable levels in the 96th Congress, amending activity moved in opposite directions for the House and Senate Budget committees as well.

31. See Bach and Smith, *Managing Uncertainty*, chap. 2.

tee in advance. Moreover, there are times when a committee's reputation within the chamber hinges on its ability to protect agreements with colleagues from floor amendments and embarrassing public exposure on the floor. Committees may seek to avoid a reputation for being easily "rolled" on the floor, even if the damage can be undone later in conference, for fear of encouraging amendments in the future.

Restrictive rules affect more than action on the floor, of course. The prospect of receiving a restrictive rule often alters strategies at stages earlier in the process. In some cases, anticipation of restrictive rules has shaped members' attitudes about modifying legislation in committee. In early 1988, for example, Judiciary Committee approval of a controversial fair-housing bill was delayed by the consideration of numerous amendments sponsored by committee Republicans. Since the prolonged committee consideration took place halfway through the second session of the Congress, the life of the measure was threatened, as some of the amendment sponsors no doubt intended. The refusal of committee Republicans to set aside their amendments led the subcommittee and full committee chairmen to promise that they would seek an open rule from the Rules Committee if the Republicans agreed to withhold some of their amendments and allow the bill to go to the floor.[32] The Rules Committee later complied with the request of the two chairmen.

More conspicuous was the role of restrictive rules in the politics of "domestic summits" between administration and congressional leaders on budget and social security matters. In the fall of 1987, for instance, executive and legislative officials managed to agree on a set of domestic and defense spending reductions that would have to be implemented in a continuing resolution and a reconciliation bill. Only by anticipating that these measures would come to the floor under highly restrictive rules could House leaders assume that controversial commitments, such as reducing cost of living adjustments for social security, would be endorsed by the House. When Rules Chairman Claude Pepper threatened that he would insist that the House vote on an amendment on the social security change, there was substantial doubt that a summit agreement could be reached. An agreement was finally reached after the negotiating team gave up on the plan for including cost of living increases in their package.[33] Once that

32. Macon Morehouse, "Floor Fight Likely over Amendments: Fair-Housing Bill Approved By House Judiciary Committee," *Congressional Quarterly Weekly Report*, April 30, 1988, pp. 1159–60.

33. Tom Kenworthy, "Hope Dims for Friday Budget Accord," *Washington Post*, November 17, 1987, p. A6; and "The Narrow Road to Deficit Accord: Benefits Fight Was Crucial," *Washington Post*, November 22, 1987, p. A1.

threat to the summit accord was removed, the two key measures, developed in consultation with Appropriations and Budget committee leaders, were assured protective special rules for floor consideration that shielded them from crippling amendments.

Conclusion

Committee power has proven to be an elusive subject. The complexities of the strategic context in which congressional committees operate make straightforward inferences from the outcomes of amending activity quite misleading. The vast majority of the policy provisions enacted into law each year still are put in legislation at the committee stage. The pattern of change in floor amending activity therefore reflects a change in degree, rather than kind. Committees remain powerful, even if not as dominant as they once were.

The vast differences in committee floor experiences since the 1950s caution against simple theories of the foundations of congressional committee power. The underlying rules governing the legislative process surely must be central to any explanation of congressional committee power, but the changes and differences in committee power since the 1950s suggest that much more than formal procedures must be taken into account. Parent-chamber indifference, the distribution of staff resources, and a variety of developments external to Congress, as well as formal jurisdictional arrangements and parliamentary procedure, must play a role in any comprehensive explanation of committee power. In some cases, a committee's autonomy appears to be a function of its small, noncontroversial jurisdiction and the parent chamber's indifference to the legislation the committee reports. In other cases, any special influence a committee exercises is the product of its full exploitation of procedural and political resources. In yet other cases, it is the support of outside groups and constituencies that gives a committee the ability to overcome the objections of its parent chamber.

The observations of this chapter reinforce and extend the arguments of the previous chapters. Those House and Senate committees with the most to lose on the floor—committees with jurisdiction over the most important and controversial legislation—indeed suffered the most from the expansion of floor amending activity. Far greater variance in committee floor experiences emerged as the suppressive norms of apprenticeship and committee deference gave way. Secondary amendments, which are employed frequently, give committees an opportunity to minimize the damage of floor amendments, but aggregate statistics on their use give no clues about their substantive significance. In the House, the committees that suffered most from the surge in amending activity turned to restrictive special rules for some relief. Thus, in the 1980s the floor experiences of the major committees of the House and Senate once again diverged. The uncertainties of floor decisionmaking have been minimized in the House but remain unchecked in the Senate.

CHAPTER SEVEN

Conferences and Committee Power

→»X«←

COMMITTEE power appears to have declined as a result of expanded amending activity on the House and Senate floors. This central inference of the previous chapters may be wrong if, at the conference stage, committees can regain everything they lost on the floor. If this were so, the significance of the developments on the House and Senate floors during the past three decades would be quite small. So the question is: Can committees compensate in conference for their losses on the floor?

The ability of committees to compensate at the conference stage is the product of three characteristics of the way differences between House and Senate versions of legislation are resolved. First, most major legislation heads to conference after initial House and Senate action because the differences between the chambers are usually too important and complex to be resolved through informal negotiations and exchange of amendments between the chambers. Second, conference committees are composed, usually exclusively, of members of the standing committees that originated the legislation. And third, once conference committees report back to the two chambers, normal procedure prevents conference reports from being amended; generally conference reports must receive a simple up-or-down vote. This parliamentary arrangement gives committee members a potential ex post veto over floor decisions as long as the conference report is acceptable to majorities in both the House and Senate.

The leverage committees gain by controlling conferences on their legislation has long been recognized to be a vital source of committee power in Congress.[1] But the point should not be pushed too far. After all, the fact that House committees sought protection from floor amendments in restrictive special rules suggests that the committees found conference power insufficient to neutralize the policy consequences of expanded floor amending activity. Still, there is no doubt that committees gain a distinct advan-

---

1. For an excellent discussion of committee power in conference, see Lewis A. Froman, Jr., *The Congressional Process: Strategies, Rules, and Procedures* (Little, Brown, 1967), chap. 9.

tage over their competitors when they dominate the conference stage of the legislative process. The purpose of this chapter is to explore the extent and nature of change in this source of committee power in Congress.[2]

Committee Autonomy in Conference

Committee power in Congress usually is addressed in terms of committee autonomy, the ability of committees to obtain legislative outcomes that reflect their own policy preferences, whether or not those outcomes are consistent with the preferences of their parent chambers. Floor amending activity threatens committee autonomy, unless that autonomy can be protected at the postpassage stage. And committee autonomy at the postpassage stage can be undermined in many ways: amendments between the houses may be used to avoid having to go to conference, committees' monopoly of conference delegations may be checked by the selective appointment of committee and noncommittee members to conferences, and the chambers can defeat conference reports if they so choose. Even the threat of such actions may be sufficient to force committee-dominated conferences to accede to the preferences of outsiders.

As simple as the notion of committee autonomy may seem, the bicameral context in which committee autonomy must be assessed severely limits the kind of inferences that can be made about it. Most obviously, the ability of the first chamber's conferees to peel away unfriendly floor amendments depends on the cooperation of the other chamber and its conferees. The other chamber's conferees may resist changes in the first chamber's bill. Furthermore, provisions adopted through floor amendments are not within the purview of the conference if both chambers adopted identical language. And when conferees strip away unfriendly floor amendments and get the conference report adopted on the floor, it may be due to the intransigence of the other chamber, rather than to the willingness of the first chamber to accept its own conferees' recommendations. Consequently, observations of committee success in reversing floor decisions do not necessarily mean that committees are autonomous at the conference stage. Unfortunately, as was noted in chapter 6, gauging committee power requires detailed information about the policy preferences of the participants at each stage. Because the true preferences of legislators are difficult to discover, the focus must be limited to observable features of the interaction between the chamber floors and committees. In this case, the focus is on evidence of floor challenges to

2. For a detailed examination of conference procedures, see Lawrence D. Longley and Walter J. Oleszek, *Bicameral Politics: Conference Committees in Congress* (Yale University Press, forthcoming).

committee autonomy at the conference stage. At best, such evidence can give only a few clues about the direction of change in committee autonomy; it does not allow any absolute judgments about the distribution of power over policy outcomes.

I measure change in committee autonomy with three indicators. The first is the changing patterns in the parliamentary management of interchamber differences. The use of nonconference mechanisms, instructions to conferees, amendments in disagreement, recommittal of conference reports, and other parliamentary alternatives yields a broad view of interaction between committee and floor at the postpassage stage. Second, the composition of conference delegations is examined to determine whether there has been any change in the extent to which senior members of the committees originating the legislation monopolize the delegations. The final indicator is the record of roll call vote challenges to conference reports on the floor since the 1950s. The expectation is that the three indicators will show declining committee autonomy at the postpassage stage, consistent with the pattern of floor amending activity that has been observed for the period since the 1950s.

Before turning to these indicators, a brief consideration of changes in formal rules is in order. Several formal rules governing conferences and the treatment of conference reports were modified during the 1970s in an effort to make conferences more accountable to their parent chambers.

Reforms of Conference Procedures

Several developments in formal procedure since the early 1970s have provided additional means for challenging committee autonomy at the postpassage stage. These developments reflect the changes in attitudes described in previous chapters. The consequences of weakened norms of apprenticeship and committee deference were not limited to floor amending activity, nor could they be; rather, they extended to the exercise of power by senior committee members in all aspects of the legislative process, including the postpassage stages. In fact, expanded amending activity and recorded voting meant that the policy preferences of the two chambers were articulated more frequently, more clearly, and in greater detail than they had been previously. Even in the absence of changes in formal rules, therefore, more direct challenges to committee domination of the postpassage stages would be expected to have occurred during the 1970s. Developments in four areas of formal rules are worth special notice: appointment of conferees, conference procedure, conference authority, and floor procedures for responding to conference reports.

Appointment of conferees is the responsibility of the Speaker of the House and the presiding officer in the Senate and is done after the chamber has voted to disagree with the other chamber and either requested or agreed to a conference.[3] The Speaker and the Senate's presiding officer generally rely on lists submitted by leaders of the committee or committees originating the legislation. The Speaker's choices can be modified only by unanimous consent, while the choices of the Senate's presiding officer can be modified by a successful motion from the floor, a motion that is debatable and must be adopted by majority vote. These lists were short and dominated by a few senior committee members in the 1950s, but expanded and reached deeper into committee and subcommittee ranks in the 1970s and 1980s.[4] Conference delegations dissolve once a chamber acts to approve or reject the conference report.

Since 1946 the Speaker and the Senate's presiding officer have been obligated to appoint conferees who have demonstrated support for the measure adopted in their chambers. Living up to the spirit of the rules is difficult, however, because members often support some but not all parts of a measure and most members' support for a measure can be expected to be tempered in some way. The rule was frequently ignored, which was not too surprising given the deference to committee members that existed and the difficulty of successfully challenging the list on the floor.

In the early 1970s, as members became less trusting of senior committee members to represent the chamber positions faithfully in conference, efforts to strengthen the formal rule were modestly successful in the House. A 1975 House rule provides that "in appointing members to conference committees the Speaker shall appoint no less than a majority of members who generally supported the House position as determined by the Speaker." The 1975 rule was further strengthened in 1977 with the additional stipulation that "the Speaker shall name members who are primarily responsible for the legislation and shall, to the fullest extent feasible, include the principal proponents of the major provisions of the bill as it passed the House." The initiative for naming conferees continues to reside with the chairman of the committee of origin in both chambers, but the new rule gives House members unhappy with a chairman's list firmer

3. On these conference procedures, see Walter J. Oleszek, *Congressional Procedures and the Policy Process*, 3d ed. (Washington: CQ Press, 1989), chap. 9. For more detail, see Stanley Bach, "Resolving Legislative Differences in Congress: Conference Committees and Amendments between the Houses," report 84-214 GOV, Congressional Research Service, December 31, 1984.

4. The norm of seniority for conference appointments apparently became well established in the late nineteenth century. See Ada C. McCown, *The Congressional Conference Committee* (Columbia University Press, 1927), p. 149.

grounds for informal appeals to party leaders. The Senate does not have a similar formal rule.

House and Senate rules say very little about parliamentary procedure within conference committees. No fixed voting procedures exist, for example. For the most part, conferences are free to operate as formally or informally as they want, subject to the requirement that a majority of each chamber's delegation must approve the conference report. Traditionally, conferences met in secret sessions that often were closed even to other members of Congress. Outsiders often could not determine why certain disputes were resolved as they were, leaving conferees in a stronger position to justify compromises on their own terms. Closed sessions may have facilitated compromises between the two chambers' delegations, but they also made conferees less accountable to their parent chambers.

After a few experiments with open conferences in 1974, the House and Senate adopted identical rules requiring conference meetings to be open to the public unless the conferees of either chamber vote in open session to close the meeting for that day.[5] The House went a step further in 1977 when it required that the House itself must approve a motion to close a conference's meetings. Since that time, such motions generally have been limited to national security matters, and the motions have explicitly permitted members of the House to attend the meetings if they wish to do so.[6] As a result, members, lobbyists, journalists, and others may observe most formal sessions of most conferences. Conferees often have found ways to circumvent the open meeting rule, such as by meeting in small rooms with space for only a few observers, relying on informal meetings of conference leaders and committee staff, or having each chamber's delegation meet separately with staff shuttling between the two groups. In fact, many conferences never hold a formal session. Nevertheless, the majority of conferences are held in public sessions where at least conferees' formal approval or objection to compromise positions can be witnessed by outsiders.[7]

5. See "Reform Penetrates Conference Committees," *Congressional Quarterly Weekly Report*, February 8, 1975, pp. 290–94.

6. For example, at the time the House agreed to go to conference on the 1988 defense authorization bill, Armed Services Chairman Les Aspin moved that "the conference committee meetings between the House and the Senate on H.R.4264 . . . be closed to the public at such times as classified national security information is under consideration: Provided, however, that any sitting member of Congress shall have the right to attend any closed or open meeting." The motion was approved, as are most such motions, on a unanimous recorded vote. *Congressional Record*, daily edition, June 10, 1988, p. H4140.

7. Also in the category of "openness" is the Senate rule, adopted as a part of the Legislative Reorganization Act of 1970, that House and Senate conferees jointly prepare an explan-

The authority of conference committees to modify legislation has long been a subject of great controversy. Conferees must be given substantial discretion to change and create legislative language if they are to find compromises that are acceptable to a majority of both sets of conferees and to floor majorities in both chambers. Rules and precedent provide that only matters in disagreement between the chambers are before the conference (are "conferenceable," in Capitol Hill jargon) and that conference negotiations are limited to the scope of the differences between the two versions. Experience has shown that these constraints are highly ambiguous and difficult to enforce. Limiting the scope of the conference became even more difficult as amendments in the nature of substitutes became more common for large, complex measures. An amendment in the nature of a substitute is adopted by a chamber in lieu of everything after the enacting clause in the other chamber's version, creating a new version that may be different in content, scope, and structure. A conference negotiating differences is given very wide discretion in crafting a new version. In 1971 the House attempted to make more explicit and stringent the constraints on conference discretion by specifying that "the introduction of any language in [the conference] substitute presenting a specific additional topic, question, issue, or proposition not committed to the conference committee by either House shall not constitute a germane modification of the matter in disagreement."[8] Despite the clear intent of the new rule to narrow the discretion of conference committees, ambiguities still arise that give conferees room to maneuver.

An issue unique to the House is the treatment of nongermane provisions attached to measures by the Senate. In 1972 the House adopted a rule that created an effective means to challenge nongermane components of legislation adopted by the Senate or by the conference. Previously, the House was forced to accept the nongermane portions of conference reports or reject the entire bill. Under the new rule, if a member makes a successful

---

atory statement for every conference report. According to the rule (Senate Rule XXVIII[4]), the statement is to "be sufficiently detailed and explicit to inform the Senate as to the effect which the amendments or propositions contained in such report will have upon the measure." Previously, the House conferees wrote the explanatory statement and the Senate relied on that version. (A parallel rule was added to the standing rules of the House as well: Rule XXVIII [1][c].) The Senate now waives this rule at the start of each Congress for reports for which the joint statement already has been printed by the House.

8. House Rule XXVIII(3). The Senate rule is less specific, allowing any provision that "is a germane modification of subjects in disagreement" (Senate Rule XXVIII[3]). In the House, conference agreements that violate the House rules may avoid points of order by receiving a special rule waiving points of order, by being brought to the floor under suspension of the rules, or by being reported as an amendment in technical disagreement. The Senate has no mechanisms for waiving points of order.

point of order that a provision violates the House germaneness rule, the House proceeds to vote separately on the provision in question. Thus the House has reserved for itself the power to consider controversial, nongermane provisions of conference reports, which only its conferees considered separately before.

In addition, the Legislative Reorganization Act of 1970 made it more likely that dissenting views would be heard during floor debate on conference reports. The previous practice in both chambers was to grant control over debate time to the chairman of the chamber's conferees. Under the new rule, debate time was divided equally between the majority and the minority. In the event that both majority and minority managers support a conference report, a 1985 House rule requires that one-third of the debate on the report be reserved for an opponent of the report.[9] The House also adopted, as a part of the 1970 reforms, a requirement that no conference report may be considered until the third day after the report and its accompanying explanatory statement have been filed and printed in the *Congressional Record*.[10] The rule gives members not on the conference committee an opportunity to review the report and mobilize opposition to it. The Senate has not adopted a similar rule.

Two aspects of these developments should be noted. First, the effort to limit conference discretion and to open conference meetings followed closely the expansion of amending activity in the House and Senate. Indeed, floor and postpassage developments should be seen as two threads of the same cloth, that is, both created more opportunities for rank-and-file members to shape legislative outcomes through action on the floor. To pursue floor amendments without concern for postpassage activity would have made little sense for noncommittee members who cared about policy outcomes. It seems reasonable to surmise that the successful reform efforts put conferees on notice that their parent chambers intended to scrutinize their behavior more closely. If that is so, conferees' behavior may have changed even if observable evidence cannot be found in conference membership or overt challenges to conference products.

Second, the House moved more vigorously to limit conference discretion than did the Senate. Perhaps senior committee members in the House had abused their privileged position in conference more than their Senate counterparts. Perhaps committee and chamber policy preferences differed more greatly in the House. Perhaps the possibility of a filibuster on the conference report compels Senate conferees to abide by a higher standard

9. The rule also applies to amendments in disagreement reported by a conference.

10. House Rule XXVIII(2). The requirement does not apply to the last six days of a session and may be waived by a special rule.

of responsiveness, producing fewer challenges to their work than to the work of their House counterparts. Or perhaps the House was simply more inclined to formalize its expectations about appropriate legislative behavior than was the Senate.

For a number of reasons, then, it is to be expected that challenges to committee autonomy at the postpassage stage increased in frequency during the mid-1970s. Moreover, if the efforts to impose formal limits on conference discretion are any indication, the increase in challenges should be greater in the House than in the Senate.

Resolving Differences between the Chambers

The natural place to begin the search for observable indications of change in committee autonomy at the postpassage stage is to survey the use of various procedural devices for resolving differences between House and Senate versions of legislation. There are two basic mechanisms for resolving interchamber differences.[11] One mechanism is to exchange amendments between the houses. In a simple exchange, the Senate amends a House bill, the Senate sends its amendments back to the House, and the House then approves the Senate amendments. Amendments between the houses are difficult to employ when the House and Senate have adopted radically different measures. The other mechanism is to create a conference committee, whose report must be approved by both chambers.[12] Along with its report on areas of agreement, a conference committee may report "amendments in disagreement," which are voted on after the conference report is approved. Before the measure can be sent to the president, the chambers must eventually approve identical versions of the amendments remaining in disagreement after the conference. In practice, the process can become quite complex when a combination of amendments between the houses, a conference committee report, and amendments in disagreement is employed in an effort to resolve interchamber differences.

Technically speaking, the ex post veto is available to a committee only if a conference is held, so the first question is the frequency with which the House and Senate create a conference committee to resolve their differ-

11. For a review of congressional procedures for resolving interchamber differences, see Bach, "Resolving Legislative Differences in Congress."

12. The initiative for the decision to go to conference usually rests with the bill manager for the committee of origin. Before 1965, a special rule was required to send a measure to conference in the House. Since 1965, House decisions to go to conference have been made on a motion from a member of the committee of origin after the motion is authorized by that committee. In the Senate, any member may make the appropriate motion, but the responsibility normally falls to the bill manager or the majority leader.

ences. Great care must be taken in drawing lessons from the frequency of conferences, however. In the first place, members not on the committee of origin may be appointed to conferences, an issue addressed below. Second, the primary alternative to a conference, exchanging amendments between the houses, may or may not involve informal negotiations between the chambers. When informal negotiations take place, they often are conducted by the same members who would have been appointed to a conference. Therefore the absence of a conference does not indicate by itself whether committee members dominated the process of resolving interchamber differences. But because amendments between the houses are normally subject to amendment when they are proposed on the House and Senate floors and conference reports are not, noncommittee members generally have a greater opportunity to shape the details of their chamber's position when amendments between the houses are employed.

The frequency of the various methods of resolving differences between the houses in five selected Congresses is shown in table 7-1. To isolate those measures subject to the most controversy, three classes of measures are identified in the table: all measures concerning public policy on which both the House and Senate adopted some version; "major measures," legislation that was considered under a special rule in the House, which generates the vast majority of amending activity; and "key vote measures," those highly important measures for which *Congressional Quarterly* identified a key vote on some amendment or motion related to the measure. Because the key vote measures are so few in number, some caution is required in drawing inferences from the pattern of change for them.

Two general features of the pattern of resolving interchamber differences are immediately visible in table 7-1. First, the percentage of all measures and major measures on which there were no differences between the chambers (because the second chamber to act accepted the first chamber's version) declined in the 1970s and 1980s. A factor contributing to this trend is the restructuring of the congressional agenda. As Congress began to consider fewer but larger measures, the chances increased that the two houses would adopt different provisions. The expansion of floor amending activity in both chambers also made it less likely that the two chambers' versions would be identical. Second, the chambers have failed to resolve their differences (thus killing the legislation) more frequently in recent Congresses than they did in the 1950s and 1960s. This may be due to the difficulty of resolving differences on large, complex bills, particularly multiply referred bills, and to the larger backlog of legislation at the end of more recent Congresses. It may reflect the difficulty of finding compromise positions that are acceptable to larger and more diverse conference delega-

TABLE 7-1. *Methods of Resolving Differences between the Chambers, by Type of Measure, Selected Congresses, 1955–86*[a]
Percent

Type of measure	Congress				
	84th (1955–56)	88th (1963–64)	92d (1971–72)	96th (1979–80)	99th (1985–86)
All measures[b]					
No differences	67.0	62.4	48.9	37.2	48.6
Amendments between the houses	20.5	24.2	24.5	37.7	31.3
One conference[c]	11.2	11.4	22.1	18.9	11.5
Two conferences[c,d]	0.2	0.5	0.7	1.0	0.7
Differences not resolved[e]	1.1	1.5	3.8	5.3	7.9
Total	100.0	100.0	100.0	100.1	100.0
N	(997)	(657)	(605)	(605)	(444)
Major measures[f]					
No differences	25.4	34.2	23.1	15.8	12.1
Amendments between the houses	27.0	31.6	23.8	18.3	32.8
One conference[c]	45.2	28.2	47.5	53.3	43.1
Two conferences[c,d]	1.6	2.6	1.9	1.7	1.7
Differences not resolved[e]	0.7	3.4	3.8	10.8	10.3
Total	99.9	100.0	100.1	99.9	100.0
N	(126)	(117)	(160)	(120)	(58)
Key vote measures[g]					
No differences	15.4	17.4	12.0	6.7	14.3
Amendments between the houses	0.0	26.1	4.0	26.7	28.6
One conference[c]	84.6	47.8	64.0	56.7	46.4
Two conferences[c,d]	0.0	4.3	8.0	3.3	0.0
Differences not resolved[e]	0.0	4.3	12.0	6.7	10.7
Total	100.0	99.9	100.0	100.1	100.0
N	(13)	(23)	(25)	(30)	(28)

a. Includes only those measures adopted in some form by both chambers, as indicated in the final *Calendars* of the House of Representatives for the selected Congresses.

b. All public bills and joint resolutions, excluding joint resolutions expressing a sense of Congress, recognizing certain events or dates, proclamations, printing resolutions, and adjournment resolutions. Concurrent resolutions providing for the congressional budget are included.

c. Includes any measure for which a conference report was approved by both chambers, including cases that also involved amendments between the houses or amendments in disagreement.

d. Includes any case in which a conference met after a conference report was filed in either chamber.

e. The effect of this is that the measures were not enacted.

f. Measures that received a special rule, or whose companion measure received a special rule, for initial consideration in the House.

g. Measures for which *Congressional Quarterly* identified a key vote on an amendment or motion related to the measure in either chamber.

tions (see below) and to less deferential parent chambers. In the early 1980s, divided party control of Congress also may have increased interchamber conflict and contributed to this trend. Whatever the cause, it is clear that interchamber differences have become proportionately more frequent and more difficult to resolve.

The proportion of measures sent to conference shows no trend, at least over the five Congresses examined, although there are important differences among the three categories of legislation. Important and controversial measures are the most likely measures to produce interchamber differences and require a conference to resolve the differences. Between one-fourth and one-third of all measures with interchamber differences go to conference, while between one-half and two-thirds of major measures with interchamber differences do so. The pattern for key vote measures is quite uneven, although the tendency is for an even higher proportion of key vote measures to go to conference than for major measures.[13] The important point is that there is no systematic trend away from the use of conferences that would suggest a reduction in the availability of the ex post veto.

The absence of a trend away from the use of conferences must be placed in proper perspective. The use of amendments between the houses has been and remains a real alternative to sending a measure to conference for many major bills, giving the chambers a vehicle for avoiding situations that make the ex post veto possible. Between one-fifth and one-third of the differences on major measures were resolved without resort to a conference. Interchamber differences on more than one in four key vote measures were settled with amendments between the houses in three of the five Congresses studied.

Furthermore, a conference sometimes is combined with amendments between the houses or amendments in disagreement. Many combinations have occurred: a conference may follow exchanges of amendments between the chambers, repeated exchanges of amendments between the chambers may occur on amendments in disagreement reported from a conference, or the conference might be reconstituted after the initial report is rejected or after sending amendments in disagreement failed to resolve the differences, to mention just some of the possibilities. Both amendments between the houses and amendments in disagreement give committee outsiders opportunities to participate by offering modifications to them on the floor. Amendments in disagreement, when not reported merely in "technical dis-

13. Key vote measures and major measures are both subsets of the "all measures" category, but not all key vote measures are major measures because some of them did not receive a special rule in the House.

agreement," often reflect the inability of a chamber's conferees to take advantage of a potential ex post veto situation because of the policy position defended by the other chamber's conferees.[14] When an amendment is reported in technical disagreement to avoid a point of order against the report, such as when authorizations are added to an appropriations bill in conference, the amendment may reflect the exercise of substantial discretion on the part of the conferees. But such an amendment is open to amendment on the House and Senate floors and so opens the door to outsiders who seek to modify the amendment on the floor. These complications mean that the frequency of conferences indicated in table 7-1 may overstate the extent to which postpassage adjustments on major issues are made autonomously by conference committees and, consequently, may mask some evidence of declining committee control of interchamber negotiations.

Indeed, there are tidbits of evidence that the parent chambers asserted themselves somewhat more frequently in the late 1970s and 1980s than previously. Instances of one of the chambers rejecting a conference report and turning to amendments between the chambers to resolve differences occurred very seldom in the 1950s and 1960s, but occurred over a half a dozen times in 1979 and 1980 alone. Similarly, instances of complex messaging of amendments reported in disagreement were very rare in the 1950s and 1960s. With only a handful of exceptions, it took only one step in each chamber to recede or insist on certain amendments after the conference report was approved to resolve the remaining interchamber differences. But in the late 1970s and 1980s, a typical Congress had half a dozen or more cases in which amendments had to be sent between the chambers two or more times after they were reported in disagreement from conference. Finally, and perhaps most noteworthy, there was an increase in the number of times a conference report was rejected, a report was recommitted to conference, or a further conference was requested by one of the chambers. During the 84th Congress (1955–56), only five reports were so treated, compared with seven in the 88th (1963–64), nine in the 92d (1971–72), sixteen in the 96th (1979–80), and twelve in the 99th (1985–86). Individually, these developments do not seem particularly large or important, but cumulatively they suggest that the parent chambers have become more willing to challenge conference recommendations and to risk a further conference or pursue nonconference alternatives.

Inferring anything about committee autonomy from these data on the

14. Amendments in "technical" disagreement is the term applied to provisions on which the conferees agreed to compromise but are reported in disagreement rather than as a part of the agreed-upon report. This is done in order to avoid points of order when the report reaches the floor, or for other reasons.

mechanisms for resolving interchamber differences is made quite treacherous by the problem of anticipated reactions, of course. Fully informed conferees could avoid postconference challenges by modifying their report in anticipation of the floor reaction and might as well do so if successful challenges are going to be made in the absence of appropriate adjustments. Thus, even if there was no increase in challenges, conferees' behavior may have changed in ways that could not be observed in the data presented here. However, the small changes that are observed suggest that only the tip of the iceberg can be seen in these data. Just how much change is hidden below the surface is not possible to quantify.

Conference Composition

A more direct way of viewing committee autonomy at the postpassage stage is to examine the membership of conference committees. The most conspicuous change in conference membership since the 1950s is the increasing size of delegations. The megaconferences of 200-plus members on the reconciliation bills of the 1980s have received considerable attention, but the trend is even more pervasive than the megaconferences suggest. In both chambers, the average size of delegations doubled between the mid-1950s and the late 1970s, even excluding megaconferences for omnibus budget measures. In the 1950s and 1960s, the typical conference was composed of five members from each chamber, usually the three senior majority members and two senior minority party members from the committee or subcommittee originating the legislation.[15] The vast majority of the delegations had seven or fewer members (see table 7-2). During the 1960s, Senate delegations began to increase in size; they greatly expanded during the 1970s. House delegations were somewhat slower to grow, but by the early 1970s most delegations were larger, often much larger, than five members. By the late 1970s, the size of House delegations generally exceeded the size of Senate delegations. If the megaconferences on omnibus budget bills are excluded, conferences now average about twelve representatives and ten senators.

Conference delegations have increased in size largely because more members from the committee originating the legislation have been appointed to conferences.[16] Nevertheless, increasing size does have implica-

15. For background on conference composition in the 1940s, 1950s, and 1960s, see David J. Vogler, *The Third House: Conference Committees in the United States Congress* (Northwestern University Press, 1971), chaps. 2, 3.

16. In the 1970s, several House committees adopted their own rules on conferee selection. These rules guide committee chairmen when they make their recommendations to the Speaker. In some cases, the rules guarantee the inclusion of members of the subcommittee of origin for the measure.

TABLE 7-2. *Size of Conference Delegations, Selected Congresses, 1955–86*
Percent

	Congress				
Number of conferees	84th (1955–1956)	88th (1963–1964)	92d (1971–1972)	96th (1979–1980)	99th (1985–1986)
House					
3	22.9	1.2	2.0	0.6	0.0
4	0.7	0.0	0.7	0.0	0.0
5	43.6	74.1	37.3	3.2	8.2
6	0.7	2.4	0.7	13.6	0.0
7	13.6	10.6	19.3	1.3	4.1
8	1.4	2.4	2.7	5.8	6.8
9	7.9	4.7	5.3	20.8	0.0
10	0.7	2.4	14.0	5.8	9.6
11–15	5.0	2.4	14.7	31.8	30.1
16 or more	3.6	0.0	3.3	16.9	41.1
Total	100.0	100.0	100.0	100.0	100.0
N^a	140	85	150	154	73
Mean	6.2	5.8	8.1	11.4	22.3
Adjusted mean[b]	6.0	5.8	8.0	10.5	11.8
Senate					
3	19.0	9.0	7.1	1.4	2.5
4	0.0	1.1	0.6	0.7	0.0
5	52.1	43.8	39.6	25.9	26.6
6	0.7	6.7	1.9	2.0	2.5
7	11.3	5.6	16.2	17.7	11.4
8	4.9	9.0	6.5	12.2	0.0
9	2.1	18.0	5.8	6.1	11.4
10	0.7	2.2	3.2	6.1	2.5
11–15	7.0	4.5	17.5	19.0	20.3
16 or more	2.1	0.0	1.3	8.8	22.8
Total	100.0	100.0	100.0	100.0	100.0
N^a	142	89	154	147	79
Mean	5.8	6.4	7.4	9.7	12.1
Adjusted mean[b]	5.8	6.4	7.4	9.2	10.1

SOURCE: *Calendar of the House of Representatives*, final editions.
   a. The number of conference delegations is not identical for both chambers because one chamber may appoint a delegation before the other chamber agrees to the conference.
   b. The mean excluding conferences that include conferees appointed for "limited purposes," as defined in the text, and so excluding the very largest conferences, such as those for reconciliation bills.

tions for conference politics and committee autonomy. At a minimum, greater size often implies greater diversity in the interests represented on the conference. For example, conference delegations are now more likely to include the sponsors of the various elements of the legislation, even if only committee members are appointed; a handful of senior committee leaders is no longer in a position to unilaterally restructure the legislation in conference. Greater size, then, reinforces the democratization of intra-committee politics that occurred during the 1960s and 1970s.[17] Moreover, greater size creates more points of access for members not appointed to the conference. The monopoly over information about what is happening, what is feasible, and what transpired in conference, once enjoyed by a few committee seniors, has been broken, making it easier for committee out-siders to evaluate conference decisions. Combined with the other changes in conference procedures, such as open meeting requirements, increasing conference size may have improved the accountability of conferees.

The 1970s also brought changes in the formal role of committee outsid-ers on conference committees. In the 84th (1955–56), 88th (1963–64), and 92d (1971–72) Congresses, only 5 of 375 House delegations included members not sitting on the committee of origin (table 7-3). In each case, the noncommittee members were appointed to the conference to represent the jurisdictional interests of another House committee. In the 84th Con-gress, for example, two members of the Committee on the Judiciary were appointed to a conference on legislation designed to crack down on the sabotage of aircraft, a measure that originated in the Committee on Inter-state and Foreign Commerce but had criminal penalties falling in the juris-diction of Judiciary. In contrast, during the 96th Congress (1979–80), after the 1975 and 1977 rules on conference appointments were in place, nearly one in seven House delegations included members not from a committee reporting the legislation.[18] About half the cases involved multiple-committee jurisdiction situations, but the other half were cases in which a noncommittee bill or amendment sponsor was appointed to the conference (data not shown in table). Such cases remained a small percentage of all conferences and normally involved the appointment of just one noncom-

17. For example, the expansion of the conference on a large continuing appropriations resolution in 1985 permitted junior members of the House Appropriations Committee to gain seats. The junior members maintained that they were crucial to maintaining the House posi-tion on antisatellite weapons. See Janet Hook, "The Season for Negotiation: In Conference: New Hurdles, Hard Bargaining," *Congressional Quarterly Weekly Report*, September 6, 1986, pp. 2080–82.

18. The increase in noncommittee appointments began in the 95th Congress (1977–78), following the adoption in 1977 of the tightened rule on appointing the "principal proponents" of major elements of legislation.

TABLE 7-3. *Conferences with Noncommittee and Limited-Purpose Conferees, Selected Congresses, 1955–86*[a]

	Congress				
Type of conferees	84th (1955–56)	88th (1963–64)	92d (1971–72)	96th (1979–80)	99th (1985–86)
House					
Noncommittee	1	0	1	10	1
Limited-purpose[b]	1	0	0	6	5
Both noncommittee and limited-purpose	1	0	1	11	19
Neither noncommittee nor limited-purpose	137	85	148	127	44
Total	140	85	150	154	69
Senate					
Noncommittee	9	9	23	1	0
Limited-purpose[b]	1	0	0	2	1
Both noncommittee and limited-purpose	0	0	0	5	10
Neither noncommittee nor limited-purpose	132	80	131	139	65
Total	142	89	154	147	76

SOURCE: *Calendar of the House of Representatives*, final editions.
a. Each cell is the number of conference delegations including conferees of the specified type.
b. Includes both exclusive and additional conferees, as explained below in text.

mittee member, but even that change represented a significant departure from past practice.

Senate delegations included noncommittee members much more frequently than did House delegations in the 84th, 88th, and 92d Congresses. Committee outsiders were present in 41 of the 385 appointed delegations. However, 38 of the 41 Senate delegations with noncommittee members involved appropriations bills. The Senate's old Rule XVI(6) provided that nine authorization committees could select one or more members to serve on appropriations conferences dealing with matters specified in the rule.[19] After the Senate rule was dropped in 1977, the number of Senate delegations with noncommittee representation fell abruptly. In the 96th Congress, when at least some observance of the new appointment rule was visible in the House, only 6 of 147 Senate delegations included any members not from the reporting committee for any purpose, and all but one of these six cases involved multiple-committee situations. Thus, just at the

19. Under the old rule, three members from each of the nine named committees were ex officio members of the Committee on Appropriations whenever the specified matters were being considered. For background on ex officio members of the Senate Committee on Appropriations, see Stephen Horn, *Unused Power: The Work of the Senate Committee on Appropriations* (Brookings, 1970), pp. 50–62.

time committee outsiders were gaining a toehold in House conference delegations, the opposite was happening in the Senate.

The 1980s represented a new era in conference politics, particularly in the House. In both chambers, the proportion of conferences with noncommittee members increased. Omnibus legislating, which reduced the total number of conferences and increased the likelihood that noncommittee members would seek appointment to the conferences on the omnibus measures, explains a part of this shift. But for recent developments in the role of noncommittee members to be evaluated, the formal ways in which the influence of noncommittee conferees can be limited must be understood. The most common way is to limit the purposes for which the noncommittee conferees are appointed, rather than making them full-fledged, regular conferees. Such limitations are identified in the order of the Speaker or the Senate's presiding officer that appoints conferees. They may take two forms.

The most common way is to identify the outsiders as "additional" conferees for a limited purpose, usually for the consideration of specified sections or subjects. Such additional conferees then serve as voting members of the conference for only those sections or subjects. On all other matters, the additional conferees do not participate, at least officially. A majority of the "general" conferees and the additional conferees is required to approve the report language for the specified sections or subjects, while a majority of only the general conferees is required for the approval of the conference report on all other matters. In this way, the outsiders are given a voice on the matters that most concern them and led to their appointment to the conference, but that voice is limited to those matters and is diluted by the votes of the committee members appointed as general conferees.

A second way to limit the influence of noncommittee members is to appoint them as "exclusive" conferees for certain sections or subjects. That is, a set of conferees is appointed for the purpose of negotiating specified sections or subjects and is the only set of conferees with authority to vote on those sections or subjects. A majority of the specified set of conferees is required for approving report language on those sections or subjects. This arrangement may increase the power of outsiders, depending on the number of committee members appointed to the exclusive subconference. Before a conference report can be filed, a majority of the appropriate set of conferees—whether the set is composed of general conferees, limited-purpose conferees, or both—must sign the report for each section identified in the order constituting the conference delegation.

Such complex conference arrangements were very rare before the late 1970s. In 1955, for example, the House appointed twelve sets of additional conferees, each from an Appropriations Committee subcommittee, to manage a large supplemental appropriations bill, with the full committee chairman and ranking minority member serving as general conferees on all matters. This conference did not involve noncommittee members, of course, but rather was designed to permit a division of labor among members of the committee of origin for a large bill. As table 7-3 suggests, the 1955 case was indeed exceptional for its time.

Complex arrangements became more common in the late 1970s. One reason was that complex arrangements proved to be a convenient way to handle measures affecting the jurisdictions of two or more committees. Sometimes new issues created jurisdictional problems for the committee system that could be managed with a complex conference arrangement. The only complex arrangement in the 94th Congress (1975–76), for example, concerned a measure on the Federal Energy Administration affecting the jurisdictions of several House and Senate committees. In other cases, nongermane Senate amendments created a jurisdictional problem for House and Senate committees. Whatever the cause, multiple-committee situations were responsible for much of the increase in complex conference arrangements in the late 1970s. In the 95th Congress (1977–78), eleven conferences involved complex arrangements for either the House or Senate delegations, six of which involved multiple-committee matters, as did a majority of the seventeen complex arrangements in the 96th Congress (1979–80). In the 1980s, complex arrangements became standard practice for omnibus multiple-committee measures on reconciliation, continuing appropriations, trade, and drugs, to name just a few.

The appointment of representatives of committees with jurisdictional claims, particularly when the appointment is for limited purposes, does not appear to threaten committee autonomy, at least at first glance. Indeed, it might properly be interpreted as preserving autonomy in circumstances that otherwise would threaten it. After all, committee representatives are appointed to protect their committees' roles as the managers of a particular jurisdiction for the parent chamber. In the House, when a favorable complex conference arrangement is combined with restrictive rules, at least for the relevant portion of the measure, a committee gains considerable insulation from outsiders. The House Committee on Ways and Means, which often has jurisdiction over tax-related provisions in measures originating in other committees, has benefited frequently from this combination of procedural advantages during the 1980s.

Committee autonomy is most carefully preserved when a committee's representatives on the conference delegation are appointed as the exclusive conferees for the matters affecting its jurisdiction. The committee's autonomy may be compromised when its representatives share responsibility as additional conferees or when members of another committee also are appointed to the same subconference. In some circumstances, shared jurisdiction among two or more committees may require a "joint" subconference, and the participating committees frequently may not appreciate the mixed company and may not believe that their interests are represented fairly on the subconference. Additional conferees often are carefully appointed so that no set of members from a single subconference is large enough to veto an overall agreement, yet a convenient division of labor still makes possible an expeditious negotiation of House-Senate differences.

For the House of the 99th Congress (1985–86), instances of additional conferees outnumbered instances of exclusive conferees by more than three to one, indicating that complex arrangements frequently compromise committee autonomy to some degree. Included among the cases of additional conferees were the two reconciliation bills, for which House Budget Committee conferees served as general conferees. Budget Committee conferees were at least as numerous as any of the sets of additional conferees representing other House committees. In practice, subconferences were run by additional conferees who were given great independence in negotiating with the other chamber. Nevertheless, the arrangement gave the Budget Committee conferees a right to participate, which they could choose to do when subconferences were deadlocked or subconference outcomes threatened an overall agreement between the chambers.

Complex arrangements also became the standard mechanism in the 1980s for incorporating in conference delegations those members who played a major role in shaping the legislation but did not serve on a committee with a jurisdictional claim. In the 99th Congress (1985–86), all but one of the thirty appointment orders providing for noncommittee representation limited the outsiders' role in some way (table 7-3). The shift in practice was greatest in the House, where only about half the conference delegations with noncommittee members had involved limited-purpose conferees a few years earlier, in the 96th Congress. In the Senate, noncommittee members were appointed more frequently in the 1980s than previously for bills other than appropriations, but they, too, found their participation restricted to certain sections or subjects as provided in the appointment orders.

Thus, while noncommittee members broke committee members' monopoly on conference delegations in the 1970s, the influence of noncommittee members has been circumscribed in the 1980s by procedural innovations in the structure of conference delegations. Committee autonomy was weakened and then achieved a partial recovery. Even Senate committee leaders managed to borrow some of the tools forged by their House counterparts. It seems reasonable to postulate that the expanded use of limited-purpose arrangements made it easier for committee members to tolerate the loss of autonomy that was reflected in the presence of outsiders on conference delegations. The sequence of lost autonomy, recuperation, and a new equilibrium is remarkably similar to the pattern observed for floor amendments and special rules in the House.

The Case of House Defense Authorization Bills

Before turning to the final indicator of committee autonomy in conference, roll call challenges to conference committees, it will prove useful to consider the most prominent illustration of a challenge to the postpassage power of a standing committee: the defense authorization bills of the 99th and 100th Congresses. The defense authorization conferences illustrate well the limits and possibilities of noncommittee influence in conference.

Defense authorization bills have exhibited a remarkable record of floor amending activity since the 1950s (see figure 7-1). An important force in increasing amending activity has been the expanding scope of the defense authorization bill, which became an annual bill in 1961. Also important were changes in congressional attitudes about defense policy and about executive branch domination of the policy field. The Vietnam War and other events led members of Congress to challenge executive recommendations more frequently and to second-guess the judgments of the Armed Services committees, which had jurisdiction over the annual bill. The annual inside game of defense policy became very much a public battle over the major elements of national security and procurement policy.[20] However, Armed Services members continued to hold seats at the conference table—with the occasional exception of including Intelligence Committee members for those few parts affecting the defense intelligence agencies—that is, until the 1980s.

The 1980s brought a dramatic increase in the volume of amending activity on the annual authorization bill. New lobbying groups became active

20. See James M. Lindsay, "Congress and Defense Policy, 1961–1986," *Armed Forces and Society*, vol. 13 (Spring 1987), pp. 371–401. Also see Robert J. Art, "Congress and the Defense Budget: Enhancing Policy Oversight," *Political Science Quarterly*, vol. 100 (Summer 1985), pp. 227–48; John Gist, "The Impact of Annual Authorizations on Military Appropriations in the U.S. Congress," *Legislative Studies Quarterly*, vol. 6 (August 1981), pp. 439–54; Edward J. Laurance, "The Changing Role of Congress in Defense Policy-Making," *Journal of Conflict Resolution*, vol. 20 (June 1976), pp. 213–53; and Herbert W. Stephens, "The Role of the Legislative Committees in the Appropriations Process: A Study Focused on the Armed Services Committees," *Western Political Quarterly*, vol. 24 (March 1971), pp. 146–62.

FIGURE 7-1. *House Floor Amendments Offered to Defense Authorization Bills, 87th-99th Congresses (1961–86)*

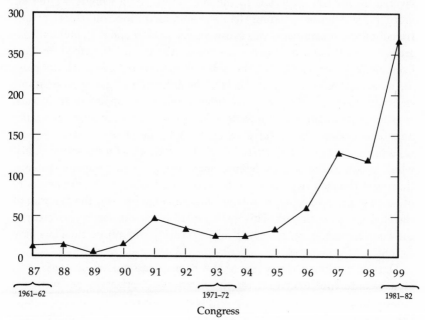

Number of amendments

87 88 89 90 91 92 93 94 95 96 97 98 99

1961–62   1971–72   1981–82

Congress

SOURCE: See appendix 2.

(the Union of Concerned Scientists, for example), providing amendments and resources to members eager to take on the defense establishment. The high public profile of defense issues and defense spending in the Reagan administration encouraged members to pursue floor amendments. And the issues themselves became more contentious and partisan, in part because of the severity of budget constraints. Like many bills of similar complexity, salience, and controversy, defense authorization bills of the 1980s have received restrictive special rules to limit and structure amending activity; but the rules have not been very restrictive, primarily because rank-and-file members of the majority party insisted on challenging the proadministration, prodefense positions reflected in the bills as reported from committee. Amendments on matters such as the strategic defense initiative, the SALT II limitations on nuclear weapons, chemical weapons development and production, antisatellite missile development and testing, procurement reform, and MX missile deployment were considered and often adopted on the House floor during the 1980s.

One of the ironies of these developments is that the move to annual authorizations, originally designed to give the Armed Services committees greater leverage over defense policy and the executive branch, also gave committee outsiders regular opportunities to challenge the defense policy favored by the committees.[21] In the late 1950s, when Congress often favored more defense spending than the administration, the threat of unfriendly floor amendments was substantially smaller and the potential hazards of annual authorizations were not on the minds of Armed Services Committee members. Rather, the committees viewed the necessity of passing an annual bill as a way of checking the discretion of the Appropriations committees, compelling executive branch officials to appeal to them each year for their budgets and programs, and guaranteeing themselves a voice in defense policy. By the early 1970s, though, the House Armed Services Committee was unambiguously more supportive of administration policy, which was pushing higher defense spending and new weapons systems, than were the majority party and often the full House.[22] And the necessity of passing an annual bill meant the committee had to run the gauntlet of the House floor each year. This was reflected in the number and content of the floor amendments, as well as in the scrutiny committee outsiders gave to conference outcomes.

During the first three years of the Reagan administration (1981–83), House conference managers for the defense authorization bill were appointed in a manner consistent with previous practice. But in 1984 conditions changed. For one thing, liberal Democrats were visibly angry about the way House conferees had compromised too much on key House amendments in 1982 and 1983. Many of them blamed those conference outcomes on half-hearted, unskilled negotiating on the part of Armed Services members. Equally important, the Democratic leadership put its weight behind the opponents of the MX missile, thereby pitting the leadership against the compromise position advocated by Armed Services member Les Aspin as well as against the Reagan administration's position. On the key vote, the MX opponents' position won by a margin of just two votes. To strengthen the hand of MX opponents in conference, Speaker Thomas P. O'Neill appointed three additional conferees for the consideration of the MX provisions: two junior members of Armed Services (Patricia Schroeder and Nicholas Mavroules) who opposed the MX and a noncommittee leader

21. For a concise review of the events leading to annual authorizations in 1961, see Raymond H. Dawson, "Congressional Innovation and Intervention in Defense Policy: Legislative Authorization of Weapon Systems," *American Political Science Review*, vol. 56 (March 1962), pp. 42–57.

22. See "Armed Services Committees: Advocates or Overseers?" *Congressional Quarterly Weekly Report*, March 25, 1972, pp. 673–77.

of the anti-MX forces, Les AuCoin. When the appointment was made, Republicans objected to this arrangement, but O'Neill's appointments could not be challenged under House rules. O'Neill appointed limited-purpose conferees for three other issues as well.[23] Reflecting the influence of the three anti-MX liberals, the House subconference refused to budge, producing a deadlock after serveral weeks of negotiations. The impasse was broken only after direct talks between O'Neill, Senate Republican leader Howard Baker, and the administration produced a compromise on the number of MX missiles and other issues.[24]

The 1985 delegation reverted to the more standard arrangement of Armed Services members plus two sets of additional conferees from two committees with jurisdiction over parts of the bill. What had changed between 1984 and 1985 was that Aspin, a fairly liberal Democrat, had successfully challenged the aging Melvin Price for the chairmanship of Armed Services. Aspin promised to be a more articulate spokesman for House Democrats on defense policy and generally had policy views more congruent with those of the majority of House Democrats, the MX issue being a notable exception. Many House Democrats hoped Aspin would do a better job of upholding the House position on key issues than had his predecessor. Nevertheless, many of them sought appointment to the conference, which Aspin actively resisted, arguing that limited-purpose conferees inhibit the bargaining across issues that is essential to a successful conference. Perhaps out of deference to the new chairman, Speaker O'Neill acquiesced to Aspin, whose only concession was to dip farther down the seniority ranking of Armed Services to include liberals Mavroules and Schroeder among the general conferees.[25]

Many House Democrats were outraged by the results of the 1985 conference.[26] Some charged that Aspin reneged on a promise to modify his position on the MX, others were more concerned about his concessions to the Republican Senate on the total spending authorized by the conference version, and yet others complained that Aspin gave in too readily to the Senate in other areas. Aspin's critics were not timid in making their views

23. *Congressional Record*, June 21, 1984, pp. 17707–08.

24. It should be noted that several members considered to be swing votes in the House on the MX issue signed a letter to the conferees insisting on the House version. See Pat Towell, "Difficult Conference Looms on Defense Issues," *Congressional Quarterly Weekly Report*, June 23, 1984, pp. 1479–83; and Towell, "Hill Leaders, Reagan Break Defense Stalemate," *Congressional Quarterly Weekly Report*, September 22, 1984, pp. 2291–92.

25. Pat Towell, "Pentagon's Buying Practices: Battle Lines Drawn," *Congressional Quarterly Weekly Report*, July 13, 1985, pp. 1369–72.

26. Pat Towell, "Budget Dealing Derails Defense Bill in House," *Congressional Quarterly Weekly Report*, August 3, 1985, pp. 1532–33.

known in raucous Democratic Caucus and whip meetings and quickly began to organize to defeat the conference report. Responding to the critics,
O'Neill devised an agreement that allowed the critics to block a defense
appropriations bill that provided for spending more than the House-passed
figure and also provided for the reconsideration of some of the disputed
issues when the defense appropriations bill came to the floor. This arrangement permitted some liberals to circumvent Armed Services, even though
many of them remained dissatisfied that the authorizations conference report would be approved.[27]

Needless to say, Aspin's argument for a standard conference delegation
did not succeed in 1986. By the time conferees were appointed in mid-
September, two of Aspin's Armed Services colleagues, Charles Bennett and
Marvin Leath, already had declared their candidacies to unseat Aspin at the
start of the next Congress, and a third, Mavroules, said that he was ready
to do so. When the conference was appointed, seven sets of limited-purpose
conferees were appointed for major issues, including five sets of exclusive
conferees, in addition to even more junior Armed Services members than
had been included in 1985.[28] The set of exclusive conferees managing the
arms control provisions included nine non-Armed Services Democrats and
nine Armed Services Democrats, including Aspin. As a group, the subconference was far more liberal than the general conferees from Armed Services. Participants reportedly believed that under the circumstances Aspin
would support a compromise on the arms control provisions only if it was
backed by the leading arms control activists on the subconference.[29] External events, such as President Reagan's Iceland summit, intervened to undermine the efforts of the arms control activists, but they ultimately were
a party to the compromise that produced a conference report.

At the start of the 100th Congress in 1987, Aspin managed to retain
his chairmanship in a four-way contest against Bennett, Leath, and Mavroules, but only after losing a preliminary up-or-down vote on his own
chairmanship. The result was seen as a victory for Democratic liberals, not
because Aspin survived, but because a message was sent and received by
Aspin about what the majority of House Democrats expected of him. One
liberal said, "You never heard such a chorus of commitments to arms reduction, procurement reform, and no spending increases."[30] In addition,

27. Pat Towell, "House Accord May Clear Way for Vote on Defense Measure," *Congressional Quarterly Weekly Report*, September 14, 1985, pp. 1798–99.

28. *Congressional Record*, daily edition, September 18, 1986, p. H7192.

29. Pat Towell, "'Pre-Summit' Snags Hill Arms Control Efforts," *Congressional Quarterly Weekly Report*, October 4, 1986, p. 2337.

30. Quoted in Jacqueline Calmes, "Aspin Makes Comeback at Armed Services," *Congressional Quarterly Weekly Report*, January 24, 1987, p. 142.

one of Aspin's chief critics and a leader on procurement reform issues, Barbara Boxer, gained a seat on Armed Services.

The 1987 conference delegation included a set of exclusive conferees to handle arms control issues such as the application of SALT II limits, funding for the strategic defense initiative, and the testing of antisatellite missiles in space. On the Democratic side, nine Armed Services members were on the subconference, including liberals Ronald Dellums, Mavroules, Frank McCloskey, and Schroeder. As in 1986, the major arms control advocates in the House also were appointed to that subconference. A clear majority of the subconference, even when the Republicans were taken into account, favored strong arms control provisions. The arms control group's clout was enhanced by the refusal of the Republican subconference members to sign any compromise report on arms control, requiring fourteen of the Democratic members of the subconference to sign the report for a majority to be obtained. The group's intransigence contributed to a long delay in resolving House-Senate differences, and the eventual outcome was considered to be a substantial victory by the arms control advocates.[31]

In 1988 Speaker Jim Wright was more receptive to Aspin's request that no subconference of outsiders be appointed for arms control issues. Perhaps the Speaker was finally convinced by Aspin's argument, after the delays experienced in 1987, that outsiders unnecessarily complicated negotiations with the Senate, whose conferees had complained about the difficulty of negotiating with a committee chairman who could not speak for his delegation. Or perhaps the arms control activists' argument that Aspin could not be trusted to defend the House position lost some force after his improved performance in 1987. Whatever the reason, no group of committee outsiders was appointed for arms control or other issues, although several subconferences were structured to handle matters affecting the jurisdictions of other committees. While Armed Services members were not pleased with the inclusion of representatives from other committees, they were pleased that the Speaker provided that the members of each of the committee-based subconferences were to be considered additional conferees so their influence could be checked by the general conferees from Armed Services.

In addition, to further enhance the procedural advantages of Armed Services' conferees, the general conferees in the 1988 delegation were made "exclusive conferees with respect to any proposal to report in total disagree-

31. Pat Towell, "Accord in Sight on Defense Authorization," *Congressional Quarterly Weekly Report*, November 14, 1987, pp. 2795–97; and Towell, "Final Amount Depends on Budget Summit: Defense Authorization Clears as Arms Control Battles Fade," *Congressional Quarterly Weekly Report*, November 21, 1987, p. 2865.

ment."[32] Designed by an aide to the Speaker and the parliamentarians, the unprecedented provision gave the Armed Services conferees the ability to report in total disagreement if they were sufficiently dissatisfied with the results of one or more of the subconferences. The provision created the possibility that Armed Services members could stop the conference and return to the House for a newly constituted delegation. The provision was not employed, but it gave Aspin and his Armed Services colleagues a source of leverage, albeit a somewhat unwieldy one, for dealing with obstructionist subconferences.

The recent history of defense authorization conferences demonstrates the potential threat to committee autonomy represented by the 1970s rules changes governing conference composition. The changes lent legitimacy to the demands of House liberals seeking to alter conference outcomes on vital defense issues. They also made it easier for other committees with jurisdictional claims on parts of the bills to gain representation on the conferences. When combined with other reforms, such as the requirement that committee chairmen stand for election at the start of each Congress, the conference reforms made it possible to hold committee leaders accountable for their conference actions to a degree that was not possible before the mid-1970s. A fair conclusion is that the autonomy of the House Armed Services Committee was indeed undermined by the changes in attitudes and formal rules of the 1970s.

Yet the defense authorization conferences were exceptional. The defense authorization bills were extraordinary for the degree to which they engendered intense conflict within the House majority party, which was frustrated with policy outcomes under a popular Republican president and Senate. The House Armed Services Committee probably was more out of step with the majority caucus than were most House committees. Furthermore, Les Aspin, who in 1984 had taken the unusual step of making a personal challenge against the incumbent chairman, probably contributed to his committee's problems by stimulating an interest in retribution on the part of some of his colleagues and raising expectations about changes in policy outcomes for others. Armed Services was much more vulnerable than other House committees.

Even in such special circumstances, the burden of proof for appointing outsiders to the conferences continued to lie with the noncommittee members. The case was made most successfully by leaders of other committees that had jurisdictional claims over parts of the legislation, often due to actions of the Senate. In only three of the eight years of the Reagan ad-

32. *Congressional Record*, daily edition, June 10, 1988, p. H4138.

ministration did outsiders with no committee-based claims manage to gain a special place in the defense authorization delegation. Nevertheless, the challenges to the Armed Services Committee autonomy reached a level that would have been inconceivable in the 1950s and 1960s.

Roll Call Vote Challenges to Conference Committees

An additional perspective on changes in committee autonomy at the postpassage stage is gained from the record of roll call votes on motions related to conferences. Several types of motions are subject to recorded votes that express chamber preferences about conference decisions: the motion to send a measure to conference (with or without instructions); the motion, in the House, to discharge a conference (permitted after the measure has been in conference for twenty days); the motion to instruct conferees or to approve a resolution that instructs conferees; the motion to recommit a conference report (with or without instructions); and the decision to approve a conference report. In the House, such motions always have been considered in the full House, rather than in the Committee of the Whole, so that the teller-voting reform did not affect, at least not directly, voting on conference-related motions. If floor amending activity and other forms of challenges to committee autonomy in conference are guides, recorded-vote challenges to conferences would be expected to have increased in the 1970s, particularly in the House.

Roll call votes are rare for several types of motions affecting conferences, even in the 1970s and 1980s. For example, motions to request or agree to a conference are routinely adopted by voice vote in both chambers. In fact, in no Congress since the early 1970s have more than one or two motions to send a measure to conference been subject to a roll call vote. In most situations, the decision to request or agree to a conference is routine and noncontroversial.

In 1972 a rare instance in which a roll call vote was requested produced the highly unusual outcome of rejecting the motion. At issue was legislation to increase the minimum wage.[33] The House had amended its committee's bill to substantially lower the proposed increase in the minimum wage and to limit the scope of minimum-wage requirements. When Education and Labor Committee Chairman Carl D. Perkins asked for unanimous consent to send the bill to conference, the sponsor of the amendment adopted by the House, Republican John N. Erlenborn, questioned the

33. For a summary of these events, see "House Vote Kills Legislation Raising Minimum Wage," *Congressional Quarterly Almanac, 1972,* vol. 28 (1973), pp. 361–70.

chairman about the list of recommended conferees he was providing the Speaker. Perkins responded that he was recommending that the ten members of the labor subcommittee that had originated the legislation be appointed as the managers for the House. Erlenborn then objected to the request, noting that the six Democratic members of the subcommittee voted against his amendment and could not be trusted to support the House position in the face of a stronger Senate bill. He argued:

> All too often . . . the House speaks its will by amending legislation from [the Education and Labor Committee] or adopting substitute bills and sending the legislation to the other body. All too often the other body passes a bill very similar to that rejected by the House. And almost without exception the conference committee members appointed by the House accede more to the provisions of the other body than they try to protect the provisions which the House had adopted.[34]

The House heeded Erlenborn's warning and on two subsequent roll call votes rejected motions to send the bill to conference, effectively killing the bill for the 92d Congress. Although the House apparently preferred some increase in the minimum wage, the House also seemed to prefer to have no bill than to have the version expected to emerge from the committee-dominated conference.

Somewhat more common than roll call votes on motions to go to conference are roll call votes on motions to instruct conferees or to recommit a report to the conference. When they are offered, both motions tend to involve controversial issues and usually are subject to requests for a roll call vote when they are offered. Roll call votes are most common on the motion to adopt conference reports, which normally is the last opportunity for members to express their support or opposition to a measure.

Some caution is required in interpreting statistics on roll call votes for conference-related motions. While the request for a roll call vote and motions such as those to instruct conferees and to recommit a report usually represent challenges to conference decisions, there are times when conferees themselves seek such votes. For example, key House managers of the 1985 conference on reconciliation legislation providing a tax on manufacturers to fund chemical waste dumps supported compromise tax language in conference but worked against adoption of the report, which included dozens of other reconciliation items as well. They hoped that the necessity of passing the reconciliation elements would lead the House to reject the report, move to strike the tax provisions at issue, and then force the Senate

34. CQ Almanac, 1972, p. 371.

to adopt the amended version.[35] In 1988 House majority party strategists on an omnibus trade bill sought a recommittal vote to allow some members to first cast a public vote to vent their displeasure with the report before being asked to vote for the adoption of the report.[36] In a few cases, a chamber's conferees endorse motions to instruct because it reinforces their own bargaining position in conference. Such strategies are the exception to the rule, however. Some qualified conclusions may be drawn about roll call voting on conference-related motions.[37]

Several features of recorded voting on conference-related motions stand out (see table 7-4). The surge in roll call vote challenges to motions to adopt conference reports in the 1970s is unmistakable, both proportionately and in absolute numbers. This surge was much greater in the House than in the Senate. Moreover, the House continued in the 1980s to have far more roll call votes on adoption motions than the Senate; challenges tapered off in the Senate and maintained a high relative frequency in the House. These general patterns deserve brief consideration before reviewing the pattern for each type of motion.

The surge of challenges to conferences coincides, as expected, with the increase in amending activity in the 1970s. A reasonable interpretation is that many of the same conditions that contributed to the upswing in amending activity—the breakdown of norms limiting participation, increasing external demands on members, increasing challenges within committees to the dominance of their senior members—contributed to the surge in roll call vote challenges to conferences as well. It seems likely that amending activity, particularly that which produces recorded votes on important issues, would stimulate challenges to the independence or decisions of conference delegations. As amending activity increased, more members, particularly those who sponsored amendments, would see a personal stake

35. Jacqueline Calmes, "Deficit-Reduction Bill Goes Down to the Wire," *Congressional Quarterly Weekly Report*, December 21, 1985, pp. 2669–72.

36. See Elizabeth Wehr, "House Vote Raises Democrats' Hopes: Congress May Yet Send Reagan a Veto-Proof Trade Measure," *Congressional Quarterly Weekly Report*, April 23, 1988, pp. 1059–60.

37. In table 7-4, motions to instruct include simple motions to instruct, motions to send a measure to conference with instructions, and motions to recommit with instructions. Motions to recommit include simple motions to recommit and motions to recommit with instructions. Thus the instruction and recommittal sets may overlap in some Congresses reported in the table. A conference report may be adopted in the form of an amendment in disagreement or an amendment in technical disagreement, as is sometimes done to avoid points of order against a report. Because the sources for the data reported in table 7-4 do not distinguish amendments in disagreement that constitute the conference agreements and other amendments in disagreement, such forms of approving the conference report are not included in the table. This has the effect of understating the frequency of roll call votes on the adoption of conference reports. Successful motions to table are included as votes on the motions.

TABLE 7-4. *Percentage of Conferences Subject to Roll Call Votes on Motions to Adopt Report, Instruct Conferees, or Recommit Report, Selected Congresses, 1955–86*[a]

Congress	House Adopt report[b]	House Instruct conferees[c]	House Recommit report[d]	Senate Adopt report[b]	Senate Instruct conferees[c]	Senate Recommit report[d]
84th (1955–56)	7.0 (10)	2.8 (4)	4.9 (7)	2.1 (3)	2.1 (3)	2.1 (3)
88th (1963–64)	22.1 (19)	7.7 (7)	7.0 (6)	1.2 (11)	0 (0)	0 (0)
90th (1967–68)	28.1 (39)	10.3 (14)	11.5 (16)	12.9 (18)	0 (0)	0 (0)
91st (1969–70)	34.0 (53)	7.0 (11)	1.9 (3)	15.4 (24)	1.2 (2)	1.3 (2)
92d (1971–72)	38.4 (58)	5.1 (8)	0.7 (1)	19.2 (29)	0.6 (1)	0.7 (1)
93d (1973–74)	47.3 (96)	4.5 (9)	5.9 (12)	23.2 (47)	3.0 (6)	4.4 (9)
94th (1975–76)	56.1 (97)	6.4 (11)	8.1 (14)	20.8 (36)	0.6 (1)	0.6 (1)
95th (1977–78)	61.2 (104)	9.7 (17)	4.7 (8)	18.8 (32)	5.6 (10)	4.1 (7)
96th (1979–80)	49.0 (70)	8.2 (13)	4.2 (6)	23.8 (34)	1.3 (2)	2.1 (3)
97th (1981–82)	40.0 (34)	4.2 (4)	4.7 (4)	27.1 (23)	0 (0)	2.4 (2)
98th (1983–84)	52.9 (45)	5.3 (5)	1.2 (1)	17.1 (14)	0 (0)	0 (0)
99th (1985–86)	52.2 (36)	6.3 (5)	2.9 (2)	15.9 (1)	2.4 (2)	1.4 (1)

SOURCES: Final *Calendars* of the House of Representatives; and the record of roll call votes provided by the Inter-University Consortium for Political and Social Research.

a. Numbers in parentheses are roll call votes on each type of motion.

b. Includes motions to adopt conference reports and motions to table motions to adopt conference reports. Does not include voting on amendments in disagreement or amendments between the houses that incorporate the text of conference agreements. The denominator for calculating the percentages is the number of conference reports filed.

c. Includes simple motions to instruct, motions to send a measure to conference with instructions, and motions to recommit with instructions. The denominator for calculating the percentages is the number of conference delegations appointed in each chamber.

d. Includes simple motions to recommit, motions to recommit with instructions, and motions to request a further conference. The denominator for calculating the percentages is the number of conference reports filed.

in the conference outcome. In addition, the chamber position would be defined more clearly, particularly on those issues subject to recorded votes, giving opponents of conference decisions a less ambiguous standard against which to evaluate and criticize those decisions. Unfortunately, because of the mutually reinforcing and compounding effects of the various influences on challenges to conferences, measuring their independent effects is not possible.

Curious interchamber differences also are apparent in table 7-4. The 1970s surge in roll call votes on conference-related motions was greater in the House than in the Senate, although there was a surge in both chambers. This is consistent with the earlier observation that the House moved more vigorously than the Senate to limit committee autonomy in conference in the 1970s, perhaps because some House committees were particularly out of step with the parent chamber.[38] But the interchamber difference is not solely a by-product of the turbulent 1970s.[39] Throughout the period under examination, the House has demonstrated a greater propensity than the Senate to cast roll call votes on conference-related motions. A definitive explanation for this difference is beyond the scope of this discussion, but a few possibilities are worth noting.

One set of considerations is related to chamber size and committee assignments. As a function of sitting on more committees and conferences, senators may be more sympathetic about the difficulties their colleagues face in conducting conference negotiations. Greater tolerance of unfavorable conference outcomes might be the result. Furthermore, because of their busy schedules, senators may be less apt to demand time-consuming roll call votes. There is no Senate tradition of minority party watchdogs forcing issues to a vote as there is in the House. And, perhaps due to the Senate's smaller size, the probability that a member will demand a roll call vote is lower there than in the House.

Procedural differences between the chambers also may affect the frequency of the three types of motions in the Senate. The motion to instruct and the motion to recommit are debatable motions in the Senate. Resolutions providing for instructions to conferees, as well as the motion to proceed to the consideration of such resolutions, also are debatable. As a re-

---

38. One prominent case occurred in the Congress just before the adoption of the open-meeting reform in 1975. On a defense authorization bill in 1973, the House adopted a floor amendment providing for a total authorization figure substantially below the figure adopted by the Senate. When the bill emerged from conference, it included a figure even larger than the Senate figure, which angered many members of the House, including the sponsor of the floor amendment, Les Aspin. See *Congressional Quarterly Almanac*, vol. 29, (1973), p. 902.

39. It might have been expected that the greater ease and speed of conducting a roll call vote with electronic voting would have produced more roll call challenges to conferences.

sult, conferees may threaten to filibuster such unfriendly motions and thereby require their opponents to muster an extraordinary majority to be successful, increasing the cost of such challenges to conference autonomy and reducing the expected value of the effort. In contrast, conference opponents have the upper hand on motions to adopt conference reports because they may filibuster. Serious threats of filibusters may produce further concessions in conference, which ultimately may lead to a report that receives broad support in the Senate. Actual filibusters prevent the Senate from voting on the motion to adopt, of course. And if a filibuster is broken by a cloture motion, the motion to adopt is anticlimactic and therefore may not be subject to a call for a roll call vote.

Consequently, the apparent ease with which the Senate accepts conference reports is a little misleading. At least as frequently as the House defeats motions to adopt conference reports, senators filibuster or threaten to filibuster conference reports.[40] Senators who object to the compromises being reached in conference, particularly those who have the support of a sizable number of their colleagues, are in a stronger position to attract the attention of conferees than are conference opponents in the House, where only a majority must be mustered to adopt a report. When the Senate gets to the motion to adopt, opponents to the report either have been accommodated, have not carried through on any threat to filibuster, or have been circumvented with a successful cloture motion.

Of the three types of motions reported in table 7-4, motions to instruct are the least threatening to committee autonomy in conference. Motions to instruct are not binding on the conferees, even though they usually are not appreciated by them.[41] In some situations, motions to instruct are intended to be nothing more than advisory, but in many other situations they are "warning shots" that put conferees on notice of the present chamber's strongly held preferences on an important issue.

The most damaging motions to instruct, generally speaking, are those that demand that the conferees accept the position of the other chamber. They are especially damaging because, if adopted, they directly undermine conferees' arguments about what provisions will or will not be acceptable to their parent chamber; they also indicate that the parent chamber's preference for the other chamber's provisions is held with some intensity. In

40. The motion to proceed to the consideration of a conference report is privileged in the Senate and so may not be filibustered, but extended debate on the report itself is permitted, in the absence of unanimous consent to limit debate.

41. In both houses, only one motion to instruct may be adopted before the appointment of conferees. In the Senate, additional instructions may be adopted at any time during a conference. In the House, additional instructions are in order only after the measure has been in conference for twenty days.

July 1988, for example, after the House had adopted a $7 billion welfare reform bill, Republican Hank Brown offered a motion that the House instruct its conferees to keep the cost of the bill to no more than the $2.8 billion figure estimated for the Senate bill and to support work requirements similar to those in the Senate bill. Despite the complaints of Ways and Means Chairman Dan Rostenkowski that "the conferees should not be bound by an arbitrary spending limit" and that "now is not the time to issue ultimatums and bottom lines," the House adopted the motion, 227–168.[42] The conference ultimately adopted a version very similar to the Senate bill.

Three months earlier, the proponents of a motion to instruct the conferees for an education measure also won an important battle. The House conferees had been instructed to accept a nongermane Senate provision banning "dial-a-porn" telephone services.[43] The House conferees opposed the ban, arguing that the courts would find it unconstitutional, and managed to get the Senate to approve a compromise allowing the services on a subscription basis. The conference outcome was unacceptable to those seeking a complete ban, including the sponsors of the motion to instruct, so they sought a special rule that allowed an amendment on the dial-a-porn provisions to the conference report. Instead of providing for an amendment to the conference report, the Rules Committee reported a rule providing for a vote on the conference report, as filed, and a vote on a separate bill providing for a complete ban. Proponents of a complete ban, believing that a separate bill would not survive in the Senate, managed to defeat the rule and pass a new bill with the education and dial-a-porn provisions, which the Senate then adopted. The House conferees, all of whom were members of the Committee on Education and Labor, simply were defeated by their parent chamber.

While certainly not an everyday occurrence, motions to instruct have been offered and adopted frequently enough to make it clear that they are an option often considered.[44] They have been offered and adopted most frequently in the House. Between 1971 and 1986, thirty-eight motions to instruct were adopted in the House, compared with just six in the Senate.

42. *Congressional Record*, daily edition, July 7, 1988, pp. H5038-44. Also see Julie Rovner, "House Orders Its Conferees to Slash Cost of Welfare Bill," *Congressional Quarterly Weekly Report*, July 9, 1988, p. 1916.

43. See Macon Morehouse, "Measure Sent to Reagan: 'Dial-a-Porn' Ban Approved As Rider to Big Education Bill," *Congressional Quarterly Weekly Report*, April 23, 1988, p. 1078.

44. Examples of successful motions to instruct House conferees to accept Senate provisions include: October 25, 1977, on H.R. 8059; November 16, 1979, on H.R. 2440; December 18, 1979, on H.R. 3919; October 20, 1987, on H.R. 5; and July 9, 1988, on H.R. 1720.

House motions to instruct often are made after the Senate adds provisions that were not considered by the House. Motions to instruct also have been offered and adopted when the first chamber to act appeared to change its position or failed to express an opinion on a provision through a vote on a floor amendment.

Motions to recommit have been offered and subject to recorded votes about as frequently as motions to instruct (table 7-4). They, too, are more common in the House than in the Senate, and they exhibit the same increase in the frequency of roll call votes during the mid-1970s as other conference-related motions. However, if adopted, a motion to recommit stands as a strong threat to conference autonomy. The motion comes after conference negotiations have been completed and a report has been filed— that is, at at time when conferees hope that they have finished their work and often are proud of the results. And, if adopted, a motion to recommit is an explicit and binding rejection of the conferees' work. Accordingly, conferees generally resist motions to recommit more vigorously than motions to instruct, which is reflected in the small frequency with which recommittal motions are adopted. In 1971–86, the House adopted only sixteen motions to recommit (25 percent of the motions made) and the Senate adopted only four (17 percent). In both chambers, the number adopted surged in the mid-1970s: fourteen of the sixteen successful House motions and three of the four successful Senate motions were adopted in 1973–80.

When motions to recommit are adopted, their proponents often are successful in forcing a change in the conference report. For example, in August 1982 the House recommitted a large reconciliation package because it included a provision, inserted at the behest of a Senate conferee, to require a government commission to recommend a congressional pay raise two years earlier than was required by law at that time. The conference reconvened and quickly removed the offending provision. The House then approved the report.[45]

Roll call votes on motions to adopt conference reports are far more common than votes on motions to instruct or recommit. Roll call votes on motions to adopt are demanded frequently because members realize that such motions usually are the last opportunity to publicly express a preference on legislation. Since the early 1970s, the House has cast a roll call vote on over half of the reports that have been filed and the Senate has done so on about a fifth of the reports.

Defeating motions to adopt a conference report is a somewhat more

45. Diane Granat, "After a Brief Panic over Pay, Congress Clears Bill Cutting Expenditures by $13.3 Billion," *Congressional Quarterly Weekly Report*, August 21, 1982, pp. 2047–48.

drastic action than recommitting the report. Defeating the motion to adopt a report not only rejects the work of the conference but also disbands the conference, forcing the appointment of a new conference if House-Senate negotiations are to be continued. For example, in December 1985 the House defeated a motion to adopt a conference report on a continuing appropriations resolution. The House requested a further conference the next day, and both chambers appointed new conference delegations. To facilitate negotiations, both chambers reduced the size of their delegations. The House delegation included the general conferees from the first delegation but dropped all of the additional conferees, whose sections of the resolution were no longer in dispute. The Senate pared back the size of its delegation from twenty-nine to thirteen. A new report was eventually approved. Not surprisingly, conference reports are rejected on motions to adopt less frequently than on motions to recommit. During the late 1970s, when the House attempted to rein in conferences, there was a brief surge in conference defeats: nine reports were defeated in the 95th and 96th Congresses (1977–80). The Senate defeated five reports on roll call votes in the same two Congresses. In the following three Congresses, only four reports were defeated on adoption motions, all in the House.

The 1985 continuing resolution demonstrated the potential utility of defeating, or threatening to defeat, the motion to adopt. House Republicans voted against the motion 55–119, objecting to both its spending totals and to the entire process of wrapping all appropriations bills into a massive continuing resolution. House Democrats also voted against the motion 115–120, with many liberals upset about the concessions made to the Senate on defense spending, several weapons programs, and other defense issues. The product of the second round of conference negotiations, which was approved by the House and Senate, was a cut of $1.3 billion from the defense budget and the adoption of a new restriction on the kinds of expenses defense contractors may charge to the government.[46]

Conclusion

Several threads of evidence suggest that committee autonomy at the postpassage stage has been challenged more frequently since the early 1970s and, at least during the 1970s, the challenges were successful more often as well. Both chambers adopted rules to encourage greater responsiveness on the part of conferees to the preferences of the parent chambers.

46. See Nadine Cohodas, "$368.2 Billion Omnibus Spending Bill Cleared," *Congressional Quarterly Weekly Report*, December 21, 1985, pp. 2665–68.

The House especially sought to reduce the distance between its preferred outcomes and those pursued by its conference managers. Small but notable increases in the use of procedures that circumvent or challenge conferences—resorting to amendments between the houses after a report has been turned down, complex exchanging of amendments in disagreement, and outright rejection of reports—occurred in the House during the 1970s. Committees lost their monopoly on conference membership in the late 1970s, and roll call vote challenges to conference decisions surged in the mid-1970s.

No single one of these developments makes a strong case for the demise of committee autonomy, but, when taken in the aggregate, they appear to represent a substantial weakening of committee autonomy at the conference stage. Autonomy was defined at the outset of this chapter as the ability of committees to obtain legislative outcomes that reflect their own policy preferences, whether or not those outcomes are consistent with the preferences of their parent chambers. The evidence suggests that during the 1970s members of both chambers, but more so in the House, became more willing to challenge committee autonomy at the postpassage stage and became marginally more successful in doing so. The difficulty of judging the policy significance of such challenges, and of actions taken by committees in anticipation of possible challenges, prevents stronger inferences from the evidence about the absolute level of damage done to committee autonomy by the late 1970s.

Committees seemed to recover to a certain extent during the 1980s. Creating separate subconferences provided a means for limiting the influence of outsiders in conferences, and floor challenges to conference reports subsided somewhat, although such challenges remained at a level substantially higher than in the 1950s and 1960s. Postpassage politics may have reached a new equilibrium. The power of standing committees is not threatened as overtly as it was in the 1970s, particularly in the House, and yet committees cannot assume that their parent chambers would defer to their recommendations as a matter of well-established norms.

Nevertheless, the more fully decentralized system of the 1950s, supported by a set of well-integrated norms and procedural obstacles to rank-and-file participation, has disappeared. Committee power is now more dependent on the active exercise of procedural advantages on the floor and at the postfloor stages. And the exercise of those procedural advantages is now more actively scrutinized by committee outsiders. The balance may have shifted back toward the committees in the 1980s, leaving them the central actors in congressional policymaking, but patterns of decisionmaking in both chambers remain far more collegial in character than they were before the 1970s.

CHAPTER EIGHT

Debate, Deliberation, and Reform

T HE STORY told in this book is one of institutional innovation and adaptation to changing conditions. A wide range of mutually reinforcing developments enhanced the role of the House and Senate floors as arenas for policymaking. More complex and controversial issues, growing constituencies, an expanding community of interest groups and lobbyists in Washington, intensifying campaign pressures, and personal policy interests motivated members to pursue issues more frequently on the chamber floors. The loosening of the stranglehold of the conservative committee chairmen and their supporting coalitions, the demise of restraining prescriptive norms, and the reform of House voting procedures lowered the barriers to participation in floor decisionmaking. By the early 1970s the political context of floor decisionmaking had changed in fundamental ways, altering the incentives for participation and transforming the nature of decisions made on the floor.

In both chambers of Congress, the process of adjustment to the new context was a highly interactive, strategic one. In the House, a remarkable change in rank-and-file attitudes about the role of the floor was complete by the mid-1970s. Building frustration with floor procedures that reinforced the power of a few senior committee chairmen and discouraged the participation of many members eventually produced a new system of recorded voting in the Committee of the Whole. The surge in floor amendments that followed the reform of voting procedures posed problems for leaders, committees, and the majority party. Leaders and committees responded in several ways: changes in rules governing floor voting procedures, strategic packaging of legislation, innovation in the uses of special rules. But members who valued their ability to contribute to policy on the floor also wanted their contributions protected in conference. This desire led to rules changes and more roll call votes to hold conferees more accountable to their parent chambers. Leaders and committees responded with creative arrangements in conference appointments.

True to form, change in the Senate tended to be less dramatic, but it was equally interactive and strategic. An escalation of floor amending activity, increasingly severe time constraints, increased use of extended debate and holds, repeated efforts to modify Rule XXII, adoption of restrictions on floor debate amendments for budget measures, and elaboration of complex unanimous consent agreements interacted to change the strategic context of Senate floor politics.

In both chambers, then, the net result of three decades of change was to shift decisionmaking processes away from the traditional centralized-decentralized continuum and toward a more collegial, floor-oriented process. Although the House has managed to moderate this shift through a variety of procedural innovations, the very necessity of procedural safeguards indicates the continuing influence of rank-and-file and minority party members who seek to alter policy on the floor. The evolutionary process continues in both chambers.

Central Arguments

In describing the process of change in House and Senate floor politics, I have made several overlapping arguments. First, change in congressional decisionmaking processes cannot be characterized in terms of movement along a simple centralized-decentralized continuum. Congress is not like a hierarchical bureaucracy or corporation whose central managers determine the appropriate location for making certain kinds of decisions. The location of congressional decisionmaking shifts not only between the standing committees and central party leaders, but also between rank-and-file members and the committees and party leaders. Nearly all important congressional decisions are constrained by the necessity of obtaining majority support on the floor, where members share equal voting power. Developments in the rules and practices of floor deliberations in the past three decades draw attention to this fundamental feature of Congress.

A second emphasis has been that the House reforms of the 1970s were much richer and more complex than the reforms of the committee system alone would indicate. Reform of the formal procedures touched on many elements of House decisionmaking, including the floor and conferences, and changes in Congress's political environment stimulated change beyond the scope generated by alterations in formal rules. In both chambers, floor challenges to committee products skyrocketed during the 1970s, transforming the strategies of all participants in congressional politics.

The importance of formal rules in molding behavior and outcomes also has been a central theme. Recorded electronic voting in the House, the necessity of obtaining unanimous consent to limit debate and amendments in the Senate, and the procedures governing the resolution of interchamber differences have great effect on the relationship among the floors, party leaders, and committees. There are many other forces that shape congressional behavior, of course, and yet the central role of formal procedure in structuring incentives for floor activity has been quite obvious.

Formal rules are important not only to the explanation of changes in congressional behavior over time, but also to the explanation of fundamental differences between the chambers. In 1967 Lewis Froman described the House as more formal, more hierarchically organized, and subject to more rigid rules than the Senate.[1] The differences seemed to fade somewhat after the floor and committee reforms were implemented by the House in the 1970s. As House reforms made House voting procedure on amendments more similar to Senate voting procedure, the pattern of amending activity in the House began to look much like that of the Senate. But the record of the 1980s reinforced Froman's basic conclusions. When the House majority party leadership shifted its tactics toward using special rules, House amending activity once again developed a distinctive cast. The House now is in a postreform period quite different from the unsettled period of the late 1970s, while Senate floor practices look much the same in the 1980s as they did in the 1970s. The House remains more majoritarian and dependent on formal rules to structure the decisionmaking practices; the Senate remains more individualistic and dependent on informally devised decisionmaking practices.

Another theme has been the complex nature of the interaction between formal rules and interparty conflict. On the one hand, rules changes often have been motivated by interparty conflict as the parties sought procedural advantages. The conflict over formal procedure is, in part, a product of a long-standing tension in Congress between the desire to air all points of view on the floor and the necessity of streamlining decisionmaking processes so Congress can manage its work load. Majority parties err on the side of streamlining the process; minority parties err on the side of open and unlimited discussion of policy alternatives. On the other hand, rules governing formal procedure often shape the character of interparty conflict. The last two decades have shown how the majority party can produce effective procedural change in the majoritarian House but still may be blocked by an aggressive minority in the more egalitarian Senate. In the House, developments in the use of the floor frequently have a distinct partisan cast. In the Senate, new rules and practices have been the product of explicit or implicit interparty negotiations and agreements; opposition to

1. Lewis A. Froman, Jr., *The Congressional Process: Strategies, Rules, and Procedures* (Little, Brown, 1967), p. 7.

reform proposals often comes from individual senators of both parties concerned about losing personal prerogatives on the floor.

The vital role of the national policy agenda in shaping decisionmaking processes within Congress also has been an important theme. New and divisive issues in the 1960s and 1970s encouraged rank-and-file members to challenge committee recommendations, turned committees against each other, and encouraged disrespect for traditional ways of doing things. In the 1980s the pervasive effects of huge budget deficits restructured the legislative packages that organized debate, stimulated innovations in special rules, and created new opportunities and constraints for standing committees and individual members. The powerful effect of the political agenda on decisionmaking processes is one of the reasons why predicting the future of congressional practices is so hazardous.

Qualifying the themes of change has been the frequent observation that important features of the decisionmaking processes in both chambers remain in place. The bulk of congressional decisions still are made in committee. And decisions made elsewhere—in party caucuses, on the floor, or in conference—are heavily influenced by committee preferences. For reasons that include the burden of a large work load and the necessity of a division of labor, the special procedural advantages of committees, and informal attitudinal norms, the standing committees remain central to most decisions on most issues. In the House, where standing committees came under severe attack in the 1970s, the committees have shown great resilience. In partnership with the majority party leadership and the Committee on Rules, the major House committees managed to reduce much of the uncertainty about floor deliberations. In both chambers, committees, with the support of party leaders, responded in creative ways to the challenges to their autonomy at the conference stage. The fact that committees and party leaders were compelled to respond in these ways indicates that the developments on the floors were important and threatening; the fact that committees were able to make some adjustments suggests that committees, particularly in the House, retained valuable political and parliamentary advantages over rank-and-file members.

Debate and Deliberation on the Floor

Improving the operations of the House and Senate floors is a subject of continuing interest. In late 1988 the House Republican Research Committee issued a report entitled "A Call for Congressional Reform," and just a week later the Senate Committee on Rules and Administration issued its

Report on Senate Operations, 1988, both of which addressed floor procedure as well as many other elements of standing rules and informal practice.[2] The House Republican report was only the latest of a series of reform documents that House Republicans have produced at the end of recent Congresses in preparation for the modification and adoption of the standing rules at the start of the next Congress. The Senate committee's report was the fifth major report by Senate committees or task forces since 1976 that included significant proposals for altering the chamber's standing rules on floor procedure. Such efforts are endemic to Congress, which is, after all, a representative assembly whose decisionmaking processes are not fixed constitutionally and thus are subject to influence from its changing political environment and from the shifting political needs of its members.

The most common approach to evaluating proposed reforms is to examine their partisan or factional implications. Partisan and factional considerations, after all, often motivate the proposals in the first place. Such evaluations tend to be short-sighted, however. As the electoral fortunes of the parties and factions within the parties change, the distribution of advantages and disadvantages created by parliamentary procedures is usually altered as well. The approach taken here is to consider the more generic functions of the chamber floors, identify the distinctive functions of each chamber's floor, and note the weaknesses of current practice as measured against the identified functions.

Debate and Deliberation

The House and Senate floors share certain basic functions. All legislation ultimately must be approved in identical form by both chambers; the chambers hear appeals of committee decisions at the floor stage; the chambers and individual members record their policy preferences and react to presidential vetoes on the floor; floor speeches are used by members to explain their votes and advertise themselves; and, what is perhaps just as important, discussion at the floor stage contributes to the sense of legitimacy and fairness of congressional decisions. And yet, as has been described in detail throughout this book, the two chambers structure floor consideration of legislation very differently. These differences reflect distinctive views about the function of floor discussion in policymaking.

2. The Republican reports generally can be found in the *Congressional Record* at the time the standing rules are adopted at the start of each Congress. For their 1988 report, see *Congressional Record,* daily edition, October 21, 1988, pp. E3655–57. For the Senate report, see *Report on Senate Operations, 1988,* Committee Print, Senate Committee on Rules and Administration, 100 Cong. 2 sess. (Government Printing Office, 1988).

Discussion is highly valued in most legislative bodies, or at least ought to be, in the view of many critics.[3] Discussion is no substitute for coalition building and bargaining, particularly in a large, complex, and decentralized institution like Congress, but even in Congress legislators regularly demonstrate a commitment to and appreciation of discussion about the merits and politics of their policy choices. Ideally, discussion among legislators is the means by which common interests are distilled from narrow interests, innovative public policy is identified and nurtured, and members and the public become educated about the substantive and political implications of the policy options they face.

Discussion comes in many forms, so it is useful to distinguish between two types that are emphasized in legislative bodies: debate and deliberation. The two terms often are used interchangeably or in tandem, as they have been to this point in this book, and they certainly are used interchangeably by most members of Congress. Reserving the terms for a more technical purpose will facilitate a more precise definition of the unique functions of the House and Senate floors, even as seen by representatives and senators themselves.

Debate refers to a verbal contest between people of opposing views. It is a contest in which emphasis is placed on coherent argument and well-developed differences of opinion. Generally, the opposing views are sufficiently crystallized that the discussion is well focused on a small set of alternatives. Debate is inherently strategic, with each side of the argument anticipating the arguments of the other side, preparing to refute those arguments and avoiding arguments that weaken one's own case. Evidence is presented to support conclusions already drawn rather than to be freshly evaluated. An underlying assumption of debate is that the best solutions can be discovered through the presentation of the strongest cases for lim-

3. My thoughts on discussion, debate, and deliberation have benefited from discussions with Jane J. Mansbridge, whose book, *Beyond Adversary Democracy* (University of Chicago Press, 1983), stimulated my thinking about the nature of congressional discussion. Also see her "Motivating Deliberation in Congress," a paper prepared for the Bicentennial Conference, "E Pluribus Unum: Constitutional Principles and the Institutions of Government," University of Dallas, October 16-18, 1986; Brian Barry, *Political Argument* (New York: Humanities Press, 1965); and two papers by Joseph M. Bessette: "Is Congress a Deliberative Body?" in Dennis Hale, ed., *The United States Congress* (Boston College, 1982), pp. 3–11, and "Deliberation in Congress," a paper prepared for the 1979 annual meeting of the American Political Science Association. Bessette notes the traditional emphasis on deliberation in several classic statements on legislatures. Also see Edmund Burke, *The Works of the Right Honorable Edmund Burke* (Little, Brown, 1894), vol. 2, pp. 95–96; Carl J. Friedrich, *Constitutional Government and Democracy: Theory and Practice in Europe and America*, 4th ed. (Waltham, Mass.: Blaisdell, 1968), chap. 17; and Woodrow Wilson, *Congressional Government* (Meridian, 1956), especially pp. 61–79.

ited, feasible alternatives. Alternatives are limited by some preliminary screening process, such as might be provided by a committee system.

Deliberation, in contrast, involves a careful consideration of all alternatives. No premium is placed on crystallized options, well-focused discussion, or rapid decision. Preliminary processes for screening alternatives are thought to undermine the essential features of deliberation. Broad participation is valued because it enhances the range of options that are identified, developed, and discussed. Reasoning together about the nature of a problem and solutions to it is emphasized over argumentation and refutation. The views of others are accorded equal validity and importance until the evidence, jointly evaluated, proves that they are untenable or must be modified. An underlying assumption of deliberation is that from a slow, cautious discussion of the issues a consensus will emerge around common interests.

The two forms of discussion have important features in common. In both forms, it is assumed that the discussion will serve to persuade at least a few participants of the appropriate course of action. This means that at least some participants remain uncommitted or capable of changing their preferences as a result of the discussion. Participants also are assumed to be sufficiently independent to make judgments based upon what they hear. And in both forms participants are assumed to have at least certain shared interests, perhaps only to see that conflict is resolved peacefully, which makes it possible to conduct discussion in a civil manner. Finally, both debate and deliberation involve more than eloquent speech. Debate and deliberation are interactive processes between speechmakers and between speechmakers and their audiences.

In neither chamber of Congress does floor discussion achieve the ideal form of either debate or deliberation. Few members are persuaded of the merits of a policy by floor discussion, particularly on matters of much importance or controversy. Much of the talk on the House and Senate floors has merely symbolic and theatrical purposes. Addressing external audiences obviously serves members' personal political goals. Less obvious is the institution's interest in reinforcing the sense of legitimacy of its decisions. And speeches aimed at colleagues may serve to educate them about the policy implications of the votes they were going to cast in any event. It is pointless to hope that the two chambers make such fundamental changes in how they conduct their business that they could achieve the ideal forms of debate and deliberation on their floors. Factors such as the important role of the president and other external agenda setters, the large congressional work load, and the size of the two bodies weigh against setting pure debate or deliberation as a standard for evaluating change and reform.

To say that floor discussion is far from ideal is not to say that little debate or deliberation takes place in Congress. To the contrary, debate and deliberation occur frequently and everywhere. A great deal of debate and deliberation transpires before most major policy decisions are made: in informal meetings between members, constituents, lobbyists, and administration officials; in committee and subcommittee meetings and hearings; in party committees, task forces, and caucuses; in the newspapers and on television; and on the floor. Indeed, a critical feature of the House and Senate floors is to provide members a final opportunity to discuss the merits of legislation before passage.

Nor should it be assumed that pure debate or pure deliberation is necessarily desirable on the chamber floors. Because of the substantial discussion that occurs before bringing legislation to the floor, floor discussion often would be redundant and inefficient. In other cases, extensive floor discussion of extremely divisive issues may so damage political relations among members and their constituencies, or perhaps so entangle the chambers in lengthy discussion about policy disputes that cannot be resolved, that it would undermine the ability of the chamber to conduct meaningful discussion on other issues. In practice, therefore, debate and deliberation must be carefully managed by legislative leaders, and perhaps judiciously regulated by formal rules, if they are to serve their intended functions.

Nevertheless, nearly all legislative bodies value floor discussion. They tend to emphasize one form of discussion over the other. The preference for either debate or deliberation may reflect the agenda-setting mechanisms in political systems. For example, American legislatures, particularly Congress, are more deliberative than parliaments in which the alternatives are structured in advance by the government. Logistical considerations also play a role. Full participation and protracted discussion of unstructured alternatives is impractical in legislative bodies that have a large membership and are burdened with large work loads. Various political considerations—the expectations of members and constituents, confidence in the expertise and judgment of agenda setters, the complexity of the issues— also shape preferences for debate or deliberation. And philosophies about what constitutes democratic procedure, affected as they may be by practical considerations, also play a role.

Central Tendencies in the House

The central tendencies in the attitudes of the two chambers of Congress are quite distinctive. The House clearly emphasizes debate over deliberation, while the Senate places much more emphasis than the House on floor deliberation. The difference between the chambers is a matter of degree, but it is so clear that any treatment of floor operations must take it into account. The difference suggests that the criteria for evaluating current practices and reform proposals should reflect the special character of each chamber.

In the House, the emphasis on debate is embodied in the standing rules that govern floor discussion and is reflected in the dramatic changes in special rules of the last decade. The standing rules provide for a highly structured discussion of legislation. Measures are considered in the Committee of the Whole on a title-by-title or section-by-section basis. Amendments must be germane to the particular title or section before the chamber; amendments to a particular title or section may not be considered after the chamber has moved on to the next title or section. The discussion of amendments is limited to five minutes a side, and pro forma amendments are seldom used to raise issues not germane to the title or section before the chamber. The standing rules allow bill managers or floor leaders to limit discussion of measures if majority support can be obtained (this is possible with the previous-question motion in the House and the motion that the committee rise in the Committee of the Whole).

Special rules make discussion in the House even more debate-oriented. A standard feature of special rules, under which most major legislation is considered, is a requirement that general debate be confined to the bill. And control over the use of time during general debate is given to the majority and minority managers of the bill. Restrictive special rules often further focus and limit discussion by limiting the number of amendments and structuring their consideration. Innovative provisions in special rules also structure discussion. For example, king-of-the-mountain rules allow the House to focus its attention on a few major alternatives without the burden of title-by-title consideration and to set debate limits more generous than those provided under the five-minute rule. So the basic thrust of restrictive special rules is the same as the standing rules—to carefully limit and structure debate and the amending process.

Although a few representatives oppose restrictions of any kind as a matter of principle, the vast majority of members have demonstrated a willingness to support special rules for controversial bills in order to limit amendments and discussion to the major alternatives that have crystallized during prefloor stages. Republican objections to restrictive rules reflect the perceived partisan advantage created by some rules, but Republicans, too, have supported efforts to limit the focus of floor activity on controversial, complex measures to the most important issues. Republican alternatives to restrictive rules proposed by the Democrats also have usually restricted amendments and debate.

House debate on limited alternatives is consistent with a process that relies heavily on a committee system. The committee system assists the House in crystallizing alternatives. The rules of the House grant substantial parliamentary advantages to committees, particularly with respect to blocking new proposals. Special rules often further enhance the privileged position of committee recommendations. These advantages, along with the resource advantages that committees still retain, help to narrow the focus and improve the coherence of floor debate.

To overstate the case a little, then, the more decentralized character of House decisionmaking fosters more coherent, efficient, and adversarial floor debate. Decentralization and active floor debate are not fully compatible, of course, since meaningful floor debate would not have a place in a purely decentralized system. The House seems to prefer a mix that combines substantial reliance on committees to set the boundaries of floor discussion with broad opportunities to debate the issues and consider alternatives within those boundaries.

Central Tendencies in the Senate

The Senate gives far greater emphasis to deliberation. The Senate's boast that it is the "greatest deliberative body in the world" reflects senators' general preference for few limits on the issues they can raise, on when they can raise new issues, and for how long they can discuss issues of their choice. Extended debate is protected by Rule XXII, the absence of a general germaneness rule, and informal practices, such as the reliance on unanimous consent to set time limits on the consideration of measures and amendments. "Debate" is the term senators use most often to describe floor discussion (except, perhaps, "speech making") but the context and details of their comments suggest that most senators lean toward a format that is much less structured and focused than is typical of the House.

Senators' views on the role of the floor were made quite explicit in the 1982 and 1986 battles over televising floor sessions and related rules changes.[4] Although senators differed greatly about the proper role of the floor, particularly in relation to the role of standing committees, both proponents and opponents of television made the quality of floor deliberations central to their arguments. In successfully opposing the 1982 reform proposals, Senator Russell Long asserted that "the Senate must be preserved as a body where a minority, be it wrong or right, has the opportunity to

4. On the 1982 debate, see Richard F. Fenno, Jr., "The Senate through the Looking Glass: The Debate Over Television," paper prepared for the Hendricks Symposium on the U.S. Senate, University of Nebraska-Lincoln, October 6-8, 1988.

make its case."[5] Long feared that the logistics of televised sessions, along with the incentives for grandstanding that the presence of television cameras would create, would force the Senate to adopt rules limiting free debate.

The leading proponent of television in 1982, Howard Baker, argued that television would have no such effect:

> The Senate is a great institution. It is the balance wheel which keeps democracy on track. It is the framework on which the Republic is constructed. It is the essence of compromise. It is the only place where there is unfettered expression of individual views. It is the last fortress that can be used to defend against the tyranny of a temporary majority. I would not change a thing about that.[6]

Baker believed not only that the Senate could retain its unique character with televised sessions, but also that televised sessions would bring senators back to the floor to listen to each other, to once again make the Senate floor the nation's most important public forum—a function, he noted, that the floor served in the period before the Civil War.[7] Both Baker and Long placed high value on the slower, less constrained discussion of issues on the floor.

The same arguments were offered in 1986 when the resolution providing for televised floor sessions was finally adopted, although the 1986 debate differed from that of 1982 in an important respect: in 1986 the television proposal was tied explicitly to a larger set of procedural reforms by its primary sponsor, Minority Leader Robert Byrd. The direct linkage of television to other rules changes, which was demanded by some tentative supporters of television, led senators to address, even more explicitly than in 1982, those specific features of Senate procedure that make its floor unique: extended debate and the lack of a germaneness rule for amendments.

The defense of extended debate was made in response to Byrd's proposal to limit debate on motions to proceed. Senator William Armstrong led the opposition, arguing that it would be "a change of drastic and fundamental nature."

> The significance [of extended debate on the motion to proceed] is not to delay the Senate but, in fact, to enhance the procedures of the Senate,

---

5. *Congressional Record*, February 8, 1982, p. 991.
6. *Congressional Record*, February 3, 1982, p. 744.
7. Fenno, "The Senate through the Looking Glass," p. 17.

because when every Senator has the right to prolong debate on a motion to proceed, then it brings every Senator into the process and the accommodations which are the day-to-day work of the Senate. For example, if a bill is coming up in which a Senator is interested, he sends a notice through his cloakroom to the leader, "Please protect my rights to be on the floor and object to a unanimous-consent request to proceed to a bill." That is a signal. It is a signal that that Senator has an amendment to offer or is opposed to the bill or wants to work something out. In 99 percent of the cases—indeed, in 99.99 percent of the cases—that is what happens: they get worked out. Only on the rarest of occasions do we actually see a filibuster on the motion to proceed.[8]

Armstrong was arguing that formal rules were required to guarantee that each senator's views were recognized and taken seriously by the leadership and all senators. Extended debate, along with the ability to object to unanimous consent requests to restrict debate, secures for each senator the opportunity to be heard and sometimes the leverage necessary to force compromises at the floor stage. As Armstrong put it, "The fact that I had a right to object and would have, had I insisted, required the leader . . . to offer a motion, which I could then debate at any length of my choosing, . . . made me a part of the action."[9]

Byrd's proposal to allow three-fifths of the Senate to bar nongermane amendments also produced resolute opposition. Senator Dennis DeConcini summarized the views of many of his colleagues:

The Senate has always differed from the House of Representatives in that it is touted as a deliberative body. Sometimes we make jokes about that because of foolishness that goes on on this floor. But, indeed, we are a body that is able to bring up things that cannot get up on the House floor. That, at least in this Member's mind, is important to this Nation. In this Chamber we take the time and have the opportunity to consider any issue that a Senator might believe is necessary and wish to raise. We can react swiftly to crisis without waiting for a break in the so-called rule that might be governing the debate. A single Senator can raise any issue on the floor if it is important enough to that Senator. We consider not just what the leadership chooses to consider, but every Senator has that right except in a few circumstances when the germaneness [requirement] is imposed.[10]

Armstrong added, "Often the lack of germaneness rules is the only means by which a minority or a single Senator can gain access to the legislative

8. *Congressional Record*, daily edition, February 19, 1986, pp. S1399–1400.
9. *Congressional Record*, daily edition, February 20, 1986, p. S1465.
10. *Congressional Record*, daily edition, February 26, 1986, p. S1661.

process and legislative vehicles." [11] And Senator Lowell Weicker reemphasized elements of deliberation:

> In this body where we have the opportunity to discuss and persuade each other, no automatic mechanisms, no diminishing of rights, no legislation to substitute for established practical experience—none of these things are going to work. It is that sense of fairness as between and among ourselves that must take hold. It is the feeling that no matter how unpopular the view of one of our colleagues, he or she should be heard because, indeed, they might be right, and if not now maybe in the future. This is what is important in the U.S. Senate. [12]

DeConcini, Armstrong, Weicker, and others believed that the ability to introduce new considerations, even if they were not germane to the measure before the Senate, was just as vital as extended debate to preserving the role of individual senators and minority factions. Both sets of reforms were ultimately dropped from the television resolution.

In discussions of procedure it is difficult to distinguish members motivated by a concern for personal advantage from members motivated by a commitment to the institution's well-being. Whatever their motives, senators opposing the rules changes believed that appeals to their colleagues phrased in the language of deliberation would be persuasive. These Senate views about the role of the floor are strikingly different from those found in the House. Even the Senate reformers' proposals were quite modest by House standards: debate was to be limited by standing rule only for the motion to proceed, and germaneness was to be imposed on amendments only by an extraordinary majority. Indeed, the reformers were compelled to argue that the regulation of excessive individualism and obstructionism could be accomplished without altering the fundamental character of the Senate as a deliberative body. In contrast to the House, the high ground in the Senate clearly belonged to opponents of restrictions on debate and amendments.

To put it differently, senators view deliberation as central to their chamber's collegial process, with its minimal restraints on floor participation and relatively weak procedural safeguards for committee recommendations. Senate committees still play a vital function in screening policy alternatives, but the Senate generally has not restricted the set of alternatives to committee recommendations that may be considered on the floor. Individual senators' ability to raise issues *de novo* on the floor encourages broad participation and the consideration of alternatives opposed or ignored by

---

11. *Congressional Record,* daily edition, February 26, 1986, p. S1662.
12. *Congressional Record,* daily edition, February 26, 1986, p. S1664.

committees. As a result, the Senate's committees do not narrow the floor agenda to the extent that House committees do, and the potential for deliberation at the floor stage is preserved.

Reform Proposals

Neither chamber is entirely satisfied with the blend of debate or deliberation reflected in current practice. Indeed, the distressing necessity of compromising discussion and participation in order to achieve a modicum of efficiency ensures that at least some members will be dissatisfied with any particular balance of floor practices. Finding the right balance is made even more difficult by the ever-changing political conditions under which floor proceedings are conducted. The desirability of extended discussion— even if eloquent, informative, and persuasive—varies greatly from issue to issue, from month to month, and from Congress to Congress. Members' interest in participating on the floor varies with the changing pressures of the budget, authorization, and electoral cycles. Rules governing debate and deliberation must be flexible enough to allow the chambers to adjust to changing conditions and expectations yet preserve the parliamentary privileges for individual members under normal circumstances. Thus anchoring floor procedure in more rigid standing rules seems counterproductive in both chambers, and reforms in that direction are unlikely to have much staying power.

While a comprehensive review of reform proposals is beyond the scope of this concluding chapter, three sets of proposals that directly affect the quality of floor debate and deliberation are worth brief mention. The first set concerns the structure of the congressional agenda, particularly on budget matters, and so affects both chambers. Proposals related to the use of special rules in the House constitute a second set. And the third set involves proposals for germaneness restrictions and debate limitations in the Senate.

Few developments in the last decade have altered floor decisionmaking in both chambers as much as omnibus measures for budget and money matters. Omnibus measures for appropriations and reconciliation swallowed large chunks of the congressional agenda throughout most of the 1980s. By themselves, such measures need not have altered the character of floor decisionmaking much. Both chambers could have preserved the quality of floor discussions on the many issues encompassed by omnibus measures by creating debate and amendment opportunities proportionate to the size and importance of such measures. However, the same factors that led to the creation of omnibus money measures—political gridlock and severe time constraints—also encouraged the two chambers to alter the way in which the measures are handled on the floor. In the House, extremely restrictive rules have drastically reduced amending opportunities, sometimes closing off all amendments. In the Senate, lengthy floor sessions have been devoted to the omnibus measures, but often at the expense of discussion on other matters of importance.

Proposals to move away from the annual budget cycle to a two-year budget cycle would improve the quality of discussion on budget measures in both chambers. If adopted, the new process would allow more time to be devoted to discussion of each biennial measure and perhaps more time could be reserved for floor consideration of other measures. Even if political stalemate can be overcome only under the guillotine of fiscal deadlines, the problem will arise less frequently. In the absence of a more reasonable timetable for considering omnibus budget measures, direct action should be taken to force more detailed discussion of the major components of omnibus measures, such as new rules that would support points of order against certain omnibus combinations or require that omnibus measures be divided into separate bills before they are presented to the president. Such rules may be overridden, of course, but the procedural advantage would shift to those members seeking opportunities to address issues buried in omnibus measures. Similar reasoning supports proposals to reduce the frequency with which other major legislation is considered on the House and Senate floors, such as a move to two-year cycles for defense authorizations.

In the House, omnibus bills have been particularly troublesome because of the highly restrictive special rules under which many of them have been brought to the floor. Most commonly, the minority party is granted an opportunity to offer a massive substitute for the majority party's version, but few other alternatives are allowed. While such rules structure debate, consistent with the basic thrust of House practices, they often unnecessarily undermine the ability of the minority party or factions within either party to have their policy alternatives debated. Reducing dependence on omnibus measures will improve minority participation in the House somewhat, but many measures other than omnibus budget measures also have received highly restrictive rules.

The problem for the House is maintaining its majoritarian character while preserving genuine floor debate. The majority party of the House may be on the verge of limiting and structuring floor discussion of policy alternatives far too much, thus undermining the opportunities for and quality of floor debate on alternatives to the policy recommendations of committees and the majority party leadership. As examples in chapter 3 indicated, Republican complaints about partisan manipulation of special rules have substantial merit. The majority party may be placing too much value on orderly and predictable floor debate. Some Democrats argue that they should be able to have their way on special rules as a means of accomplishing majority policy goals. This argument ignores the effects of agenda manipulation on policy outcomes—that is, that special rules can and do determine *which* majorities get recognized during multidimensional, multifactional conflict over complex legislation. It is fair to assume that restrictive rules are used so frequently because the Rules Committee and the majority party leadership believe these rules make a difference.

A reasonable approach to protecting the rights of the minority party and minority factions would be to require an extraordinary majority, say three-fifths, to support the adoption of special rules that include certain kinds of restrictive provisions. Prime candidates for such treatment are rules that include self-executing provisions, eliminate the minority party's ability to offer a motion to recommit with instructions,[13] waive germaneness or other restrictions for bills and amendments, or close parts of the legislation to amendments.[14] Some rules may be best presented in two parts, one to bring a measure to the floor and the other to establish the ground rules for amending action. Small minority factions could not stand in the way of a large majority seeking to streamline floor consideration to implement majority views, but a cohesive minority party normally could prevent the majority from imposing rules that bar floor debate and votes on key issues.

Requiring extraordinary majorities for certain types of special rules would cut to the core of the majoritarian tradition of the House. Majority parties, Democratic or Republican, are unlikely to find the approach acceptable. Perhaps more acceptable would be a rule providing for a longer layover period for special rules. Under the current rule, a special rule must lay over one day before a member may be recognized to ask for its consideration. Extending the layover period to two or three days would give opponents of particularly restrictive rules more time to explain their position and attract support. The layover period could be waived by a two-thirds vote, as under current rules.

The problem in the Senate is just the reverse of that in the House. The absence of effective limits on discussion and amendments has sometimes prevented any action on legislation favored by sizable majorities, often by

13. A motion to recommit with instructions gives the minority party the ability to propose amendments (instructions) just before final passage in the House.

14. The House Republican Research Committee proposed similar reforms in the fall of 1988 and incorporated them in H. Res. 599. See *Congressional Record*, daily edition, October 21, 1988, pp. E3655–57.

empowering individual senators with effective means of obstruction. Such excesses often produce repetitive or trivial deliberation on the issue subject to the obstructionism and reduce the quantity and quality of deliberation on other issues. The absence of effective limits on debate and amendments also has meant that speeches often are unfocused, successive speakers address unrelated issues, and amending activity moves back and forth among unrelated sections of the legislation. The problem for the Senate is how to limit the excesses of individualism, devise means for more orderly consideration of legislation, and also foster and protect collegial, deliberative decisionmaking on the floor.

Collegial, deliberative decisionmaking requires that opportunities to express new points of view and expose previously unnoticed weaknesses in committee recommendations be preserved, but it does not obligate the Senate to tolerate unchecked procedural obstructionism. A quite modest step in the right direction would be the adoption of standing rules providing for limited restrictions on debate and amendments, on a case-by-case basis, by a vote of an extraordinary majority.[15] Possible restrictions include a limitation on debate after a substantial period of unstructured debate has transpired, a requirement that amendments be printed a day in advance, a requirement that amendments be germane,[16] and provision for section-by-section consideration of a measure for the purpose of amendment.[17] At a minimum, the Senate should impose a tight restriction on debate for the purely procedural motion to proceed to the consideration of a measure. Such restrictions would lend greater order to floor consideration without unduly limiting the ability of minority parties and factions to raise issues of their choosing.

In both chambers, then, the problem is controlling the excesses of their fundamental, and legitimate, methods of floor decisionmaking. In the House, meaningful debate and majoritarianism are difficult to sustain and balance in the face of a large, cohesive majority party. In the Senate, quality deliberation and collegial decisionmaking are difficult to preserve in the face of unrestrained individualism and unrelenting obstructionism. The struggle to achieve meaningful and effective floor discussion and meet the political challenges facing the institution, the parties, and the individual members will continue.

15. A three-fifths majority would be consistent with the cloture rule.

16. Germaneness restrictions would be effective only if the Senate also adopted a rule making it more difficult to overturn germaneness rulings of the presiding officer.

17. A germaneness test or a weaker test, relevancy, must be applied to amendments in order for section-by-section consideration to be meaningful. A relevancy test might also be applied to debate, either for an entire bill or on a section-by-section basis.

A New Equilibrium?

Even after all the necessary qualifications are taken into account, including the observation that the House and Senate are very different legislative institutions, the inescapable conclusion must be that the House and Senate floors are now far more important arenas for policymaking than they were in the 1950s. The proposition is supported by a variety of indicators: more issues were raised, more members participated, and more decisions were made on the chamber floors of the 1970s and 1980s than in the 1950s and 1960s. In fact, it has been suggested that a new equilibrium may have been established in congressional decisionmaking practices in the 1980s, comparable to that observed for the 1950s and early 1960s. By way of concluding, I can now address the appropriateness of that depiction.

Cautioning against an equilibrium view is the danger of exaggerating the extent of stability and balance in decisionmaking patterns before the 1970s. The "textbook" Congress was a composite drawn from Huitt's and Matthews's work on the Senate, Fenno's work on appropriations politics, and a few other works focusing on the 1950s and early 1960s.[18] Regular patterns of participation and a distinctive distribution of power, reinforced by widely recognized prescriptive norms, yielded a picture of a fully mature, stable institution. But this view was becoming dated even as the literature recording it was published, a possibility that most of the authors of that literature fully appreciated and expressed in their writing. Change was constant in the post–World War II Congress. The elaboration of the subcommittee system began in the late 1940s and continued into the 1970s, amending activity was expanding during the 1950s, traditional norms restraining participation were questioned in the mid- and late 1950s, the autocratic control of several committee chairmen was challenged successfully in the 1950s and 1960s, and so on. Even by the late 1950s, the behavior of leaders such as Senate Majority Leader Lyndon Johnson and House Speaker Sam Rayburn had changed greatly as they were forced to respond to the demands of rank-and-file members. It is true that many of these patterns and developments peaked in the early 1970s, some of which were institutionalized in the reform of formal rules, but to assume that the

18. On the textbook view, see Kenneth A. Shepsle, "The Changing Textbook Congress," in John E. Chubb and Paul E. Peterson, eds., *Can the Government Govern?* (Brookings, 1989), pp. 238–66. See Ralph K. Huitt, "The Morse Committee Assignment Controversy: A Study in Senate Norms," *American Political Science Review*, vol. 51 (June 1957), pp. 313–29; Huitt, "The Outsider in the Senate: An Alternative Role," *American Political Science Review*, vol. 55 (September 1961), pp. 566–75; Richard F. Fenno, Jr., *The Power of the Purse* (Little, Brown, 1966); and Donald R. Matthews, *U.S. Senators and Their World* (Vintage Books, 1960).

Congress of the 1950s and early 1960s was a well-equilibrated system probably exaggerates the stability that was present.

There also is great danger in asserting that a new equilibrium, a new era of stability, has arrived. Any equilibrium is the product of many forces beyond the control of Congress—including partisan control of Congress and the White House and the policy problems facing government. Such forces influence the motivations of the members of Congress and the nature of the political conflict Congress is asked to resolve. In turn, Congress's methods for resolving political conflict are likely to reflect the character of its members and the conflicts it faces. Republican control of the White House, relative domestic tranquility, the persistence of budget deficit politics, and the stability of the party system made the 1980s Congress look about as stable as the 1950s Congress. It seems hazardous to predict that this confluence of external forces will remain in place for long.

Although the notion of an equilibrium is difficult to apply to Congress, it is clear that the modal decisionmaking processes have changed since the 1950s and the roles of the floors in the two chambers differ considerably. The majority party in the House has developed general strategies for managing the uncertainties and dangers of floor amending activity. Restrictive rules, omnibus legislating, creative conference appointments, and other strategies became standard features of House decisionmaking in the 1980s. The net effect of these innovations was to halt the degeneration of the role of standing committees relative to that of the floor and to enhance the role of the majority party leadership. In contrast, the strain of unpredictable Senate floor activity in the 1980s produced a constant rumble among senators for procedural reform. Efforts to respond to the demands, with the exception of the 1986 rule providing for televised sessions and thirty hours of postcloture debate, were blocked by filibusters or threatened filibusters.

The stability of these patterns is quite uncertain. In the House, considerable tension is built into the current arrangements. While little of the steam of the reform movement of the 1970s remains, there is also little evidence that rank-and-file members share the traditional norms restraining participation that were held by their predecessors of the 1950s. Both rank-and-file members and the leaders of authorizing committees have objected to the use of continuing resolutions, the former because of the way the resolutions limit opportunities for rank-and-file members to contribute and the latter because of transgressions of legislative jurisdiction. Rank-and-file Democrats have tolerated highly restrictive rules as a necessary evil in the face of a popular opposition president, but such rules may not be so readily accepted under other circumstances. And rather than imposing a distinctive pattern of decisionmaking, the budget politics of the 1980s have produced ever-changing ad hoc arrangements in the timing and locations of major decisions that have made planning difficult for committees and individual members alike. In short, the acceptance of leadership strategies for managing difficult circumstances in the early and mid-1980s should not be read as universal or unconditional approval of those strategies, even within the majority party.

The Senate's struggle to manage floor activity continues. Ad hoc arrangements for making major decisions are nothing new in the Senate, of course, as the history of the use of unanimous consent agreements attests. The 1980s, therefore, represent a much less distinctive period for floor practices in the Senate than in the House. Nevertheless, the struggle to adapt is taken seriously. In late 1988 the Senate Committee on Rules and Administration proposed a set of reforms for floor procedure that initially received mixed reviews. The prospects for these proposals are unclear, but the record of the past three decades indicates that reforms as significant as germaneness restrictions will be difficult to put in place. Adoption of the full package of reforms would have significant effects on the volume and structure of amending activity in the Senate, thus altering the strategies of leaders, committees, and individual senators in dramatic ways.

Whatever reforms or informal strategies are adopted in either chamber, they will not resolve the problems inherent to decisionmaking in legislative bodies in which the members are formally equal. Accommodating the legitimate demands of members seeking a voice in policymaking, while ensuring that sufficient expertise and coherence are reflected in policy decisions, breeds conflicting conceptions of the appropriate arrangement of congressional decisionmaking structures. The same members demanding a role in shaping major policy decisions can be heard calling for order out of the chaos that is the result of unrestrained participation.

Introduction to Floor Procedure

T HE HOUSE and Senate have developed quite different rules and practices for bringing legislation to the floor, considering amendments, and voting. This appendix provides a brief introduction to those rules and practices.[1]

The House

The House of Representatives has a particularly complex set of rules and precedents governing floor consideration of legislation. These rules and precedents have evolved to avoid the potential chaos of over 400 members seeking to affect policy on the floor without undermining minimum standards of fair play and democratic decisionmaking. Simply put, the House system is majoritarian. Rules are established by simple majorities, and the majority party, if cohesive, is in a position to structure the decisionmaking process to its own liking. Majority party leaders assume responsibility for scheduling floor activity. Far more emphasis is placed on controlled debate and efficient processing of legislation in the House than in the Senate.

Legislation reported by House committees is placed on one of several calendars, depending on the nature of the legislation. The standing rules provide that a measure is to be considered in the order it was placed on the appropriate calendar. The exception is privileged legislation on appropriations, budget, rules, and a few other matters that may be called up directly on the floor.[2]

In practice, minor legislation tends to be handled in one of three ways:

1. For a general treatment of congressional rules and procedure, see Walter J. Oleszek, *Congressional Procedures and the Policy Process*, 3d ed. (Washington: CQ Press, 1989). More detailed discussions are available in two reports by Stanley Bach, "The Amending Process in the House of Representatives," report 87-778, Congressional Research Service, September 22, 1987; and "The Amending Process in the Senate," report 83-230, Congressional Research Service, December 7, 1983.

2. Privileged status is reserved for matters in which the House has a special interest, often because of constitutional provisions.

(1) it is placed on one of several special calendars that are considered periodically and that provide for quick action; (2) it is brought to the floor by unanimous consent; or (3) it is called up and voted on under a motion to suspend the rules and pass the legislation. Under the first two procedures, amendments are allowed but very seldom offered. Motions to suspend the rules are debated for no more than forty minutes, are not subject to amendment, and require a two-thirds majority for adoption. A successful motion to suspend the rules permits a bill's sponsors to bypass the Rules Committee and to avoid floor amendments.

Major legislation normally requires a special rule to pull it from a calendar and to set the ground rules for floor consideration. Rules usually specify the length of general debate and identify the members who will control the time during general debate. They often limit and structure the way a bill may be amended, sometimes prohibiting amendments altogether. Special rules also may make it possible, by waiving points of order that might be raised on the floor, to consider legislation and amendments that would violate the rules of the House. Rules may be very simple, providing for floor consideration and general debate with no other provisions, or very complex, identifying the amendments that will be allowed and the order of consideration as well as waiving points of order. Proponents of privileged legislation, particularly certain appropriations and budget measures, also may seek a special rule to gain protection from points of order or amendments. Complex rules have become far more common since the 1970s. The responsibility for scheduling legislation on the floor, once the Rules Committee reports a special rule, belongs to the majority party leadership.

Special rules must be approved by the House, which requires a simple majority. Most rules are approved without much opposition, but rules have been amended or defeated outright and sent back to the Rules Committee. Once the rule is adopted, the House may resolve into the Committee of the Whole to conduct general debate and consider amendments, as provided in the special rule. The Committee of the Whole is the full House operating under a somewhat different set of rules. For example, the quorum required to conduct business is smaller in the Committee of the Whole, making it easier to conduct business while committee meetings are being conducted, and the amending process is speedier in the Committee of the Whole. Once the amending process is complete, the measure is reported by the Committee of the Whole back to the House, which must approve amendments adopted in the Committee of the Whole and vote on final passage.

Unless a special rule provides otherwise, amending activity in the Committee of the Whole is conducted under the "five-minute rule." That is, the sponsor of the amendment and an opponent each may speak for five minutes before a vote on the amendment. In practice, other members may gain the floor by offering pro forma amendments to obtain time to speak, but what they say must be germane to the amendment on the floor. Legislation is read section by section for amendment, unless the governing special rule makes some other provision. A special rule may dispense with the actual reading of each section, or the Committee of the Whole may do so by unanimous consent. Amendments may be offered only after the relevant section is read, but not after the reading of the next section begins. Amendments sponsored by the committee of origin are considered first for each section of the bill. Committee amendments often make technical corrections in the bill, but sometimes they are offered in anticipation of unfriendly amendments.

House rules permit four types of amendments: (1) an amendment to the measure; (2) an amendment to the first amendment; (3) a substitute to the first amendment; and (4) an amendment to the substitute amendment. Once an amendment to the measure has been offered, an amendment to it and a substitute amendment are in order. If a substitute amendment is offered, an amendment to it is in order as well. If all four types are offered, as happens occasionally, the House first votes on the amendment to the first amendment. Then the House votes on the amendment to the substitute, followed by a vote on the substitute itself. Finally, the House votes on the first amendment, as it may have been modified by the other amendments. The order of voting can be important to members seeking to defeat or dilute the effects of unfriendly amendments. The five-minute rule on debate applies to each amendment offered.

The rules and precedents governing amending activity in the Committee of the Whole are quite strict. Normally, amendments must be in writing and must be offered from the floor by the sponsoring member. The amendment sponsor may not withdraw or modify his or her amendment without unanimous consent, and a rejected amendment cannot be offered again in the same form. And what is perhaps most important, amendments must be germane; that is, they must be relevant to the subject at hand. The germaneness rule is interpreted restrictively in most circumstances. For example, an amendment must be germane to the particular section open to amendment, only the actual text of the section (as opposed to related conditions or implications) is considered when assessing germaneness, and the amendment must be related in both purpose and method of the proposition to which it is offered. The restrictiveness of House rules and precedents, especially with respect to germaneness, often leads amendment sponsors to seek exemptions in a special rule.

Voting procedures in the Committee of the Whole were changed in vital ways in 1971 and 1973. Before 1971, the rules provided no mechanism for recording individual members' votes in the Committee of the Whole. Voice, standing division, and teller votes were the only methods permitted.[3] In a teller vote, members pass by two tellers, one for the "yeas" and one for the "nays," at the rear of the chamber to be counted without a record of who passed by which teller. Beginning in 1971, recorded teller votes were allowed upon the request of twenty members. On a recorded teller vote, members signed green (yea) or red (nay) cards and dropped them in a box at the front of the chamber. Voting by electronic device began in 1973, essentially supplanting teller voting. All recorded voting, whether in the Committee of the Whole or in the House, usually is called "roll call" voting. The House adopted a rules change in 1979 to require that twenty-five members call for a recorded vote in the Committee of the Whole.

After the amending stage is complete, the Committee of the Whole votes to report the bill and any approved amendments to the House. In most cases, the House then approves the amendments en bloc by voice vote, although a separate vote on one or more amendments may be requested. Furthermore, a recorded vote may be requested on the amendments. In any case, only those amendments approved by the Committee of the Whole are before the House, with no further action permitted on those amendments that were rejected.[4] Moreover, amendments to amendments, substitute amendments, and amendments to substitutes may not be reconsidered.

Special rules may modify this process. They may set longer limits on the debate for particular amendments or motions, for example. They also may alter the permissible relationships among amendments and the order in which voting occurs. And they may provide for House reconsideration of amendments rejected in the Committee of the Whole. Once adopted, a special rule ordering the consideration of amendments cannot be changed, even by unanimous consent. Not surprisingly, special rules may shape policy outcomes in some situations.

3. Technically, a roll call vote could occur if a quorum was not present for the division or teller vote and a point of order was raised. In that case, an "automatic" roll call occurred, with the bells ringing in the House office buildings. Very few such roll calls occurred in the period under study.

4. The prohibition on reconsideration of amendments rejected in the Committee of the Whole is a consequence of a standard feature of special rules, namely, that the previous question is considered as having been ordered when the bill is reported to the House. When a measure is considered without a special rule, the bill manager is routinely recognized to offer a motion calling for the previous question (before defeated amendments are reconsidered), which normally is easily adopted.

The Senate

The Senate's floor procedures are less complex and far less rigid than those of the House. They reinforce, and are reinforced by, the Senate's tradition of protecting the privileges of the individual senator. The key rule is the cloture rule, which now requires a three-fifths constitutional majority to stop the extended debate of a minority. As a result, the Senate usually requires a substantial consensus to proceed to the consideration of controversial legislation. Since obstructionism, even by a single senator, can create delays and cause a backlog of legislation awaiting floor consideration, the majority leader tries to anticipate problems and devise solutions in advance of bringing up the bill. If successful, the majority leader will then seek and receive unanimous consent to call up the bill. Unanimous consent agreements often contain provisions structuring floor debate. Such agreements are the closest mechanism the Senate has to the special rules employed by the House.

Unanimous consent agreements setting the terms of floor debate often are labeled "time-limitation agreements," reflecting their primary function. They may set a time to begin consideration of a bill and a time for completion of debate and amending activity. In the "usual form," they also prohibit nongermane amendments, identify the senators who will control the time on the floor, and even may indicate the order of consideration and time limits on debate on certain amendments. They sometimes waive points of order against certain parts of a bill or amendments, and they may prohibit even germane amendments to certain parts of the legislation or on certain subjects. As the name suggests, they require unanimous consent, and unanimous consent is also required to modify such an agreement after it is adopted.

In the absence of a unanimous consent agreement providing otherwise, Senate rules do not limit time for debate on legislation and amendments. Similarly, in the absence of a consent agreement to the contrary, debate and amendments may be unrelated to the bill, no five-minute rule limits debate on amendments, amendment sponsors may withdraw or modify their own amendments without approval, and amendments to any section of the bill are in order. Such a process is very unpredictable on controversial bills, so floor leaders push for unanimous consent to structure the amending stage, even if they must do it on a day-to-day basis. Most senators, of course, appreciate the predictability of a fixed schedule, but all members are aware that any schedule can be altered by unanimous consent at any time.

In exchange for its relative simplicity and flexibility, the Senate suffers filibusters and threatened filibusters, in which amending activity often plays a crucial role. Filibusters take many forms and occur at many stages. Sometimes they occur on the motion to proceed to the consideration of the bill, sometimes they occur on the bill or some amendment, and sometimes they take the form of extended amending marathons. Without a sufficiently large majority to invoke cloture, filibusters prevent adoption of the legislation. And even when cloture can be invoked, it is a time-consuming process that may not be worth suffering for legislation of modest importance or with poor prospects in the House.

The Senate's Rule XXII governing cloture has changed four times in recent decades. In 1959 the old rule requiring a two-thirds majority of the entire Senate for invoking cloture was changed to allow a two-thirds majority of those present and voting to do so. This modest change had little effect on the number of successful cloture motions. A three-fifths majority of the entire Senate was, and still is, required under a more effective rule adopted in 1975, but senators began to employ a "postcloture filibuster" strategy. Under the 1975 rule, senators still could call up amendments offered before cloture was invoked and could delay action by making various parliamentary motions. A one-hundred-hour limit on postcloture debate, one hour per senator, was adopted in 1979, with time devoted to parliamentary motions counted against the limit. Frustration with that limit led to the adoption of a thirty-hour limit in 1986 as a part of the resolution providing for televised floor sessions.

Proposed rules changes may be subject to a filibuster, of course, preventing simple majorities from imposing new procedures to overcome the obstacle of large minorities. The 1975 rules provided that a two-thirds majority of those present and voting is required to invoke cloture on proposals to amend the Senate's rules. The threat of filibusters, along with the possibility that the associated introduction of television would be thwarted, killed several proposed rules changes in 1986. The cloture rule, then, is the linchpin of individual prerogatives in the Senate.

Voting in the Senate, including voting on amendments, can take one of three forms: voice, division, and roll call votes. The Senate has not employed a teller voting procedure and has not adopted electronic voting, although it considered electronic voting in 1986. Recorded voting in the Senate continues to be conducted with a name-by-name call of the roll. A roll call vote can be demanded by only eleven senators, one-fifth of the quorum of fifty-one, and even that requirement is very seldom constraining as senators readily grant colleagues' requests for a recorded vote. The basic outline of Senate voting practice has remained the same for many decades.

Relations among amendments, and the order of voting on amendments, are different in the Senate from those in the House. In the Senate, the four types of amendments listed above for the House can be applied to either a bill or an amendment in the nature of a substitute for the entire bill, the latter being considered the same as a bill for amending purposes. When an amendment in the nature of a substitute is pending, an amendment to the original bill and an amendment to that amendment may be offered. Thus, counting the amendment in the nature of a substitute and the four amendments thereto, as well as the amendments in two degrees to the original bill, the Senate permits seven amendments to be pending at one time. Complexity and confusion is the obvious price of flexibility.[5]

The logic, however, is not too complex. Amendments in the nature of the substitute usually are committee amendments seeking to rewrite and restructure most of the bill. Since these amendments are likely to be adopted, if anything is, the Senate makes available to members the full array of perfecting and substitute amendments. In the House, the full array is not available on committee amendments in the nature of substitutes unless a special rule provides otherwise, as it often does.

A central difference between the two chambers, then, is the method by which major legislation is brought to the floor. In the House, nearly all major bills are considered under special rules, which are reported by the Rules Committee and are adopted by a simple majority vote. In the Senate, major legislation is called up by unanimous consent or, if necessary, through a cloture vote to break a filibuster. Complex unanimous consent agreements are crafted by party leaders. Both House special rules and Senate unanimous consent agreements set aside standing rules for the purposes of considering particular legislation.

5. For more complete discussion and examples, see Stanley Bach, "Parliamentary Strategy and the Amendment Process: Rules and Case Studies of Congressional Action," *Polity*, vol. 15 (Summer 1983), pp. 573–92.

Notes on Data Collection

SEVERAL documentary sources were used to gather data on amending activity and unanimous consent agreements. I included all floor amendments for the selected Congresses: first-degree amendments, amendments to pending amendments, substitute amendments, and amendments to substitute amendments. I excluded motions to "strike the amending clause," pro forma amendments such as those to "strike the last word," previously noticed amendments not actually offered on the floor, amendments withdrawn by their sponsors, amendments ruled out of order, and committee amendments. Amendments were identified by using the index to the *Congressional Record* and outcomes were determined by examining the debate reported in the *Record*. Each member's floor amendments are listed in the index. The compilation is dependent on the accuracy of the index.

I collected amendment data for only selected Congresses. For the House, I examined every other Congress between 1955 and 1969 and every Congress between 1969 and 1986, with the exception of the 97th (1981–82) and 98th (1983–84). Data for the 97th and 98th Congresses were not collected because of the difficulty of using the unbound daily edition and monthly indexes of the *Congressional Record* to identify members' amendments.

A rough estimate of the number of floor amendments can be made based on the historical relationship between floor amendments and recorded votes. The linear relationship between the number of floor amendments and the number of recorded votes for the 93d–96th and the 99th Congresses is given by the equation: number of amendments = 391.5 + 0.82 (number of recorded votes), with $R^2 = 0.82$ (F is significant at $p = 0.03$).

Based on this equation, the estimated number of floor amendments for the 97th Congress is 1,057 and for the 98th Congress, 1,134. The estimated number of amendments for the 97th and 98th Congresses is substantially lower than for the 96th Congress (1979–80), consistent with the inferences drawn in chapter 3 about the effects of budget politics and the move to restrictive rules.

For the Senate, I examined five Congresses: the 84th (1955–56), 88th (1963–64), 92d (1971–72), 96th (1979–80), and 99th (1985–86). The linear equation for the relationship between recorded votes and floor amendments for these five Congresses yields unreliable estimates: number of amendments = 227.5 + 1.42 (number of recorded votes), with R^2 = 0.67 (F not significant at p = 0.09). Ignoring the unreliability of these estimates, the number of floor amendments the equation predicts for the 97th Congress is 1,579 and for the 98th Congress, 1,183, also a decrease from the Congresses of the late 1970s.

The content of all complex Senate unanimous consent agreements was coded for five Congresses: the 84th, 88th, 93d, 96th, and 99th. The content of agreements for key vote measures was coded for nine Congresses: the 84th, 86th, 88th, 90th, 92d, 94th, 96th, 97th, and 98th. Agreements were identified in the Senate *Journal* and coded from the descriptions of the agreements provided in the *Journal*. For the purposes of judging the complexity of agreements, the present or absence of the following provisions was counted:

—a limit on debate for the measure;
—a limit on debate for amendments;
—a separate limit on debate for second-degree amendments;
—a limit on debate for motions, points of order, or appeals;
—control of time on the measure;
—a time certain for a vote on the measure;
—a time certain for a vote on amendments;
—a time certain for a vote on motions, points of order, or appeals;
—provision for some amendments, but not excluding others;
—provision for only certain amendments;
—provision for unspecified leadership amendments;
—provision for self-executing committee amendments;
—provision for other self-executing amendments;
—a bar on amendments on certain subjects;
—a bar on amendments to certain parts of the measure;
—a bar on second-degree amendments;
—a bar on motion to recommit;
—a bar on intervening motions;
—a bar on tabling motions;
—a bar on nongermane amendments;
—a bar on nongermane second-degree amendments;
—specified exceptions to the germaneness requirement;
—a bar on all amendments;
—a provision explicitly waiving statutory or rule restrictions.

Index

➤➤✂︎✂︎➤

Albright, Robert C., 105n, 135n
Alexander, Bill, 65, 66
Allen, James, 105n, 154
Alternative substitutes, 71–73, 74
Amending activity, 12–13; apprenticeship norm and, 136–39; committee deference norm and, 141–45; committee power, indicator of, 176–83; secondary amendments, 29–30, 183–87, 195. *See also* House amending activity; Senate amending activity
Amendments between the houses, exchange of, 204, 205, 207, 208
Amendments in disagreement, 204, 207–08
Amendment trees, 171–72, 173
Apprenticeship norm, 23, 130–34; amending activity and, 136–39; committee deference norm and, 139; demise of, 133–35, 139, 161, 175; interchamber differences, 137–38, 159; partisan differences, 146–51
Appropriations Committee (House), 146, 173, 211n; amending activity on committee's measures, 177, 180; appropriations riders, 59, 62; omnibus legislating, 57, 58; special rules pertaining to, 188, 190, 191
Appropriations riders, 59–62
Arieff, Irwin B., 157n
Arms control issues, 220–21
Armstrong, William, 112n, 243–45
Art, Robert J., 216n
Ashbrook, John, 34, 155, 156
Asher, Herbert B., 135n, 141n, 146n
Aspin, Les, 2, 201n, 218, 219–20, 221, 222, 227n
AuCoin, Les, 219

Austen-Smith, David, 174n
Axelrod, Robert, 131n

Bach, Stanley, 3n, 37n, 38n, 39n, 43n, 44n, 61n, 62n, 69n, 70n, 71n, 72n, 74n, 75n, 81n, 163n, 183n, 188n, 193n, 200n, 204n, 253n, 259n
Baker, Bobby, 99n
Baker, Donald P., 156n
Baker, Howard H., Jr., 108–09, 111–12, 219, 243
Baker, John W., 139n
Baron, David P., 173n
Barry, Brian, 238n
Bauman, Robert, 32n, 34, 45, 46n, 67, 156
Beeman, Richard R., 94n
Beilenson, Tony, 68n, 79
Bennett, Charles, 220
Bentsen, Lloyd M., 126
Bessette, Joseph M., 238n
Bibby, John F., 26n, 141n
Boggs, Hale, 22
Bolling, Richard, 26, 28, 40, 42, 43–44, 75–76n, 78
Boren, David L., 90n
Boxer, Barbara, 221
Bradley, Shannon, 120n
Brown, Hank, 229
Brown, William Holmes, 183n
Buchanan, James M., 120n
Budget politics (House): appropriations riders, 59–62; budget process, 50–52; committees, role of, 50, 57–59, 62; reconciliation instructions, 51, 52. *See also* Omnibus legislation
Budget politics (Senate), 122–25
Bullock, Charles S., III, 177n
Burke, Edmund, 238n

Burke, James, 22–23n

Burton, Dan, 76n

Byrd, Robert C.: cloture rule, 94n, 96, 97; complex unanimous consent agreements, 103n, 105–08, 110n, 111; germaneness requirements, 120, 124; televising of floor sessions, 243

Calmes, Jacqueline, 59n, 73n, 94n, 103n, 113n, 124n, 220n, 225n

Caro, Robert, 99n

Carter, Jimmy, 40, 51

Centralized decisionmaking, 3–4, 11, 83–84

Chubb, John E., 250n

Cigler, Allan J., 7n

Civil Rights Act of 1964, 24, 145

Clapp, Charles L., 134n

Closed rules, 28, 45. See also Special rules

Cloture rule, 86–87, 94–97, 101, 120, 257, 258

Cohen, Richard E., 8n, 42n, 106n, 125n

Cohodas, Nadine, 231n

Collegial decisionmaking, 4–5. See also Floor decisionmaking

Committee deference norm, 23, 130, 131; amending activity and, 141–45; apprenticeship norm and, 139; demise of, 140–41, 175; interchamber differences, 140, 141, 143–45, 159; partisan differences, 146–51; specialization norm and, 140–41

Committee of the Whole (House), 21, 25, 27, 29, 36, 147, 172, 254–56

Committee power: amending activity on committees' measures, 176–83; chairmen's control of amending activity, 21–23, 46–47; committee rankings, 180–81; complex unanimous consent agreements and, 172; deterioration in, 170, 175–76; difficulty of assessing, 169–70; extraprocedural resources, 174; negative forms, 171–73, 174–76; norms and, 174; omnibus legislation and, 57–59, 173–74; parent chamber control, 168–69, 198; policy agenda of committee and, 176–83, 191, 195; positive forms, 171, 173–75; at postpassage stage, 198–99, 204, 209, 214–16; procedural resources, 173–74, 199–204; retention of, 84, 85, 236; secondary amendments

and, 183–87, 195; sources of, 170–76; special rules and, 172, 188–95; staffs and, 174. See also Conference committees

Committee Reform Amendments of 1974, 25, 70

Complex unanimous consent agreements (Senate), 98–99, 257; advance notice of, 104, 107, 108; amending activity, effect on, 110, 119; amendment restrictions, 118–19; Baker's use of, 108–09, 111–12; Byrd's use of, 105–08, 110n, 111; changes in, 113–19; committee power and, 172; compared with special rules, 127–28; debate limitations, 115–18; Dole's use of, 109–10, 112–13; holds, 104, 110–13; Johnson's use of, 99–101; on key vote measures, 113, 115, 118; Mansfield's use of, 101–04, 106; motions to table and, 106–07; time-limitation requests, 99–101, 106–07, 108, 109, 115

Conable, Barber, 53

Conference committees: alternatives to, for resolving interchamber differences, 204–09; appointment of conferees, 200–201; authority to modify legislation, 202–03; defense authorization conferences, 218–23; floor procedures for responding to conference reports, 203–04; frequency of conferences, 204–05, 208; jurisdictional problems, 214–15; noncommittee members appointed to, 211–16, 221–22; nongermane provisions of conference reports, House treatment of, 202–03; parent chambers' willingness to challenge conference recommendations, 208; parliamentary procedure within, 201; proportion of measures sent to conference, 207; relation to committee power, 172–73, 197–204, 209, 211, 213–16, 222–25, 228–32; roll call voting on related motions, 223–31; size of delegations, increase in, 209–11

Congressional Budget and Impoundment Control Act of 1974, 25, 50

Congressional Research Service, 10, 126

Conservative Opportunity Society (COS), 65–66, 67, 68, 157

Conte, Silvio, 56

Continuing resolutions (CRs), 54–55, 56, 58–59, 122, 123–24, 125
Contra legislation, 77
Cook, Timothy, 64n, 65n
Cooper, Ann, 36n, 38n
Cordtz, Dan, 135n
Counteramendments. *See* Secondary amendments
Cranford, John R., 52n, 182n
C-SPAN, 63, 64, 127

Danforth, John C., 90n, 125
Davidson, Roger H., 8n, 25n, 26n, 29n, 70n, 168n
Davis, Joseph A., 182n
Dawson, Raymond H., 218n
Debate, 238–40; in House, 240–42; in Senate, 242–46
Decentralized decisionmaking, 3–4, 5, 11, 47, 83–84
Decisionmaking processes in Congress, 3–6, 11, 47, 83–84
DeConcini, Dennis, 244
Deering, Christopher J., 9n, 25n, 42n, 168n, 176n, 177n
Defense authorization bills, 1–2, 216; amending activity regarding, 216–18; conference committee consideration of, 218–23
Deliberation, 239–40; in House, 240–42; in Senate, 242–46
Dellums, Ronald, 221
Democratic Study Group (DSG), 23
Democrats: defense authorization bills and, 218–22; electronic voting and, 33–34; norms of floor participation, 146–51; suspension motions and, 37–40; televised floor sessions, partisan use of, 65–67
Deschler, Lewis, 183n
Dewar, Helen, 97n, 126n, 127n
"Dial-a-porn" telephone services, legislation on, 229
Division votes, 21–22, 32
Dodd, Lawrence C., 51n, 94n, 176n
Dole, Robert, 109–10, 112–13, 124
Donovan, Robert J., 134n
Dove, Robert, 101n
Durenburger, David F., 112n
Dyson, James W., 176n

Eagleton, Thomas, 95n, 97
Ehrenhalt, Alan, 54n, 69n, 112n, 154n
Electronic voting for recorded votes: effects of, 28–35, 137; introduction of, 27–28; Senate consideration of, 86, 123n
Ellwood, John W., 51n
Equilibrium view of congressional decision-making, 250–52
Erlenborn, John N., 223–24
Evans, C. Lawrence, 167n
Evans, Daniel, 89–90
Evans, Rowland, 99–100, 101
Ex post vetoes, 172–73, 204, 207. *See also* Conference committees

Feld, Scott L., 121n
Felton, John, 77n, 90n
Fenno, Richard F., Jr., 126n, 132n, 134n, 140n, 141n, 176n, 177n, 182n, 242n, 243n, 250
Ferejohn, John A., 173n
Filibusters, 86–87, 94–98, 258; reforms targeting, 96, 101, 120; success rates, 97
Fiorina, Morris P., 43n
Fishel, Jeff, 146n
Floor decisionmaking: assessing importance of, 12; as collegial versus centralized or decentralized decisionmaking, 4–6, 11, 47; committee reforms and, 8–10; external changes promoting, 6–8; hours devoted to floor sessions, 7–8; increased importance since 1950s, 1, 5–6; individual participation in, 130–32, 166, 167; internal changes promoting, 8–11; parties' role in, 13; rules on, 10–11; staff resources and, 10. *See also* House amending activity; Reform of floor procedures; Senate amending activity
Foley, Michael, 8n, 133n, 140n
Foote, Joe S., 65n
Friedrich, Carl J., 238n
Froman, Lewis A., Jr., 23–24, 27n, 119–20, 197n, 235
Fuerbringer, Jonathan, 110n

Garay, Ronald, 62n, 63n, 68n
Garn, Jake, 182
General Accounting Office, 10
Germaneness requirement for floor amendments, 98, 100, 103, 120, 249
Gertzog, Irwin, 146n

Gingrich, Newt, 66, 67
Gist, John, 216n
Glass-Steagall Act of 1933, 182
Gold, Martin, 101n
Graham, Bob, 182
Gramm-Rudman-Hollings procedure, 52, 122
Granat, Diane, 64n, 65n, 66n, 67n, 112n, 230n
Green, Elizabeth, 101n
Greenaway, Roy, 101n
Grofman, Bernard, 121n
Gross, H. R., 34, 153, 155

Haas, Lawrence J., 58n
Haeberle, Stephen H., 25n
Hale, Dennis, 238n
Hall, Richard L., 167n
Heinz, H. John, 182
Helms, Jesse A., 154, 155
Hildenbrand, William, 101n, 106n
Hoffman, Clare, 155n
Homans, George C., 131n
Hook, Janet, 59n, 79n, 97n, 211n
Horn, Stephen, 212n
House amending activity, 1–2, 15, 233; on appropriations bills, 56–57, 59–62, 81; on budget bills, 56–57; committee chairmen's control of, 21–23, 46–47; committee power, effect on, 47; "hyperactives," involvement by, 153, 155–58; institutional position of a member, influence on, 161–63, 166; omnibus legislation, effect of, 55–59; partisan character, 33–34; on politically significant legislation, 17, 24, 81; proportion of measures affected, 17–18; rules and precedents governing, 254–56; Senate amending activity, comparison with, 92, 93, 127–29, 130, 153, 235; under special rules, 78–83; success rates of amendments, 18–19, 81–82, 83; suspension of rules, 37–40; televising of floor sessions and, 46n, 62–65; turnout on the floor, 22–23, 31–32; types of amendments permitted, 255. See also Amending activity; Recorded voting (House); Secondary amendments; Special rules
House committees: Agriculture, 191; Armed Services, 180, 181, 216, 218, 219–23; Banking, 190; Budget, 51, 146, 188, 190, 193n, 215; budget politics, role in, 50, 57–59, 62; Education and Labor, 181–82, 190, 223–24, 229; Energy and Commerce, 181, 188, 190; Foreign Affairs, 180, 190; Government Operations, 191; Interior, 191; Interstate and Foreign Commerce, 211; Judiciary, 190, 191, 194, 211; Merchant Marine and Fisheries, 191; Post Office and Civil Service, 191; Public Works and Transportation, 182n; reforms of 1970s, impact of, 8–10, 25. See also Appropriations Committee (House); Committee power; Conference committees; Rules Committee (House); Ways and Means Committee (House)
House of Representatives, decisionmaking styles, 83–85. See also House amending activity; House committees; House rules; Speaker of the House
House Republican Research Committee, 236–37, 248n
House rules, 253–56; on quorum calls, 32n; Rule XXVIII(2), 203; Rule XXVIII(3), 202
Huitt, Ralph K., 99n, 139–40n, 153, 154n, 250
Humphrey, Hubert H., 105n, 121
Hynes, Michael, 62n, 81n
"Hyperactives" in amending activity, 153–58

Institutional position, influence on amending activity, 159–61, 167; in House, 161–63; in Senate, 163, 166
Interest groups, 7

Johnson, Lyndon B., 99–101, 250
Johnston, J. Bennett, 120n, 125, 126
Jones, Charles O., 151n, 158n

Keith, Robert, 98n, 105n, 106n
Kennedy, Edward M., 154
Kenworthy, Tom, 58n, 125n, 173n, 194n
Kephart, Thomas, 70n
Key vote measures, amending activity on, 17, 81, 88, 89; under complex unanimous consent agreements, 113, 115, 118; resolution of interchamber differences, 205, 207
King, Anthony, 141n

King, Larry L., 99n
King-of-the-mountain rules, 76–77, 241.
    See also Special rules
Krehbiel, Keith, 170n, 171n, 173n

LaFalce, John, 40–41
Laurance, Edward J., 216n
Leath, Marvin, 220
Legislative Reorganization Act of 1946, 20
Legislative Reorganization Act of 1970, 25,
    27, 201n, 203
Legislative riders, 59
Lew, Jack, 76n
Limitation amendments, 59–62
Lindsay, James M., 216n
Long, Gillis, 42
Long, Russell, 242–43
Longley, Lawrence D., 198n
Loomis, Burdett A., 7n

McCloskey, Frank, 221
McCormack, John, 20
McCown, Ada C., 200n
MacKay, Buddy, 58n
MacNeil, Neil, 155n
Madden, Ray, 36
Madden, Richard L., 155n, 156n
Malbin, Michael J., 7n, 17n, 55n
Mann, Thomas E., 7n, 17n, 33n, 35n, 55n,
    68n, 127n
Mansbridge, Jane J., 238n
Mansfield, Mike, 96, 101–04, 106
Martin, Joe W., Jr., 133–34
Matthews, Donald R., 1, 132, 133, 139,
    167, 250
Mavroules, Nicholas, 218, 219, 220,
    221
Metzenbaum, Howard, 113, 154, 182
Michel, Robert H., 64, 66, 77, 157
Miller, Clem, 139n
Miller, George, 58n
Miller, Norman C., 154n
Minimum wage legislation, 223–24
Montgomery, G. V. "Sonny," 36
Morehouse, Macon, 194n, 229n
Morse, Wayne, 153, 154
Motion to table, 106–07
Multiple-committee bills, 70–71, 72
Murphy, Thomas P., 134n
Murray, Alan, 6on
MX missile issue, 218–19

Nickels, Ilona B., 126n
Nixon, Richard M., 121
Norms, 23, 166–67; committee power and,
    174; recorded voting and, 143–44, 147;
    specialization, 132, 139, 140–41; types
    of, 131–32. See also Apprenticeship
    norm; Committee deference norm
Novak, Robert, 99–100, 101
Novak, William, 21n
Nutting, Brian, 126n, 127n

O'Donnell, Jayne, 29n
Oleszek, Walter J., 8n, 25n, 70n, 114n,
    168n, 198n, 200n, 253n
Omnibus legislation: amending activity, ef-
    fect on, 55–59; committee power and, 57–
    59, 173–74; conference committees, effect
    on, 209, 213; continuing resolutions,
    54–55, 56, 58–59, 122, 123–24, 125;
    reconciliation bills, 53–54, 56, 57, 123,
    124; reform proposals regarding, 246–
    47; special rules to limit amendments,
    56–57, 247
O'Neill, Thomas P. "Tip," Jr., 16, 60; con-
    ference committees, 218–19, 220; re-
    corded voting, 26, 27; special rules, 42,
    78, 79; suspension motions, 38; televising
    of floor sessions, 63, 64, 66; teller voting,
    21n, 24n
Oppenheimer, Bruce I., 51n, 94n, 95n, 96n
Ornstein, Norman J., 7n, 8n, 9n, 10n, 17n,
    21n, 23n, 25n, 26n, 32n, 33n, 35, 55n,
    56n, 68n, 99n, 127, 128, 132, 140n,
    141n

Parker, Glenn R., 99n, 132n
Peabody, Robert L., 99n, 132
Pepper, Claude, 78–79, 194
Perkins, Carl D., 223–24
Peterson, Paul E., 250n
Plattner, Andy, 79n, 109n, 112n
Political action committees, 7
Polsby, Nelson W., 99n, 134n
Postpassage stage of legislation, for resolv-
    ing interchamber differences, 204–09.
    See also Conference committees
Price, Melvin, 219
Proxmire, William, 125, 126–27, 153,
    154, 155, 182
Proxy-sponsored amendments, 91–92

Quillen, James, 81

Rapp, David, 169n
Ray, Bruce A., 142n
Rayburn, Sam, 20, 250
Reagan, Ronald, 51, 59n
Reconciliation bills, 53–54, 56, 57, 123, 124
Recorded voting (House), 256; electronic voting, 27–35, 137; introduction of, 25–26; norms, effect on, 143–44, 147; partisan conflict resulting from, 33–34, 35; rules changes regarding, 36; on secondary amendments, 184–86; turnout and, 31–32
Recorded voting (Senate), 86, 123n, 184–86
Reform of floor procedures: to change budget cycle, 246–47; to limit omnibus bills, 246–47; to limit Senate debate, 119–23, 248–49; to limit special rules in House, 247–48; reports on, 236–37
Reid, T. R., 67n, 157n
Republicans: electronic voting and, 33–34; norms of floor participation, 146–51; special rules, attitude toward, 44–45, 81, 241; suspension motions and, 37–39; televised floor sessions, partisan use of, 65–68; watchdog function, 34, 155–58
Restrictive rules. See Special rules
Rhodes, John, 156
Riddick, Floyd M., 101n, 184n
Rieselbach, Leroy N., 25n
Riker, William H., 174n
Ripley, Randall B., 101n
Robinson, James A., 43n, 70n
Robinson, Michael J., 68n
Rockefeller, Nelson, 121
Roe, Robert A., 182n
Rohde, David W., 21n, 23n, 26n, 43n, 69n, 99n, 132, 135n, 139n, 140
Roll call voting. See Recorded voting (House)
Rosenthal, Andrew, 65n
Rostenkowski, Dan, 229
Rousselot, John H., 34, 45n, 156
Rovner, Julie, 229n
Rudman, Warren, 125n
Rules, formal, 10–11; behavior and outcomes, effect on, 234–35; interparty conflict and, 235–36

Rules Committee (House), 20, 61, 146; recorded voting, 36; Speaker's influence on, 25, 78–79; special rules, 42–43, 70–71, 72, 73, 75–76, 78–81, 188, 190, 194, 229, 248; televising of floor sessions and, 68
Rundquist, Paul S., 126n
Russell, Mary, 40n, 42n

Sachs, Richard C., 61n
Salisbury, Robert H., 7n
Schattschneider, E. E., 35n
Schick, Allen, 51n, 53n
Schofield, Norman, 121n
Schroeder, Patricia, 218, 219, 221
Schulze, Richard T., 45n
Secondary amendments, 29–30, 183–87, 195
Seconding motions, 39
Self-executing provisions, 71, 73–74, 248
Senate amending activity, 2, 88–92, 233–34; budget politics and, 122–25; germaneness requirement, 98, 100, 103, 120, 249; House amending activity, comparison with, 92, 93, 127–29, 130, 153, 235; "hyperactives," involvement by, 153–55; institutional position of a member, influence on, 166; on politically significant legislation, 88, 89; proportion of measures affected, 88–90; proxy-sponsored amendments, 91–92; restrictions on, 87; rules and precedents governing, 257–59; success rates of amendments, 90–91. See also Amending activity; Complex unanimous consent agreements; Secondary amendments
Senate committees: Appropriations, 177, 180, 193n, 212n; Armed Services, 180, 181, 216, 218; Banking, 182; Budget, 169n, 193n; Finance, 177, 180, 191n; Foreign Relations, 180; Labor and Human Resources, 181; rank-and-file members' participation in, 9–10; Rules and Administration, 120–21, 236–37, 252. See also Committee power; Conference committees
Senate rules, 257–59; constitutional provision regarding, 121–22; Rule V, 98; Rule V(2), 121n; Rule XII, 98n; Rule XVI(4), 122n; Rule XVI(6), 212; Rule

XXII (*See* Cloture rule); Rule *XXVIII(1)(c)*, 202n; Rule *XXVIII(3)*, 202n; Rule *XXVIII(4)*, 201–02n
Shepsle, Kenneth A., 131n, 173n, 250n
Shull, Steven A., 17n
Sinclair, Barbara, 88n, 96n, 97n, 137n, 153n
Sinclair, Ward, 113n
Smith, Steven S., 9n, 25n, 42n, 44n, 69n, 70n, 71n, 72n, 74n, 75n, 81n, 105n, 142n, 163n, 168n, 173n, 176n, 177n, 188n, 193n
Soule, John W., 176n
Speaker of the House: conference committee members, appointment of, 200; reforms of 1970s and, 25; special rules design, 78–79; suspension motions, 37, 38
Specialization norm, 132, 139, 140–41. *See also* Committee deference norm
Special-order speeches, 66–67
Special rules (House), 82–83, 254–55; amending activity under, 78–83; anticipation of, 194–95; closed rules, 28, 45; committee leaders' amending activity, effect on, 162–63; committee power and, 172, 188–95; conditions underlying move to, 40–44, 69–71; debate, effect on, 241–42; design of, 78–79; "domestic summits," role in, 194–95; intercommittee conflict and, 70–72; king-of-the-mountain rules, 76–77, 241; legislative text, specified by, 71–74, 248; for omnibus legislation, 56–57, 247; for politically significant legislation, 17, 81–83; reform proposals regarding, 247–48; Republican attitude toward, 44–45, 81, 241; role of Speaker, 78–79; specificity in, 74–77; success rate of amendments, effect on, 80, 82, 83
State Department authorization bill of 1987, 89–90
Stenholm, Charles W., 58n
Stephens, Herbert W., 216n
Stevens, Ted, 112n
Stewart, John G., 99n, 105n
Stangeland, Arlan, 182n
Subcommittees, 9–10, 25
Sundquist, James L., 8n, 25n, 169n
Suspension of the rules, 37–40
Symms, Steven, 156

Tate, Dale, 53n, 54n
Televising of floor sessions (House): amending activity and, 46n, 62–65; audience for, 63; awareness of floor activity and, 62, 68–69; campaign use of taped speeches, 64; local-station use of taped debates, 63–64; by national networks, 65; partisan use of, 65–68
Televising of floor sessions (Senate), 125–27, 242–43
Teller voting, 21, 22–23, 24, 256; electronic recorded voting, 27–35; recorded voting, 25–27
Time-limitation requests, 99–101, 115
Tolchin, Martin, 154n
Towell, Pat, 219n, 220n, 221n
Tullock, Gordon, 120n

Unanimous consent agreements (Senate), 98. *See also* Complex unanimous consent agreements (Senate)
Ungar, Sanford J., 105n

Vanderleeuw, James M., 17n
Vogler, David J., 209n
Voice votes, 31

Walker, Jack L., 7n
Walker, Robert, 66, 67, 68, 157
War Powers Resolution of 1973, 25
Ways and Means Committee (House), 54, 146, 214; amending activity on committee's measures, 177, 180, 191n; special rules pertaining to, 28, 43, 45, 188, 190
Wehr, Elizabeth, 56n, 57n, 122n, 225n
Weicker, Lowell, 245
Weingast, Barry R., 131n, 172n, 173n, 184n
Weiss, Ari, 43n, 44, 78n
White, William S., 140n
Whitten, James, 56
Wildavsky, Aaron, 134n
Wilson, Woodrow, 1, 238n
Wolfinger, Raymond E., 94n
Work load of Congress, increase in, 7–8
Wright, James C., Jr., 58–59, 64, 65, 79, 221

Zwebin, Murray, 101n